The Theatre of Meyerhold

Revolution and the
Modern Stage

EDWARD BRAUN

Methuen · London

First published in this paperback edition in 1986 by Methuen London Ltd,
11 New Fetter Lane, London EC4P 4EE
Reprinted 1986
Originally published in hardback by Eyre Methuen Ltd in 1979
Copyright © 1979, 1986 by Edward Braun

ISBN 0 413 41120 6

Printed in Great Britain by
R. Clay Ltd, Bungay, Suffolk

To Sarah

Contents

List of Illustrations

Introduction

Over the last hundred years the function of the stage director has so increased in scope, coherence, and self-awareness that at its best it has become an art as much creative as interpretive and has been as vital to the advance of modern drama as the contribution of any dramatist. The difficulties involved in reconstructing so ephemeral a phenomenon as a theatrical performance are daunting, yet the interest of a wide public has been such as to stimulate the publication of studies of most of the major innovators ranging from the Duke of Saxe-Meiningen through to Jerzy Grotowski. However, until recent years the crucial contribution of Vsevolod Meyerhold was recorded only in fragments, and in the West he remained a blurred, legendary figure. After the pioneering accounts by Huntly Carter in the 1920s, there was little but the occasional excited reports from those enthusiasts who made their way to Moscow in the 'thirties, such as Edward Gordon Craig, Harold Clurman, Jay Leyda, Norris Houghton, and André van Gyseghem.* Whereas Stanislavsky and the Moscow Art Theatre visited Europe as early 1906 and the United States in 1923, and Tairov and the Kamerny Theatre spent seven months touring in Germany and France in 1923, the Meyerhold Theatre was denied permission to travel until 1930, by which time it had passed its zenith.

The fact and circumstances of Meyerhold's execution in 1940 were long suppressed, and such references as were made to him in Soviet publications did nothing but vilify and discredit him. On 26 November 1955 he was officially rehabilitated by the Military Board of the Soviet Supreme Court. Thereafter, *de facto* rehabilitation proceeded with extreme caution, the first brief and highly tentative study of his work (by Boleslav Rostotsky) appearing in 1960. In the same year, the director Nikolai Petrov published the first theatrical memoirs to contain lengthy and sympathetic references to Meyerhold. These were followed by the reminiscences of a number of his pupils, assistants, actors, and designers,

---

* The details of all the published material cited in this introduction are to be found in the bibliography on pp. 287–291.

notably Igor Ilinsky, Sergei Eisenstein, Yury Yuriev, Sergei Yutkevich, Alexander Golovin, Boris Zakhava, and Erast Garin. In addition, two former assistants of the director have done much to restore their mentor's reputation: Alexander Fevralsky, with a series of scrupulously documented factual essays (and a recent autobiography), and Alexander Gladkov with a number of collections of aphorisms and other recorded utterances by Meyerhold. Finally, in the last ten years there have appeared four monumental works which leave no doubt that alone amongst Soviet directors Meyerhold is ranked once more on a level with Stanislavsky: first, the six-hundred-page anthology of memoirs and criticism *Encounters with Meyerhold* (Vstrechi s Meyerholdom) published in 1967 in an edition of 100,000; second, the two-volume thousand-page edition of Meyerhold's writings, lectures, interviews, rehearsal notes, etc., which contained much unpublished archive material (principal editor Fevralsky, published 1968); third, the first full-length critical study *Meyerhold the Director* (Rezhissyor Meyerhold) by Konstantin Rudnitsky (1969), a work of great balance and perception; lastly, in 1976 a finely annotated collection of some 535 letters between Meyerhold and his contemporaries (*V. E. Meyerhold – Perepiska*, ed. V. P. Korshunova, M. M. Sitkovetskaya).

Unfortunately, the first retrospective work on Meyerhold to appear in the West, Yury Yelagin's *The Dark Genius* (in Russian under the title *Tyomny genii*, New York 1955), is rendered worthless by blatant tendentiousness and a quality of scholarship which varies between carelessness and sheer distortion. Two works by the Italian Angelo Maria Ripellino are in an altogether different category: *Majakovskij e il teatro russo d'avanguardia* (Turin, 1959), whilst devoted principally to Mayakovsky's contribution to the Russian theatre, discusses Meyerhold at length and in particular his important collaboration with the poet; *Il Trucco e l'Anima* (Turin, 1965) is composed of long essays dealing with Stanislavsky, Tairov, Vakhtangov, and Meyerhold, in which Ripellino vividly re-creates the sensation of their productions and the cultural environment of the period, drawing widely on eye-witness accounts.

It was a Czech scholar, Dr Karel Martínek, who in 1963 produced the first serious full-length study of Meyerhold (*Mejerchold*, Prague). A year earlier the first collection of his writings and utterances appeared in Italian (*La Rivoluzione teatrale*, translation G. Crino, Rome, 1962). Since then collections have been published in France, Spain, Hungary, West Germany, Great Britain, and the United States. My own anthology *Meyerhold on Theatre* (London–New York, 1969) was drawn from all the material published in the USSR prior to the appearance of the two-volume anthology in 1968.

The book which follows is a considerably expanded and revised version of my unpublished doctoral thesis *The Dramatic Theory and Practice of Vsevolod Meierkhol'd*, submitted to the University of Cambridge in 1970. I have taken account of all material published since that time, notably the Soviet works cited above. For my original thesis I drew as far as possible on published eye-witness accounts of Meyerhold's work together with the critical studies published in his lifetime, notably Nikolai Volkov's two-volume biography *Meyerhold* (Moscow–Leningrad, 1929) and Boris Alper's appraisal of his productions in the first Soviet decade (*Teatr sotsialnoy maski*, Moscow–Leningrad, 1931). My further indebtedness is conveyed in the footnotes and bibliography.*

What follows is not intended as a biography; I refer to Meyerhold's non-professional life only where it is necessary to sustain narrative coherence or where it has a direct bearing on his work in the theatre. My principal aims are to trace the major influences on Meyerhold during his formative years as a director, to assess the viability of his theories in practice, to establish the coherence of his ideas from the Theatre-Studio in 1905 right through to the productions of the late 'thirties, and to locate his artistic activities in their aesthetic and social context. I have largely resisted making comparisons with the work of other similar-minded directors such as Craig, Vakhtangov, Piscator, Brecht, Planchon, Brook, or Lyubimov. Certainly the parallels are there, but each one would require a lengthy treatise to do it justice. There seems little point in drawing attention merely to Richelieu swinging from a chandelier in Planchon's *Three Musketeers*, to the circus tricks of Puck and Oberon in Brook's *Dream*, to Brecht and Piscator's projected titles. Far more important, I feel, is to convey by implication a sense of Meyerhold's central role in the creation of an anti-illusionistic 'theatrical' theatre synthesising all the arts, his pursuit of the grotesque as the expression of modern man's sense of philosophical disinheritance, his advancement of the stage as a platform for revolutionary propaganda, and as a focus for the attention of all sections of society.

My work on Meyerhold has stretched with intervals over thirteen years. In that time I have benefited from the generous help and encouragement of more people than I can possibly record. Those who must be

---

* Some sections of the present book, mostly relating to the post-revolutionary period, incorporate passages from my commentary in *Meyerhold on Theatre*. In every case they have been revised in the light of any relevant Russian source material published since 1968. Chapter Eight (*The Government Inspector*) and the section of Chapter Five covering Meyerhold's work in the cinema remain substantially similar.

mentioned are Professor Elizabeth Hill, Isaac Schneidermann, Irina Meyerhold, Maria Valentei, Marina Ivanova, Nikolai Abramov, and above all Alexander Fevralsky.

Finally, I am indebted to my wife Sarah and to Martin White for their many helpful comments on my manuscript.

All translations are my own except where otherwise indicated.

E. B.

Revolution on the
Modern Stage

1. 1874–1905
From Naturalism to Symbolism

In the second half of the nineteenth century the small town of Penza, some 350 miles to the south-east of Moscow, was a rapidly expanding trading centre and a popular haven for dissident writers and intellectuals expelled from Moscow and Petersburg. Prominent amongst its solidly affluent middle-class was the German family of Meyerhold, of which the father Emil Meyerhold was a distiller and the owner of four substantial properties in the town. The eighth and last of his children was born on 28 January 1874* and christened Karl-Theodor-Kasimir. He was considered of little account by his father, who was concerned more about the proper schooling of the two eldest sons, the likely successors to the family business. In consequence, Karl grew up under the influence of his mother Alvina Danilovna, and came to share her passion for music and the theatre. He circulated freely in the varied society of the busy little town, being on easy terms with his father's workmen and more than once falling in with 'socialists' who offended his father's Bismarckian rectitude.[1]

In 1895, after graduating with some difficulty from the Penza Second Gymnasium, the youngest Meyerhold entered Moscow University to read law. That year he renounced his family's Lutheran religion in favour of the Orthodox faith and took the Russian name and patronymic of Vsevolod Emilievich. This was not so much a decision of conscience as a means of avoiding conscription into the Prussian army. It also facilitated his marriage the following year to a Russian girl, Olga Munt.

In Moscow Meyerhold soon tired of his law studies and found his fellow students shallow and obsessed with back-stage intrigues at the Operetta and other trivia. His visits to the theatre were frequent but seldom measured up to his expectations. After seeing *The Power of Darkness* at the Korsh Theatre he wrote '. . . the actors no more resembled the peasants of Tolstoy's play than I do the Emperor of China'.[2]

* All dates before October 1917 are according to the old-style Julian calendar.

One production stood out; in January 1896 he paid his first visit to the
Moscow Society of Art and Literature to see Stanislavsky's production of
Othello. The following day he recorded his impressions:

> . . . Stanislavsky is highly gifted. I have never seen such an Othello,
> and I don't suppose I ever shall in Russia. . . . The ensemble work is
> splendid; every member of the crowd truly lives on stage. The setting
> is splendid too. With the exception of Desdemona, the other actors
> are rather weak.[3]

By this time Meyerhold had already taken the decision to leave University
and the possibility of a career in the theatre was stirring in his mind. Back
home in Penza, he joined the open-air Popular Theatre, a company
organised for the specific purpose of establishing links between the
intelligentsia and the working-class. After performing regularly throughout the summer, mainly in plays by Ostrovsky, he returned to Moscow
in the Autumn resolved to become an actor.

His sister-in-law was already a student at the drama school of the
Moscow Philharmonic Society, and spoke highly of her teacher on the
acting course, Vladimir Nemirovich-Danchenko, who at thirty-eight
was a successful dramatist. For his audition Meyerhold read Othello's
speech to the Senate in an interpretation which was evidently based on
Stanislavsky. Deterred neither by this plagiarism nor by the young
candidate's angular appearance and nervous movements, Nemirovich was
sufficiently impressed to offer him a place on the second-year course.

In the mid-'nineties the Russian stage bore few signs of its imminent
flowering. The Imperial theatres remained dominated by illustrious
actors who made their own laws and admitted no change. The director
was a mere functionary who supervised rehearsals; stage design was non-
existent, settings being taken from stock and costumes selected by the
performers themselves. The few commercial theatres in Moscow and
Petersburg merely pandered to current fashions, and such hope as there
was for the future lay in the two independent, partly amateur theatre
clubs attached to the Societies of Art and Literature of Moscow and
Petersburg. With Stanislavsky as principal director and leading actor, the
Moscow theatre opened in 1888, one year after Antoine's Théâtre Libre
in Paris. The repertoire was unremarkable, relying heavily on the classics,
but the level of production set new standards, especially after the second
Russian tour of the Meiningen Players in 1890, whose scrupulous
naturalism and studied ensemble work left a deep impression on Stanislavsky.

Russia's first introduction to the modern European repertoire came in

1895 when the millionaire newspaper proprietor, critic, and dramatist, Alexei Suvorin, opened a similar theatre in Petersburg. During its first season it staged plays by Ibsen, Maeterlinck, and Rostand, together with the Russian premiere of Tolstoy's *The Power of Darkness* after a ban of nine years. But the level of production was indifferent and the theatre's sense of adventure short-lived; it soon became a predominantly commercial enterprise and as such survived up to the Revolution.

At this time of theatrical stagnation Meyerhold and his fellow-students at the Philharmonic were singularly fortunate to have in Nemirovich-Danchenko a teacher who was alive to the advance of naturalism in the Western theatre and its implications for the art of acting. According to Meyerhold, he 'gave the actor a literary grounding (a proper regard for the text and metre), and also taught him the analysis of character. Above all, he was concerned with the internal justification of the role. He demanded a clearly outlined personality.' [4]

By the end of two years Meyerhold was firmly established as the Philharmonic's outstanding student, and on graduating in March 1898 he was one of two to be awarded the Society's silver medal, the other being Olga Knipper, the future wife of Chekhov. His final report from Nemirovich-Danchenko makes impressive reading:

> Amongst the students of the Philharmonic Academy Meyerhold must be considered a unique phenomenon. Suffice it to say that he is the first student to have gained maximum marks in the history of drama, literature and the arts. It is seldom that one encounters such conscientiousness and seriousness amongst male students. Despite a lack of that 'charme' which makes it easy for an actor to gain his audience's sympathy, Meyerhold has every prospect of winning a leading position in any company. His principal quality as an actor is his versatility. During his time here, he has played over fifteen major roles, ranging from old men to vaudeville simpletons, and it is hard to choose between them. He works hard, comports himself well, is skilled at make-up, and shows all the temperament and experience of an accomplished actor. [5]

That same winter the firm of Meyerhold and Sons in Penza finally went bankrupt, leaving Meyerhold déclassé and penniless. He needed to find work as an actor in order to support his wife and the first of the three daughters they were to have. The inducements to accept the lucrative and secure commercial offers which he received were strong, but the appeal made by Nemirovich-Danchenko to his idealism was far stronger. Plans for the inaugural season of the Moscow Art Theatre were well advanced;

1. Meyerhold in 1898.

Meyerhold, Knipper, and nine more of the Philharmonic's young graduates were invited to join the company.

II

The founders of the 'Moscow Popular Art Theatre', as it was initially titled, were first and foremost men of the theatre, but they also shared that sense of responsibility towards the underprivileged which character-ised the Populist movement in post-emancipation Russia.* More explicitly than their forerunners in the independent theatre movement in Paris, Berlin, or London, they announced their commitment to social

* The Emancipation of the Serfs became law in 1861.

problems. At the opening rehearsal in June 1898 Stanislavsky said in his address to the company:

> What we are undertaking is not a simple private affair but a social task. Never forget that we are striving to brighten the dark existence of the poor classes, to afford them minutes of happiness and aesthetic uplift, to relieve the murk which envelops them. Our aim is to create the first intelligent, moral, popular theatre, and to this end we are dedicating our lives.[6]

As his letters to his wife at this time indicate, Meyerhold was not over-impressed by these lofty sentiments. With two summers behind him spent bringing the theatre to the people in Penza, he clearly demanded a more concrete definition of aims, and indeed a readiness to take sides. The following January when Stanislavsky was rehearsing *Hedda Gabler*, Meyerhold wrote:

> Are we as actors required merely to act? Surely we should be thinking as well. We need to know *why* we are acting, *what* we are acting, and whom we are instructing or attacking through our performance. And to do that we need to know the psychological and social significance of the play, to establish whether a given character is positive or negative, to understand which society or section of society the author is for or against.[7]

Not only did Meyerhold object to Stanislavsky's failure to take account of the play's social implications, he was also critical of the production's lack of form; some years later he recalled: 'In *Hedda Gabler* breakfast was served during the scene between Tesman and Aunt Julie. I well recall how skilfully the actor playing Tesman ate, but I couldn't help missing the exposition of the plot.'[8]

This indiscriminate naturalism, the obsession with external detail, was typical of the Moscow Art Theatre in its early days and clearly bespoke the influence of the Meiningen Players on Stanislavsky. It was a continuing source of contention between the company and Chekhov. Meyerhold recalls in his diary Chekhov's reaction to an early rehearsal of *The Seagull* in September 1898:

> . . . one of the actors told him that offstage there would be frogs croaking, dragon-flies humming and dogs barking.
> 'Why?' – asked Anton Pavlovich in a dissatisfied tone.
> 'Because it's realistic,' replied the actor.
> 'Realistic!' repeated Chekhov with a laugh. Then after a short pause

he said: 'The stage is art. There's a genre painting by Kramskoy in which the faces are portrayed superbly. What would happen if you cut the nose out of one of the paintings and substituted a real one? The nose would be "realistic" but the picture would be ruined.'

One of the actors proudly told Chekhov that the director intended to bring the entire household, including a woman with a child crying, onto the stage at the close of the third act of *The Seagull*. Chekhov said: 'He mustn't. It would be like playing pianissimo on the piano and having the lid suddenly crash down.' 'But in life it often happens that the pianissimo is interrupted by the forte,' retorted one of the actors. 'Yes, but the stage demands a degree of artifice,' said A.P. 'You have no fourth wall. Besides, the stage is art, the stage reflects the quintessence of life and there is no need to introduce anything superfluous onto it.' [9]

This was the first time that Meyerhold met Chekhov in person, but *The Seagull* was a play which he and his fellow students at the Philharmonic had discovered through the enthusiasm of Nemirovich-Danchenko and had come to regard as their own. They saw the character of the young writer, Konstantin Treplev, as the very embodiment of the rising generation of artists and intellectuals of the 1890s, and they identified

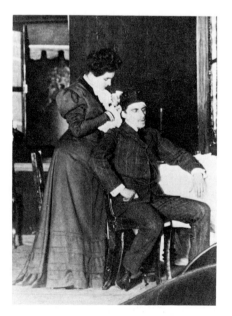

2. The Seagull *at the Moscow Art Theatre. Meyerhold as Treplev with Olga Knipper as Arkadina.*

with his restless desire for change and with his exasperation at the smug routines of his elders. The casting of Meyerhold as Konstantin in the Art Theatre's historic production was a foregone conclusion, and predictably he played the part to the life. Few could have guessed at the time that the very man playing Konstantin would in a few years be the one to respond to his demand: 'What we need is a new kind of theatre. We need new forms, and if we can't get them, we'd be better off with nothing at all.' [10]

Up to his death in 1904 Chekhov followed Meyerhold's progress with friendly concern, and Meyerhold regularly sought his advice on theatrical matters. From Chekhov, Meyerhold learned what the directors of the Art Theatre were slower to grasp: the need for economy and artifice. There is a clear link between Meyerhold's experiments as a director and the laconic style of Chekhov's latter years.

III

Stanislavsky shared Nemirovich-Danchenko's high opinion of Meyerhold, and in the first season Meyerhold was entrusted with eight roles, ranging from Treplev through Prince Ivan Shuisky in Alexei Tolstoy's *Tsar Fyodor Ioannovich* and Tiresias in Sophocles' *Antigone* to the Prince of Aragon in *The Merchant of Venice* and the Marquis of Forlipopoli in Goldoni's *La Locandiera*. The following season he took over the part of Ivan from Stanislavsky after the first few performances of Alexei Tolstoy's *The Death of Ivan the Terrible* and played the leading role of Johannes Vockerat in Hauptmann's *Lonely People* when the theatre gave it its Russian premiere on 16 December 1899. At this time Hauptmann ranked with Chekhov in Meyerhold's estimation, and the following summer he translated Hauptmann's *Before Sunrise* into Russian. Something of what he admired in Hauptmann is conveyed by this extract from Meyerhold's notebook, dating from 1901:

> Hauptmann is criticised for rejecting the drama of the individual in favour of the everyday, domestic drama. But how can one possibly dream of perfecting the spiritual life of separate units of the masses when the masses themselves are still unable to free themselves from the oppression which makes human existence impossible? [11]

It is easy to see how this conviction shaped Meyerhold's interpretation of the role of Baron Tusenbach in *Three Sisters* which he created in the Art Theatre's production in January 1901. There is in the character a contradiction, all too familiar in Chekhov, between on the one hand an urgent desire to be of use to the community, and on the other a resigned acceptance that whatever one does, nothing will change. The essential irony of the part seems to have eluded Meyerhold, and more than one critic was reminded of his portrayal of Konstantin in *The Seagull*. But Maria Andreeva, who played Irina, recalled later:

> It's impossible to imagine a better Tusenbach. Later I played opposite Kachalov, but I'm bound to say that despite his appalling hatchet face and rasping voice, Meyerhold was better than Kachalov.[12]

Andreeva, soon to join the Bolshevik Party and become the mistress of Gorky, was part of the left-wing faction that was clearly emerging in the Art Theatre company, and this may well have biased her in favour of Meyerhold. Certainly as Russian society entered a new volatile phase, political factors could no longer remain divorced from artistic judgment.

Three Sisters received its premiere in Petersburg on 31 January 1901, and it was during the company's visit that Meyerhold witnessed the brutal suppression by the police and military of a mass demonstration of students in front of the Kazan Cathedral. Shortly afterwards he wrote to Chekhov:

> I feel frankly outraged at the police tyranny that I witnessed in Petersburg on 4th March, and I am incapable of devoting myself quietly to creative work while blood is flowing and everything is calling me to battle.
>
> I want to burn with the spirit of the times. I want all servants of the stage to recognise their lofty destiny. I am disturbed at my comrades' failure to rise above narrow caste interests which are alien to the interests of society at large.
>
> Yes, the theatre can play an enormous part in the transformation of the whole of existence.[13]

In the same letter Meyerhold described the audience's reaction to the Art Theatre's performance of *An Enemy of the People* on the day of the demonstration. The cast were nonplussed when line after line was interpreted as an overt political statement by the many academics and students in the audience. In *My Life in Art* Stanislavsky, who played Doctor Stockmann, recalled:

> Up on the stage we had no thoughts of politics. On the contrary, the demonstration provoked by the play took us completely by surprise. For us, Stockmann was neither a politician nor a public orator; he was simply an honourable idealist, a just man, a friend to his country and his people such as any true and honest citizen should be.[14]

Stanislavsky conveys the essentially non-partisan attitude of his theatre at this time, an attitude which left Meyerhold and those who thought as he did in increasing isolation. To make matters worse Tusenbach had been his only new role of any significance in the 1900–1901 season.

The following autumn it was decided to stage Gorky's first play *Philistines*, a work which contrasted the pettiness of the Russian lower-middle classes with the vigour and optimism of the 'new man' of proletarian stock. Meyerhold was cast in the major part of the ex-student Peter. But mainly because of objections from the censor the premiere was repeatedly delayed. Meanwhile, in December 1901 the theatre put on Nemirovich-Danchenko's new play *In Dreams*. Bitterly frustrated, Meyerhold wrote to a friend:

> The theatre is in a fog. It is a mistake to put on Nemirovich's play: it is uninspired, superficial and falsely heroic. It is all in the style of Boborykin:* the author's attitude to the social milieu, the petty dialogue, the style of writing. It's shameful that our theatre is stooping to such plays. And because of this Gorky's play is held up. That is what is so infuriating.[15]

Meyerhold's opinion of the play must have been well known, for he was accused of organising the barracking which occurred on the opening night. Rightly or wrongly, Stanislavsky seemed convinced of Meyerhold's involvement, and refused even to grant him an interview to discuss the matter.[16] It seemed now only a matter of time before Meyerhold parted company with his once admired mentors. The reasons were confused and various; the following summer Nemirovich wrote to Olga Knipper:

> The Meyerhold movement has subsided, thank God! It was a muddle, a crazy mixture of Nietzsche, Maeterlinck, and narrow liberalism verging on gloomy radicalism. The devil knows what! An omelette with onions. It was the muddle of someone who unearths several new truths every day, each one jostling the next.[17]

This is probably a fair description of Meyerhold's confused state of mind at that time, but the times themselves were confused and Meyerhold was deeply concerned to define the changing position of himself and of the theatre in general. That is something that the Art Theatre itself was most reluctant to do. Meyerhold's early doubts were confirmed: both Stanislavsky and Nemirovich-Danchenko shied away from outright commitment, and in consequence Gorky was compelled to offer his more contentious plays such as *Barbarians* and *Summer Folk* to other companies.

* Pyotr Boborykin (1836–1921), minor Russian genre dramatist.

The 1901–1902 season was an unhappy one both for the Art Theatre and for Meyerhold: the company enjoyed not a single success and the repeated postponements of *Philistines* left Meyerhold with only minor parts in *The Wild Duck* and *In Dreams*. Early in 1902 it was decided to reorganise the theatre as a joint-stock company with sixteen shareholders, several of them actors in the company. Despite Chekhov's objections, Meyerhold was not amongst those invited, and on 12 February he resigned from the company. A few days later he and Alexander Kosheverov, a fellow-actor, stated in a letter to the press that their 'resignation from the company was totally unrelated to considerations of a material nature'.[18]

The true reason was a combination of the personal and the political, greatly exacerbated by his growing frustration as an actor. In four seasons he had played a total of eighteen roles, but in the public eye at least, nothing had quite lived up to the early promise of his Konstantin. High as the regard of Chekhov and Stanislavsky remained, Nemirovich-Danchenko had lost all faith in him and it seems unlikely that he would have retained a leading place in the company.

From Meyerhold's frustration as an actor there emerged the resolve to work independently as a stage-director. On the stage it was invariably Meyerhold's intelligence rather than his natural talent that impressed the shrewdest observers. Chekhov remarked: 'You wouldn't call him an infectious actor, but you listen to him with pleasure because he understands everything he says.'[19] Similarly, the leading Petersburg critic, Alexander Kugel, assessed his ability:

> I recall Meyerhold at the very beginning of his stage career – purely as an actor. Even though he caught one's eye; it wasn't so much his acting talent, which is open to question, but rather something unrelated to acting, a most striking intellectual quality which stood out even in the company of the Art Theatre . . . He engraved the part, so to speak, on one's theatrical perception with the pressure of his intellect. His intellect far outstripped his powers of expression, and for this reason it was entirely natural that he should progress quickly from acting to directing.[20]

Soon after the announcement of Meyerhold and Kosheverov's resignation from the Art Theatre it was revealed that a month earlier they had arranged to hire the municipal theatre of Kherson in the Ukraine for the 1902–1903 season. Kosheverov seems to have had no previous professional experience in production, whilst Meyerhold's had been limited to helping Nemirovich-Danchenko revive two Philharmonic student productions at the Society of Art and Literature in January 1899. Meyerhold remained with the Art Theatre until the expiry of his contract. His last engagement with the company was on tour in Petersburg in March 1902, when he finally played Peter in the long delayed premiere of *Philistines*. The fear of demonstrations was so great that the occasion was attended by elaborate precautions including burly militia thinly disguised as theatre ushers. But such was the mutilation wrought on the text by the censor and so tentative was the production, that the play's significance was obscured and the event proved a mild anti-climax.

IV

Kherson is a port on the River Dnieper close to the Black Sea, which at the turn of the century numbered some 35,000 inhabitants. The 'troupe of Russian dramatic artists under the direction of A. S. Kosheverov and V. E. Meyerhold', as it was modestly titled, began rehearsals there in mid-August 1902. But there was nothing modest about the company's aspirations; from the start it was made known that they were a far cry from the provincial barnstormers who had inhabited the municipal theatre in previous years, seldom performing the same play twice in a season. Five weeks were set aside for uninterrupted rehearsals, the repertoire was cut by half to seventy-nine items (a quarter of them one-act plays),[21] and the customary seasonal budget was more than doubled. It seemed a foolhardy undertaking in a remote town with no worthwhile theatrical tradition. Illarion Pevtsov, an actor with the company, has put the maximum number of local theatregoers at two-thousand, of whom no more than three hundred could be regarded as regulars.[22] What is more, Meyerhold and Kosheverov had virtually no assets of their own and were obliged to raise a loan to cover the initial costs. Chekhov feared the worst, writing anxiously to Olga Knipper: 'I'd like to see Meyerhold and cheer him up. It isn't going to be easy for him in Kherson. There's no public for plays there; all they want is more travelling shows. After all, Kherson isn't Russia or even Europe.'[23]

On 22 September, Meyerhold and Kosheverov sent a telegram to Chekhov: 'Season opened today with your *Three Sisters*. Huge success. Beloved author of melancholy moods! You alone give true delight!'[24]

Within six weeks, *Ivanov*, *The Seagull*, and *Uncle Vanya* were added to the repertoire, with Meyerhold playing Tusenbach, Ivanov, Treplev, and Astrov. The style of production was scrupulously naturalistic and clearly indebted to the Moscow Art Theatre. In later years Meyerhold re-called:

I began as a director by slavishly imitating Stanislavsky. In theory, I no longer accepted many points of his early production methods, but when I set about directing myself, I followed meekly in his footsteps. I don't regret it, because it was a short-lived phase; besides, it served as excellent practical schooling.[25]

On 17 February 1903 the season ended as it had begun, with *Three Sisters*. The company was in no positon to scorn altogether the staple provincial repertoire of farce, melodrama, and the ever-popular domestic comedies of Ostrovsky, but equally they had put on the four Chekhov plays, *Drayman Henschel*, *Lonely People*, *The Sunken Bell*, and *Michael Kramer* by Hauptmann, *The Wild Duck*, *Hedda Gabler*, and *An Enemy of the People* by Ibsen, *The Power of Darkness* by Tolstoy, *Thérèse Raquin* by Zola – and Gorky's *Philistines*. One notable success was a little-known melodrama of circus life, *The Acrobats*, by the contemporary Austrian dramatist Franz von Schönthan, jointly translated by Meyerhold and another member of the company. What impressed the local critics was the authentic depiction of the backstage scenes, on which Meyerhold lavished particular attention. But of equal importance for him was his own performance as the ageing and failing clown Landowski.

The modern transformation of the once rollicking clown Pierrot had begun with Deburau père at the Théâtre des Funambules in the 1830s. Over the years he became the new Everyman, the hapless butt of every cruel jest that an inscrutable fate chose to play on him. Successively he has been taken up by Leoncavallo, Picasso, Stravinsky, Chaplin, Carné, Fellini, Bergman. But, as we shall see, the genealogy would be far from complete without the name of Meyerhold, so this early acquaintance with Schönthan's Landowski should not go unmarked.[26]

By Moscow standards both production methods and repertoire were well-tried, but in Kherson they were a revelation and the season showed a handsome profit which financed a tour of neighbouring towns in the spring. At Sevastopol in May they presented *The Lower Depths*, *The Lady from the Sea*, and 'an evening of new art' comprising *The Last Masks* by Schnitzler and *The Intruder* by Maeterlinck. It was Meyerhold's first production of the Belgian symbolist.

In the summer of 1903 Meyerhold became the sole director of the Kherson company and renamed it 'The Fellowship of the New Drama'. It was a calculated indication of the new artistic policy which he intended to pursue, the term 'new drama' being synonymous with symbolist drama. By 1903 the impact of Western Symbolism had been fully absorbed by Russian literature, and Alexander Blok was already engaged in the

3. Meyerhold as Landowski.

composition of his early masterpiece, the poetic cycle *Verses on the Beautiful Lady*. In the theatre, whilst no Russian symbolist drama of any consequence had appeared, isolated attempts at staging Maeterlinck had been made and both his plays and his theoretical writings had appeared in translation, notably *Le Trésor des humbles*, containing his essay 'Everyday Tragedy', in 1901. The following year in Diaghilev's journal, *The World of Art*, Valery Bryusov had submitted the methods of the Moscow Art Theatre to symbolist scrutiny in a long essay entitled 'The Unnecessary Truth'.* But meanwhile, the practical problems posed by symbolist drama remained unsolved.

Meyerhold's plans for the new season included three works by Maeterlinck, four by Schnitzler, and four by the Polish Decadent dramatist, Stanislaw Przybyszewski. As the Fellowship's literary manager he engaged the young symbolist poet, Alexei Remizov, a friend from his Penza days, where Remizov had been a political exile. Describing their aims, Remizov wrote:

* Bryusov's article is discussed in the chapter on the Theatre-Studio on pp. 38–39 below.

> The theatre is not amusement and relaxation; the theatre is not an imitation of man's impoverishment. The theatre is an act of worship, a mass whose mysteries conceal perhaps redemption . . . It is of such a theatre that the 'New Drama' dreams.
>
> Its repertoire is composed of works whose words have cast a new light into the interminable nights of life, have smashed the gloomy, mouldering nests of mankind, have discovered new lands, sent forth strange calls, kindled new desires.[27]

The sentiments behind Remizov's portentous phrases were soon to become a familiar part of symbolist aspirations in Russia. Leading theorists and poets of the movement such as Vyacheslav Ivanov, Georgy Chulkov, and for a time Blok as well, sought a reunion of 'the poet' and 'the crowd' through a theatre delivered from the hands of its élitist audience and restored to its ancient origins in Dionysiac ritual.[28] For those like Meyerhold and Remizov with left-wing leanings this programme had the populist aims of repairing the separation of the intelligentsia from the people and of turning the theatre into a means for the transformation of society. This was to be achieved not by making the stage a platform for political oratory, but by creating a shared experience so compelling that it revealed the ineffable truths beneath the tawdry and illusory surface of everyday life.

This was the theory, but for the present Meyerhold and Remizov had to come to terms with a public scarcely disposed towards transformation. Still under the sign of Stanislavsky, the Fellowship opened its season on 15 September 1903 with Gorky's *Lower Depths*. This was followed by a sequence of works with serious social content: Hauptmann's *Before Sunrise*, *Peace Celebration*, and *Colleague Krampton*, Ibsen's *A Doll's House*, *Ghosts*, and *Little Eyolf*, and Sudermann's *The Homeland*, *St John's Fire*, and *The Last Days of Sodom*.

It was with Przybyszewski's *Snow* (19 December 1903) that Meyerhold took his first tentative steps away from the verisimilitude of the Moscow Art Theatre. In the words of Remizov the production 'reflected the considerable artistic flair of the director Meyerhold, who used tone, colours, and plasticity to blend the symbolism of the drama with its realistic plot'; it was '. . . a symphony of snow and winter, of consolation and irrepressible longing'.[29] Whatever the vision, it was lost on the Kherson public; its baffled and scornful response to the single performance of *Snow* encouraged no further experiments that season.

The season's final production on 4 February 1904 was of Chekhov's last play *The Cherry Orchard*, less than three weeks after its premiere at the

Moscow Art Theatre. As well as directing, Meyerhold played the part of Trofimov. It is a measure of Chekhov's regard for Meyerhold that he released the play to him and the Art Theatre simultaneously; in fact, the text performed in Kherson differed in places from the version which Chekhov finally agreed with Stanislavsky and Nemirovich-Danchenko. Soon after the close of the Kherson season Meyerhold saw the Moscow production and disliked it thoroughly. In his opinion, the play revealed an advance in Chekhov's style which the Art Theatre had failed to recognise. On 8 May he wrote to Chekhov:

> Your play is abstract, like a Tchaikovsky symphony. Above all else, the director must get the *sound* of it. In Act Three, against the background of the mindless stamping of feet – it is this 'stamping' that must be heard – enters Horror, completely unnoticed by the guests: 'The cherry orchard is sold.' They dance on. 'Sold' – still they dance. And so on, to the end. When one reads the play, the effect of the third act is the same as the ringing in the ears of the sick man in your story *Typhus*. A sort of itching. Jollity with overtones of death. In this act there is something Maeterlinckian, something terrifying. I use the comparison only because I can't find words to express it more precisely.[30]

There is a close resemblance between Meyerhold's analysis and the one published shortly before in the Moscow symbolist journal *The Scales* by Andrei Bely, who saw the guests in Act Three as 'incarnations of worldly chaos' who 'dance and posture whilst the family drama is being enacted'.[31]

However, there seems to have been little trace of the symbolist influence on Meyerhold's actual production of *The Cherry Orchard* in Kherson. His prompt copy of the play survives and apparently the annotations indicate that the treatment was similar to his earlier productions of Chekhov.[32] Furthermore, the local correspondent of the Petersburg journal *Theatre and Art* saw nothing remarkable in the production and dismissed it as 'somewhat commonplace'.[33] This is hardly surprising; in mid-season Meyerhold had little time to rehearse what is an extremely complex play, and besides, he would not have wanted to risk a further fiasco after *Snow*, least of all with his beloved Chekhov.

Nevertheless, this should not detract from the fact that in his letter to Chekhov, Meyerhold envisaged a production in which music and movement would be used not simply as components of a lifelike scene, but as the means of pointing theatrically what is truly significant in the action, the sub-text, the unspoken dialogue of emotions, what Chekhov had called 'the quintessence of life'.* As we shall see, this concept of the

* See p. 24 above.

expressive power of music and movement provided the foundation for the dramatic aesthetic that Meyerhold was to develop over the next few years.

Meyerhold's second season at Kherson ended on 8 February 1904 with the third performance of *The Cherry Orchard*. By now he was mentally and physically exhausted by the continual struggle to advance artistic standards whilst maintaining financial solvency. In the space of two five-month seasons the Fellowship had presented no fewer than 140 different productions, most of them staged by Meyerhold, and he himself had played forty-four major roles. So small was the potential audience and so resistant to change, that few plays could be staged more than twice in a season. The exception was *A Midsummer Night's Dream*, which with Mendelssohn's incidental music was presented six times.

For a time Meyerhold was thought by his doctor to be suffering from tuberculosis and was ordered to rest in the country throughout the spring and summer. But in the autumn his fortunes took a new turn. Ever since the previous year he had been pressing Chekhov to use his influence to secure the Fellowship of New Drama an engagement for a season in a more theatrically conscious town, like Rostov or Chekhov's own birthplace Taganrog. When Chekhov died on 2 July 1904 in Badenweiler, Meyerhold lost a precious friend and protector, but by now his reputation as a practitioner of the new drama was beginning to speak for itself.

In May 1904 he was invited to join the new permanent company which had been formed in Petersburg by the actress Vera Komissarzhevskaya.* Interestingly enough, Meyerhold declined the offer because it made no mention of acting, for – as he explained to Chekhov – 'No matter how interesting directing might be, acting is far more interesting. For me, working as a director is interesting to the extent that it raises the artistic level of the whole ensemble, but no less because it contributes to the improvement of my own artistic personality.'[34] In fact, Meyerhold did not give up working as an actor until after 1917.

Rather than accept Komissarzhevskaya's invitation, Meyerhold sought backing for a theatre of his own in Moscow, 'a theatre of fantasy, a theatre conceived as a reaction against naturalism'.[35] However, money could not be secured so he took his company to the Georgian capital, Tiflis, where they were offered a secure long-term engagement at the new and well-equipped theatre of the Artistic Society. With a large number of prepared productions and hopes of a more discerning public, Meyerhold could now afford to be more selective in his repertoire. The

* See p. 57 below.

season opened on 26 September with a revival of *Three Sisters*. A local critic wrote:

> . . . the public was intrigued by various rumours that the Fellowship of the New Drama was going to give them something 'new', something Tiflis had never seen before. . . . When the eagerly awaited something new was presented, it was found to consist mainly of a remarkably painstaking production of the play, with a host of minor details inspired by the desire to create an impression of the greatest possible illusion.[36]

The 'something new' was actually revealed a few days later when Meyerhold staged his previous year's production of *Snow*. Fragmentary reports suggest that the entire action was played in semi-darkness, baffling public and critics alike. So confusing was the effect that some of the audience refused to leave at the end, arguing that the play couldn't possibly be over since it was still entirely incomprehensible. The local correspondent of *Theatre and Art* commented laconically '. . . if one is going to acquaint our public with the new trends in contemporary drama (an unquestionably laudable aspiration in itself) one must proceed with great caution and certainly not begin with ultra-violet snow'.[37]

For a time this débâcle had an alarming effect on attendances at the Artistic Club and once again Meyerhold reluctantly abandoned his experiments. But whilst remaining within the limits of orthodox theatre, he contrived to introduce the works of a number of dramatists who at that time were little known in Russia, still less in Georgia; they included *The Father* by Strindberg and *The Concert-Singer* by Wedekind, which Meyerhold himself translated. On 15 February 1905 he staged Gorky's *Summer Folk*, barely five weeks after the Bloody Sunday massacre in Petersburg and immediately following Gorky's release from prison for his involvement in that event. After this single performance the play, together with *An Enemy of the People* and Alexander Kosorotov's *Spring Torrent*, was summarily banned by the Russian authorities.

The season ended on 27 February 1905 – once again with *Three Sisters*. The Tiflis public was finally well satisfied with its new company, but Meyerhold had good cause to regret his refusal of Vera Komissarzhevskaya's invitation. Even though the Fellowship could draw on the repertoire which they had built up in Kherson, they were still obliged to stage some eight new productions a month to sustain the box-office. It was clear to Meyerhold that whether in the Ukraine or in Georgia, there was no future for experimental theatre outside Moscow and Petersburg.

2. 1905 The Theatre-Studio

———————◆———————

At the beginning of 1905 Stanislavsky determined finally to realise his long-cherished idea of a second company attached to the Moscow Art Theatre. It was to be the first of several such companies which would consist mainly of young actors graduated from the drama courses run by the Art Theatre. Each company would prepare a different repertoire of some ten plays in Moscow and then perform alternately in a number of major cities throughout the provinces. In this way many young actors would be guaranteed employment and the high artistic ideals of the Art Theatre would gradually be disseminated throughout Russia. But much more important initially than this missionary task was the opportunity that a second company would afford for experiments in new theatrical forms.

By the end of 1904 both Stanislavsky and Nemirovich-Danchenko were forced to acknowledge that the Art Theatre had exhausted its potential. Following the premiere in 1901 of *Three Sisters* their work had relied consistently for its success on external realism, reaching its nadir in 1903 with a leaden, historicist version of *Julius Caesar*, in which Stanislavsky suffered acute personal embarrassment in the role of Brutus.[1] Finally, in January 1904 there was no escaping the mournful truth that even the long-awaited *Cherry Orchard* had somehow eluded the company's grasp. Many years later Nemirovich-Danchenko wrote:

> There is no denying that our theatre was at fault in failing to grasp the full meaning of Chekhov, his sensitive style and his amazingly delicate outlines. . . . *Chekhov refined his realism to the point where it became symbolic,* [N.D.'s italics] and it was a long time before we succeeded in conveying the subtle texture of his work; maybe the theatre simply handled him too roughly.[2]*

It was Chekhov who shortly before his death suggested that the theatre might extend its range by staging Maeterlinck's trilogy of one-act plays *The Blind*, *The Intruder*, and *Inside*. In *My Life in Art* Stanislavsky describes

* Cf. the comments of Meyerhold and Bely on p. 33 above.

how he sought to embody the spirit of the latest music, poetry, painting, and sculpture in a style of acting that would somehow overcome the grossness of the human form and convey the ineffable mystical truths of symbolism.[3] But he could not free himself from his naturalistic perception of the external world, and the production which opened the new season in October 1904 turned out to be an uneasy hybrid, a mixture of over-literal symbols and obscure gestures. The critic Sergei Glagol wrote: 'I cannot recall another occasion when there was such total incomprehension in the theatre, such absolute disharmony between the audience and the stage.'[4] The press was unanimous in endorsing Maeterlinck's own opinion that his plays were unstageable.

But the challenge of symbolism had still to be met; as Meyerhold had shown in the Ukraine and Georgia, there was a rich repertoire of new drama, 'The New Drama' as it now came to be called, waiting to be brought to the Russian public. In March 1905 Stanislavsky and Meyerhold met in Moscow to discuss the projected 'Theatre-Studio' (the name was coined by Meyerhold), and it was agreed that Meyerhold should become its artistic director, with Stanislavsky and Savva Mamontov* as co-directors. Stanislavsky writes:

> At this time of self-doubt and exploration I met Vsevolod Emilievich Meyerhold, a former pupil and artist of the Moscow Art Theatre. During the fourth year of our enterprise's existence he had left us for the provinces where he assembled a company and set out in search of a new, more modern form of art. Between us there was the difference that whereas I was merely striving towards something new and as yet did not know the ways and means of attaining it, Meyerhold seemed already to have discovered new methods and devices but was prevented from realising them fully, partly by material circumstances and partly by the weak composition of his company. Thus I found the man I needed at this time of exploration. I decided to help Meyerhold in his new work which, it seemed to me, accorded largely with my own dreams.[5]

Whereas Stanislavsky and Meyerhold had completely resolved their differences and henceforth were to remain on terms of mutual respect, Nemirovich-Danchenko bitterly resented Meyerhold's return to the Art Theatre. Not only did he claim that Meyerhold had usurped his own ideas on symbolist staging which Stanislavsky had persistently ignored, but he also complained that Meyerhold had deliberately set Stanislavsky against him. Stanislavsky's dismissal of these accusations was curt and to

* See p. 40 below.

the point: Meyerhold's personal motives were of no concern to him; he needed him as an artist to create the new company.[6] Understandably, Nemirovich remained antagonistic towards the whole enterprise, and the hostility between him and Meyerhold continued to smoulder for many years, fuelled at intervals from both sides. Nemirovich frequently condemned Meyerhold's innovations as mere modishness, whilst Meyerhold blamed Nemirovich for stifling Stanislavsky's innate theatricality by confining him within the bounds of psychological realism.[7]

II

The Theatre-Studio company and directors met for the first time on 5 May 1905. Stanislavsky, Meyerhold, and Mamontov all spoke, but it was left to Stanislavsky to articulate the new theatre's policy, and he took the opportunity to emphasise its social function:

> At the present time when social forces are stirring in our country the theatre cannot and must not devote itself to art and art alone. It must respond to the moods of society, elucidate them to the public, and act as its teacher. And not forgetting its lofty social calling, the 'young' theatre must strive at the same time to achieve its principal aim – the rejuvenation of dramatic art with new forms and techniques of staging.[8]

The reminder was timely, coming as it did less than four months after the events of Bloody Sunday in Petersburg; but it must be said that as the summer progressed artistic experiment was more evident than social conscience as the driving force for Meyerhold and his company.*

Initially it was agreed to aim at a repertoire of ten productions, of which the first four (all directed by Meyerhold) would be *The Death of Tintagiles* by Maeterlinck, Hauptmann's *Schluck and Jau*, Ibsen's *Love's Comedy*, and Przybyszewski's *Snow*. Other dramatists in view included Verhaeren, Hamsun, von Hofmannsthal, Strindberg, Vyacheslav Ivanov, and Valery Bryusov. Repertoire planning was placed in the hands of a 'literary bureau' headed by Bryusov. His appointment was in itself significant: not only was he the author of one of the first symbolist plays in Russian (*Earth*, 1904), but as we have seen, in 1902 he had published a crucial article 'The Unnecessary Truth' which was generally recognised as the first formulation of the 'New Theatre's' case against stage naturalism.[9] It is worth quoting at some length, since Meyerhold acknowledges it as the theoretical basis for his experiments at the Theatre-Studio and later with Vera Komissarzhevskaya in Petersburg.[10] Bryusov writes:

* But see Meyerhold's later interpretation of *The Death of Tintagiles* on p. 145 below.

The subject of art is the soul of the artist, his feelings and his ideas; it is this which is the *content* of a work of art; the plot, the theme are the *form*; the images, colours, sounds are the *materials*. . . . [Bryusov's italics]

An actor on the stage is the same as a sculptor before his clay: he must embody in tangible form the same content as the sculptor – the impulse of his soul, his feelings. . . . The theatre's sole task is to help the actor reveal his soul to the audience.

Citing the Russian poet Tyutchev's dictum 'A thought expressed becomes a lie', Bryusov defines the eternal paradox of the theatre:

The subject of art lies always in the conceptual world, but all the means of art lie in the material world. It is not possible to overcome this fatal contradiction; one can only make it as painless as possible by sharpening, refining, spiritualising art.

And this, he maintains, is what naturalistic theatre (and in particular the Moscow Art Theatre) fails to recognise; on the contrary, it strives to reproduce the material world in as concrete terms as possible. But in this too it fails because of its refusal to recognise the insurmountable conventionality of the theatre. It is not possible to reproduce life faithfully on the stage. The stage is essentially based on conventions. All one can hope to do is to replace one convention with another. It is as much a convention for the actors in Chekhov to remove their fur coats and boots on entering as it was for the characters from afar in Greek tragedy to enter stage-left. In both cases the spectator is aware that the actors have come on from the wings.

On being confronted with an exact representation of reality, our first reaction is to discover how it is achieved, our second is to discover the discrepancies with reality. Only then do we begin to respond to it as a work of art, and when we do it is because we have accepted the *convention*. The more exact the representation, the less scrutable will be the convention and the more delayed our response to it as a work of art.

Such conventions, says Bryusov, are dictated by necessity, and we must reject them in favour of the 'deliberate convention' which '. . . furnishes the spectator with as much as he requires to picture most easily in his imagination the setting demanded by the play's story'. As a model he cites the theatre of Ancient Greece where 'Everything was totally conventionalised and totally life-like: the spectators watched the action, not the setting, for tragedy – in the words of Aristotle – is the imitation not of people but of action. . . .' And in conclusion he says:

I call for the rejection of the unnecessary truth of the contemporary stage and a return to the deliberate convention of the antique theatre.

Even though it was Stanislavsky who invited Bryusov to work at the Studio, it is doubtful whether he anticipated the complete rejection of accepted methods which was soon to take place there. Meyerhold recalls Stanislavsky saying at the inaugural meeting:

> Obviously the Art Theatre with its naturalistic style does not represent the last word and has no intention of remaining frozen to the spot; the young theatre, together with its parent, the Art Theatre, must continue the process and move forward.[11]

But Meyerhold quickly showed that he was not content to 'continue the process and move forward'; in his account of the Studio he writes: 'the Theatre-Studio had no desire to uphold and further the interests of the Art Theatre, but straightaway devoted itself to the construction of a new edifice, building from the foundations upwards'.[12]

To do Stanislavsky justice it must be added that, far from opposing Meyerhold's experiments, he actively encouraged them and staunchly defended him against his detractors within the Art Theatre. Anxious to allow the young company artistic freedom, he soon left for the south to prepare his own production of Hamsun's *Drama of Life* which was due for rehearsal in the main theatre later on in the summer.

III

The month following the inaugural meeting of the Studio was devoted exclusively to the preparation of designs for the new productions in the repertoire. For the first time Meyerhold had the chance to work with true artists rather than artisan scene-painters.

Since the 1880s theatre design had begun to emerge as a creative art in Russia. The man chiefly responsible was Savva Mamontov, railway tycoon, singer, sculptor, stage director, dramatist, and munificent patron of the arts. On his estate at Abramtsevo near Moscow he created his 'Private Opera' in which the performers were amateurs, but the designers the leading painters of the day. There and later at the professional 'Moscow Private Russian Opera' (1885–1904) such artists as Apollinarius and Victor Vasnetsov, Konstantin Korovin, and Mikhail Vrubel created a dazzling series of settings and costumes which embodied the traditional motifs and colours of Russian folk art in a highly stylised and uncompromisingly theatrical manner. The result was a fully integrated spectacle whose every element – setting, costume, gesture, movement, music, and dialogue – played an equal part.

In time, Mamontov's example helped to effect a similar transformation in the Imperial operas and ballets of Moscow and Petersburg, especially after 1900 when they began to employ artists of the 'World of Art' group, among them Alexander Benois, Leon Bakst, and Alexander Golovin. A few years later, their work was to astonish Western audiences at the first of Diaghilev's Russian Seasons in Paris.[13]

Meanwhile, the status and function of the designer in the dramatic theatre remained unaltered. The Moscow Art Theatre was virtually alone in recognising and exploiting the visual aspects of the drama. But, although Stanislavsky was a great admirer of Mamontov's productions and himself performed at Abramtsevo, it was the painstaking verisimilitude of the Meiningen Players which he and Nemirovich-Danchenko took as their model. From 1898 to 1906 every major production at the Art Theatre (including all Chekhov's plays) was designed by Victor Simov, and in subsequent years too he was responsible for many more. His work was distinguished by its impeccable authenticity and its revolutionary use of the stage area. He aimed to present a complete view of life in progress, frequently in a whole series of rooms at varying levels seen, as if by chance, from an oblique angle. In terms of stage realism, the theatre today has made no significant advance on what Simov first accomplished eighty years ago – which is perhaps a measure both of the achievement and of the limitations of his method.

Amongst the young artists who joined Meyerhold and his fellow stage-directors* at the Art Theatre's model workshop in May 1905 were Nikolai Sapunov and Sergei Sudeikin. Both had worked under Korovin: Sapunov as his assistant at the Bolshoi Theatre and Sudeikin as his pupil at the College of Painting, Sculpture, and Architecture in Moscow. Jointly they were entrusted with the designs for Meyerhold's production of *The Death of Tintagiles*. In a short time they had refused flatly to conform to the accepted practice in the naturalistic theatre of constructing true-to-life models of the exteriors and interiors specified in the play. Following the already accepted practice in opera and ballet, and in any case inexperienced in three-dimensional work, they produced a series of pictures inspired by the theme and atmosphere of *The Death of Tintagiles* and designed for translation into scenic terms in collaboration with the director and scene-painters.

Their fellow designers quickly followed suit, likewise rejecting the model in favour of the impressionistic sketch:

In Act One of [Hauptmann's] *Krampton* (the artist's studio), instead of a full-sized room with all its furnishings, Denisov simply depicted a few

* Alexander Kosheverov, Sergei Popov, Vladimir Repman.

bright areas, characteristic of a studio. When the curtain rose, the studio atmosphere was conveyed by a single huge canvas occupying half the stage and drawing the spectator's attention away from all other details; but in order that such a large picture should not distract the spectator with its subject, only one corner was completed, the rest being lightly sketched in with charcoal. In addition, there was the edge of a big skylight with a patch of sky, a step-ladder for painting the canvas, a large table, an ottoman (necessary to the play's action), and a number of sketches strewn over the table. This marked the introduction of the principle of stylisation.[14]

4. Costume and make-up design by Nikolai Ulyanov for Schluck *and* Jau.

Meyerhold defines his conception of the term 'stylisation' at that time:

> With the word 'stylisation' I do not imply the exact reproduction of the style of a certain period or of a certain phenomenon, such as a photographer might achieve. In my opinion the concept of 'stylisation' is indivisibly tied up with the idea of convention, generalisation and symbol. To 'stylise' a given period or phenomenon means to employ every possible means of expression in order to reveal the inner synthesis of that period or phenomenon, to bring out those hidden features which are deeply rooted in the style of any work of art.[15]

The convention was pursued to its extreme in *Schluck and Jau*, directed jointly by Meyerhold and Vladimir Repman with designs by Nikolai

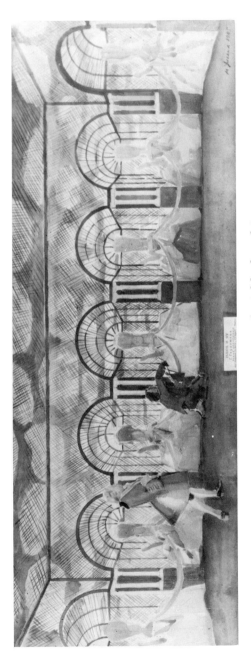

5. Set design by Ulyanov for Schluck and Jau.

Ulyanov. Hauptmann's 'ironical masque' about two vagrants ennobled for a day to amuse the gentry was transferred from its original setting in medieval Silesia to a stylised abstraction of the 'periwig age' of Louis XIV.* Here Meyerhold describes the treatment of the third scene:

> The mood of idleness and whimsy is conveyed by a row of arbours resembling wicker baskets and stretching across the forestage. The back curtain depicts a blue sky with fluffy clouds. The horizon is bounded by crimson roses stretching the entire width of the stage. Crinolines, white periwigs, and the characters' costumes are blended with the colours of the setting into a single artistic design, a symphony in mother-of-pearl with all the charm of a painting by Konstantin Somov. The rise of the curtain is preceded by a duet in the style of the eighteenth century. It rises to disclose a figure seated in each arbour: in the centre is Sidselill, on either side – the ladies-in-waiting. They are embroidering a single broad ribbon with ivory needles – all in perfect time, whilst in the distance is heard a duet to the accompaniment of harp and harpsichord. Everything conveys the musical rhythm: movements, lines, gestures, dialogue, the colours of the setting and costumes. Everything which needs to be hidden from the audience is concealed behind stylised flats, with no attempt to make the spectator forget that he is in a theatre.[16]

Meyerhold's comparison with Konstantin Somov is apt, for he was a prominent member of the 'World of Art', and it is that movement's conception of a unity of the arts which is reflected in the interpretation of *Schluck and Jau* – to the exclusion of all traces of 'unnecessary truth'.

IV

Just as the original Moscow Art Theatre company had done seven years earlier, the Theatre-Studio started rehearsals on 3 June 1905 in a barn near Pushkino some miles outside Moscow. The company was composed largely of graduates of the Art Theatre School and ex-members of the Fellowship of the New Drama, plus three graduates from the Alexandrinsky Theatre School in Petersburg.

By this time Meyerhold was firmly committed to the principle of stylisation, and he was faced with the problem of creating a style of acting

* Apparently this was at Stanislavsky's suggestion after he had visited Diaghilev's brilliant exhibition of eighteenth-century portraits at the Tauride Palace in Petersburg. The exhibition's setting by Bakst was conceived as a dramatic unity of a garden with arbours, trellises, and pavilions to set off the paintings.[17]

consistent with it. Before approaching *The Death of Tintagiles* he acquainted himself with all the available literature on the play.[18] He found the key to its interpretation in Maeterlinck's *Everyday Tragedy*. Originally conceived in 1894 as a preview of Ibsen's *The Master Builder*, Maeterlinck's essay dealt far less with Ibsen than with his own conception of the theatre and exerted a considerable influence on the work of Lugné-Poe at the Théâtre de l'Oeuvre in Paris.[19] Now its lessons were to be assimilated far more fully by Meyerhold in Russia.

Maeterlinck[20] begins by rejecting the truth revealed in 'le tragique des grandes aventures' as superficial and suggests that the truly tragic is to be found in the simple fact of man's existence:

Is it absolutely necessary to cry out like the Atridae before an eternal God reveals himself in our life? Does he never come and join us in the stillness of our lamplight? Is it not tranquillity, when we reflect on it with the stars looking down, which is most terrible? When does the meaning of life manifest itself – in tumult or in silence? . . .

I admire Othello, but to me he does not seem to lead the august daily life of a Hamlet, who has time to live because he does not act. . . .

I have come to believe that the old man seated in an armchair, simply waiting in the lamplight and listening unconsciously to all the eternal laws which preside about his house, interpreting without realising it all that which is contained in the silence of the doors and windows, and in the small voice of the lamplight, enduring the presence of his soul and its destiny, bowing his head a little, never suspecting that all the powers of this world watch and wait in the room like attentive servants, unaware that the little table on which he leans is held in suspense over the abyss by the sun itself, unaware that there is not a star in the sky, not a part of the soul, which remains indifferent to the lowering of an eyelid or the waking of a thought – I have come to believe that in reality this motionless old man leads a life which is more profound, more human and more significant than the lover who strangles his mistress, the captain who is victorious in battle, or the husband who avenges his honour.

Such a static theatre, argues Maeterlinck, is wholly practicable: consider the absence of direct action from Greek tragedy. The beauty and grandeur of Aeschylus and Sophocles resides in their dialogue; that is, not in the 'external, necessary dialogue' which advances the plot, but in the implicit, unvoiced, 'internal dialogue'. This internal dialogue determines the tragic moments of human existence when the spoken word conceals the truth:

What I say often counts for little; but my presence, the attitude of my soul, my future and my past, what is yet to be born of me, what lies dead within me, my secret thoughts, the planets which vouchsafe their approval of me, my destiny, the thousand upon thousand of mysteries which bound my existence and yours: at the moment of tragedy it is all this which speaks to you and which is contained in your reply to me.

It is this mystical dialogue, says Maeterlinck, whose echo is sometimes captured by Aeschylus and Sophocles, and which, he implies, underlies the still surface of his own 'tragédies immobiles'.

Prompted by Maeterlinck's essay, Meyerhold saw *The Death of Tintagiles* as 'above all a manifestation and purification of souls', '. . . a chorus of souls singing softly of suffering, love, beauty, and death'. He glimpsed the style of their realisation in the art of Il Perugino where 'the contemplative lyrical character of his subjects, the quiet grandeur and archaic splendour of his pictures could be achieved only with composition whose harmony is unmarred by the slightest abrupt movement or the merest harsh contrast'.[21]

To this end a style of diction was developed incorporating 'a cold coining of the words, free from all tremolo and the customary sobbing. A total absence of tension and lugubrious intonation.' Conventional histrionic gestures were replaced by 'The inner trembling of mystical vibration [which] is conveyed through the eyes, the lips, the sound and the manner of delivery: the exterior calm which conceals volcanic emotions, with everything light and unforced'.[22]

But, above all, Meyerhold exploited the expressive power of the actor's body. In his music-drama Wagner conveys the protagonists' true emotions, the inner dialogue, through the medium of the orchestral score which is frequently in counterpoint – emotional as well as musical – to the sung libretto. In *The Death of Tintagiles* Meyerhold tried to employ movement, gestures, and poses in precisely the same manner in order to suggest the inexorable tragedy of the little Prince trapped and destroyed by the unseen Queen.*

The *truth* of human relationships is established by gestures, poses, glances and silences. Words alone cannot say everything. Hence there must be a *pattern of movement* to transform the spectator into a vigilant observer. . . . The difference between the old theatre and the new is that in the new theatre speech and plasticity are each subordinated to their own particular rhythms and the two do not necessarily coincide.[23]

* Compare Meyerhold's interpretation of *Tristan and Isolde* (pp. 92 ff. below).

In order to achieve these effects, Meyerhold left as little as possible to chance, prescribing every possible detail, visual and oral, in his prompt copy, often sketching in desired gestures and poses. In this respect, his method was strikingly similar to Stanislavsky's in his early productions of Chekhov, and reflects the same wish for absolute control over the actors.

Valentina Verigina, herself a member of the Theatre-Studio company, has recorded some vivid impressions of *The Death of Tintagiles*:

> In this production statuesque plasticity was employed for the first time: the hands with fingers together, certain turns and inclinations of the head, were typical of primitive painting. But Meyerhold never copied poses or groupings from actual pictures; he imbued them with his own powerful imagination, making a splendid composition in the original style and appropriate to the actor in question. When I first saw the picture 'Madonna at the Strawberry Bed' (by an unknown Middle-Rhenish master in the museum at Solothurn), I immediately recalled Tintagiles and his sister Ygraine, even though there were no such poses and no such mise-en-scène in *The Death of Tintagiles*. I was reminded of the Theatre-Studio production of Maeterlinck's play because at certain moments the head of the little Tintagiles bent towards his shoulder just like Christ's in the picture, and his hand was raised with the fingers together in the same way. Ygraine and Bellangère pensively bent their heads like the Virgin in the picture. When I recall the production I see everything in one place, even though the characters sometimes moved around and made exits and entrances. They did it inconspicuously, simply appearing then disappearing. Right from the first act, but especially later, one sensed the sisters' anxiety for their little brother in every phrase they uttered, every gesture of their submissive hands. But most of all one felt it in the moments of silence; one felt energy concentrated in their frozen poses. In this way an almost unbearable dynamism was created beneath an outward calm. The Queen's three maidservants entered one after the other, their index fingers hooked like claws, their faces hidden by grey hoods. One recalls them motionless: unlike the other characters, they never once altered their pose. The voices of these dreadful executors of the will of fate echoed sinister yet melodious. First they all spoke in unison on one note: 'They are sle-eeping. . . . No need to wa-it now. . . .' Then separately: 'She wants everything done in secret. . . .' and so on.[24]

In 1902, the company of Otodziro Kawakami, the first Japanese actors ever to be seen in the West, performed in Russia. Their repertoire was largely western and their style a modernised version of Kabuki: rigidly formal, yet revelatory in its emotive power. Above all, the critics praised the virtuosity of Kawakami's wife, Sada Yakko.[25] Seven years later, Meyerhold recalled her performance: '. . . Sada Yakko demonstrated the meaning of true stylisation on the stage, the ability to economise with gestures, to reveal all the beauty of the composition'.[26]

Even though Meyerhold makes no reference to the Japanese theatre in his account of the Theatre-Studio, it seems likely that his first experiments in stylised movement and gesture were influenced by the example of Sada Yakko. Certainly as late as 1925 he was still describing her performance in detail to his company.[27]

V

When Meyerhold described to Chekhov his interpretation of *The Cherry Orchard* in 1904, he compared the third act to a symphony, in which the actual music of the Jewish band was merely one part.* Significantly, he wrote: 'In this act there is something Maeterlinckian, something terrifying.' Although more overtly stylised, his production of *The Death of Tintagiles* a year later was remarkably similar in conception. Consider his description of Ilya Sats' music which accompanied the play throughout:

> Both the external effects of the scenario of Maeterlinck's play (such as the howling of the wind, the beating of the waves, and the buzzing of voices) and all the points of the 'inner dialogue' picked out by the director were conveyed with the help of actual music (orchestra and choir *a capella*).[28]

Just as with *Schluck and Jau*, the aim was a production whose every element was strictly bound by a musical scheme. But whilst it was easy enough to synchronise gestures and movements with the musical score, the actors found it impossible to rid their diction entirely of lifelike intonation and to think in purely rhythmical terms. As Meyerhold says, their task might have been easier had there existed some form of notation to record the required variations in tempo, pitch, volume, and expression, thereby ensuring their consistency from one performance to the next.[29] But the root of the trouble lay in the actors' previous training in the realist tradition: as the tension of the drama mounted they would begin once more to 'live' their roles and all thoughts of musical discipline would vanish.

The extent of the actors' failure to master the new style of declamation did not become apparent while they were at Pushkino, and rehearsals

* See p. 33 above.

there proceeded in an atmosphere of general optimism. On 12 August Meyerhold revealed the extent of his company's progress to Stanislavsky, who by now had returned to Moscow. Immediately afterwards, Stanislavsky wrote to Sergei Popov, the Studio's administrative director:

> Yesterday brought me great joy. It went off splendidly. Unexpectedly, the entire Art Theatre company attended. Gorky and Mamontov turned up, so the parade was graced by the generals. *Schluck* made a splendid impression and I was delighted for Vladimir Emilievich [Repman]. *Tintagiles* caused a furore and I was happy for Vsevolod Emilievich. *Love's Comedy* was weak but I think I know the solution and can offer some good advice. But the main thing which became clear yesterday is that *there is a company*, or rather good material for one. This question has tortured me all summer and yesterday I was reassured. Yesterday the pessimists began to believe in the possibility of success and conceded the first victory of the Studio over prejudice.[30]

A week later the Studio moved to its permanent theatre in Moscow. Stanislavsky had hired the former Nemchinov Theatre, a seven-hundred seat auditorium in Povarskaya Street, which at considerable expense had been renovated in a style befitting the lofty ambitions of the enterprise. As Konstantin Rudnitsky describes it, 'The Studio was furnished with taste and elegance, as though the very blue and white front-of-house décor was a polemic directed at the deliberate unpretentiousness of the dull green and grey of the Art Theatre's interior.'[31]

For the first time the new productions were rehearsed on a full-sized stage with music and scenery, and this revealed a number of serious problems, beginning with the difficulty in *The Death of Tintagiles* of synchronising the actors' voices with Sats' score. Worse still, Sapunov and Sudeikin now showed themselves incapable of translating their brilliant atmospheric sketches into three-dimensional scenic terms. Not only did they introduce crude naturalistic details which marred the overall impression of stylisation, but they had failed to allow for the effects of stage lighting, and it altered their original designs beyond recognition.

At the beginning of October the first dress-rehearsals took place. Nikolai Ulyanov describes what happened:

> On stage semi-darkness, only the silhouettes of the actors visible, two-dimensional scenery, no wings, the back-drop hung almost level with the setting line. It's novel, and so is the rhythmical delivery of the actors on stage. Slowly the action unfolds, it seems as if time has come

to a standstill. Suddenly Stanislavsky demands 'light!' The audience
starts; there is noise and commotion. Sudeikin and Sapunov jump up
protesting. Stanislavsky: 'The audience won't stand for darkness very
long on stage, it's wrong psychologically, you need to see the actors'
faces!' Sudeikin and Sapunov: 'But the settings are designed to be seen
in half-darkness; they lose all artistic point if you light them!' Again
silence, broken by the measured delivery of the actors, but this time
with the lights full up. But once the stage was lit, it became lifeless,
and the harmony between the figures and their setting was destroyed.
Stanislavsky rose, followed by the rest of the audience. The rehearsal
was broken off, the production rejected.[32]

To Stanislavsky the problems went deeper than settings and lighting
design. Recalling the dress rehearsal in *My Life in Art*, he writes:

Everything became clear. The young inexperienced actors, aided by a
talented director, were fit to show their new experiments to the public
only in short extracts; when it was a question of coping with plays
of profound inner content, with a subtle structure and, what is more,
a stylised form, the young people revealed their childlike helplessness.
The director tried to use his own talent to obscure the faults of artists
who were simply clay in his hands for the modelling of beautiful
groups and ideas. But with actors deficient in artistic technique he
succeeded only in demonstrating his ideas, principles and explorations;
there was nothing and nobody with which to realise them in full, and so
the interesting concepts of the Studio turned into abstract theories and
scientific formulae. Once again I became convinced that a great
distance separates the dreams of a stage-director from their fulfilment,
that above all else the theatre is for the actor and cannot exist without
him, that the new drama needs new actors with a completely new
technique. Once I realised that such actors were not to be found at the
Studio, its sad fate became plain to me. Under such conditions it might
have been possible to create a studio for the stage director and his
mises-en-scène, but by that time the director interested me only
insofar as he could assist the creative art of the actor, and not for his
ability to camouflage the actor's inadequacy. For this reason the
director's studio, no matter how splendid, could not satisfy my dreams
at that time, particularly in view of the fact that by then I had become
disenchanted with the designers' work – with their canvas, their
colours, their cardboard, with all the external means of production
and the tricks of the director. I invested all my hopes in the actor and
the development of a firm basis for his technique and creativity.[33]

The opening of the Studio was put back, first to 10 October and then to the 21st. But by then Russia was in the grip of a general strike, and on 14 October all cultural life in Moscow was disrupted by a fresh and violent wave of revolutionary disturbances. Practically all theatres closed and the Art Theatre was turned into a casualty station with actresses from both companies serving as nurses. Five days later, after an imperial manifesto had proclaimed a constitutional monarchy, normal theatrical activities were resumed. However, the opening of the Studio was postponed indefinitely, and very soon Stanislavsky decided to cut his losses by liquidating the enterprise. At a personal cost of 80,000 roubles, which represented half his entire capital, he paid off every member of the company up to May 1906. It was partly to recover this loss that the Art Theatre embarked on its first European tour in February 1906.[34]

Nemirovich-Danchenko's reaction to the Studio's failure was predictable; after the disastrous dress-rehearsal he wrote to Stanislavsky:

> If you had only shown me what I saw yesterday before seeking my advice on what you should do, I would have said: the sooner you put an end to this, the worst mistake of your life, the better it will be for the Art Theatre, for you personally, and for your reputation as an artist.[35]

However, even those most passionately committed to the ideals embodied in the Studio's experiments quickly became reconciled to its closure. For, as Valery Bryusov said, 'it demonstrated to everyone who made its acquaintance that it is impossible to reconstruct the theatre on old foundations: either we must continue to build the theatre of Antoine and Stanislavsky or begin again from the beginning'.[36]

In October 1905 the Theatre-Studio must have seemed a dismal fiasco to all concerned, but its failure stemmed not so much from the fallaciousness of its aims as from the deep-rooted habits and prejudices which frustrated their complete realisation: in effect, stylisation failed because it was not stylised enough. Nevertheless the lessons learnt at the Studio equipped Meyerhold with the experience to achieve the successes which were soon to follow in Petersburg and which led to the establishment of a new tradition in the Russian theatre, a tradition to which the Moscow Art Theatre itself remained committed and to which it was soon to contribute with a series of productions culminating in 1911 with the *Hamlet* of Edward Gordon Craig.

In January 1906, Meyerhold wrote to his wife Olga, summing up his reactions to all the momentous events of the past year:

. . . Actors divide their calenders into seasons. Just as landowners calculate their resources by what they sow and what they reap, so actors reckon their successes by the season. This year I lost a season because I wasn't acting, or so it would seem. But that is only how it looks from the outside.

As I was climbing into the train to start the new season, I found myself looking back and I realised how much I had gained from the last one. This year something new was born in my soul, something which will put out branches and bear fruit; the fruit will ripen, and my life is certain to flourish abundantly. Somebody said recently that the life of a creative artist follows a curve – twenty-five years up, thirty years down and then another thirty-five years up. Well this year has been part of an upward curve for me, or so it seems. In May there was the work in the model-workshop alongside artists who helped to realise what had never before been realised, and my spirit gave birth to a new world. Summer revealed the theatre of Maeterlinck, and for the first time the Primitives were given living form on the stage. The collapse of the Studio was my salvation – it wasn't what I wanted, not what I wanted at all. It is only now that I realise how fortunate its failure was.

Then the Moscow revolution. I often found myself trembling, not from fear but from a sudden realisation of the truth. I found myself drawn out onto the streets when other people were sheltering in their homes. It wasn't the danger which drew me, as it draws neurotics to throw themselves from church-towers or under trains. I was drawn by the desire to see the transfigured world. I still remember the square lit by a single lamp at one corner and looking as though it was on a slant. The unlit side fell away and was swallowed up in the darkness where a lonely bell-tower gleamed white. I was drawn by the desire to run from street-corner to street-corner and watch the other dark figures scurrying along against the background of white snow, unlit by street-lamps but giving light enough of its own. I was drawn by the desire to listen to those hurrying figures as they told each other in whispers where it was safe to go. I was drawn by the desire to freeze when a bullet whistled past – dry, malevolent and cold, yet at the same time hot. From this *terrible* week there has remained within me something which will give me strength to feel something later, but not yet. How the soul of a creative artist trembled! It trembled so much, but nobody even noticed, and still nobody knows. . . .[37]

3. 1906–1907
With Vera Komissarzhevskaya

Meyerhold did not leave the Art Theatre immediately after the closure of the Studio. Almost at once he was persuaded by Stanislavsky to recreate his original role of Treplev in the revival of *The Seagull*. 'This was meant' – says Meyerhold – 'as a kind of bridge which might lead to my return to the Moscow Art Theatre, or so Konstantin Sergeevich indicated. But there were also obstacles: Vladimir Ivanovich's [Nemirovich-Danchenko] reaction to the suggestion was cool, to say the least. And I didn'ı know what I wanted either: I was completely disorientated. But the decision was made for me by the total absence of any friendly contact backstage between myself and my former fellow-actors in the cast: they irritated me, and I seemed strange to them.'[1]

So at the end of 1905 Meyerhold left the Moscow Art Theatre for the last time and moved to Petersburg. There he met the leading figures of the capital's artistic and intellectual circles at the regular Wednesday soirées held in the 'Tower' flat of Vyacheslav Ivanov, the leading theorist of Russian symbolism. It was at this time that Georgy Chulkov enlisted the aid of a number of symbolist poets (among them Bely, Blok, Bryusov, Remizov, Sologub, and Vyacheslav Ivanov) to realise the familiar dream of a 'mystical theatre' which would revive the spirit of Dionysus in a communal ritualistic drama. Meyerhold was seen as the natural choice for artistic director and it was proposed to build a company round a nucleus of the best actors from the Theatre-Studio. 'The Torches' (*'Fakely'*), as the company was called, never materialised because no backer could be found for such an esoteric and idealistic venture at a time when Russia was still in ferment after the traumatic disturbances of 1905. Likewise, a similar project involving Sergei Diaghilev came to nothing.[2] After almost four months of inactivity as a director, Meyerhold could not afford to remain idle, so at short notice he seized the opportunity to revive the Fellowship of the New Drama. Leaving Olga and their three daughters,

Maria, Tanya, and Irina, in Kuokkala outside Petersburg, he travelled
south to hastily prepare a repertoire for the remainder of the season in
Tiflis. The opening presentation on 20 February 1906 was a double bill
comprising Ibsen's *Love's Comedy* and an adaptation of Chekhov's short
story, *Surgery*. After five weeks in Tiflis the company went on tour for a
month to Novocherkassk and Rostov, closing there at the end of April.

Once more, Meyerhold found the provincial public unsympathetic
towards innovation and he was obliged by financial considerations to
include a large proportion of pot-boilers in his repertoire. Nevertheless,
he did contrive to further his propagation of modern drama by introducing such works as Ibsen's *Love's Comedy* and *Ghosts*, Hauptmann's
Assumption of Hannele, Strindberg's *Miss Julie*, Gorky's *Children of the Sun*,
and, at last, *The Death of Tintagiles*. His production of Maeterlinck's play
differed considerably from the Theatre-Studio version; here is his
description of the first performance on 19 March:

> I staged all the acts within a frame holding a gauze-cloth, behind which
> the action took place. The frame was covered in dark-green cloth.
> Sats' score was played on a harmonium at the beginning and the end of
> each act and during some of the long pauses (for example the prayer in
> Act One, the fight against sleep in Act Three, and the groaning in Act
> Four). As at the Studio the costumes were light in colour. In con-
> sequence of this the entire production was interpreted not in the style
> of the Primitives but in the colours of Böcklin. So clear was the
> resemblance to Böcklin that it was spotted by absolutely every one.
> For me the production was not ideal, but valuable for its coherence.[3]

Thus, despite the need to school a new and largely inexperienced company and the struggle to overcome the philistinism of the Tiflis public,
Meyerhold succeeded in testing and modifying in actual performance
some of the ideas which he had first explored at the Theatre-Studio.

But Tiflis in 1906 was little more than a staging-post in Meyerhold's
career: before the start of the season there he had been invited once more
by Vera Komissarzhevskaya to join her Petersburg theatre, and in May
he signed a contract with her as artistic director and actor for the 1906–
1907 season. Meanwhile, the Fellowship's engagement in Tiflis was
renewed for a further year, with Meyerhold agreeing to continue as
artistic director *in absentia* on the understanding that he would rejoin the
company on its summer tour to prepare the principal new productions for
the following season.

It was about this time that Meyerhold first read Georg Fuchs' *The
Stage of the Future*,[4] a work which, as he himself admitted, made the

deepest impression on him.[5] Like the symbolist poets of Vyacheslav Ivanov's circle, Fuchs called for the restoration of the theatre as a festive ritual, involving performers and spectators alike in a common experience which would reveal the universal significance of their personal existence. The drama, he writes, has no life except as a shared experience: 'By virtue of their origins the player and the spectator, the stage and the auditorium, are not opposed to each other, they are a unity.'[6] Modern theatres, with their tiers of boxes and their peep-show stages are 'crude imitations of the ballet-houses of baroque courts' in which the performer is confined beyond the barrier of the footlights at a respectful distance from the spectator.[7] Instead Fuchs proposes a steeply raked amphi-theatre capable of accommodating a large audience in the closest possible proximity to the stage. The stage itself is to be wide rather than deep and divided into three ascending strips joined by shallow steps of the same width. The low forestage is located in front of the proscenium opening, extending in a shallow arc into the auditorium. The middle stage is in effect a narrow bridge joining two walls, between which the aperture is normally closed with a backcloth. In the event of the middle stage being used (for crowd scenes or to facilitate rapid scene changes), a painted backdrop may be hung behind the rear stage, but in order to furnish a flat decorative background rather than to create an illusion of distance or perspective. The main action is concentrated on the shallow plane of the forestage where the performers are meant to stand out against the back-ground like the figures in a bas-relief.[8]

In this way, says Fuchs, all attention is focused on the most profound means of dramatic expression: the rhythmical movement of the human body in space. He reminds the actor that his art 'has its origins in the *dance*. The means of expression employed in the dance are equally the natural means of expression for the actor, the difference being merely one of *range*.'[9] Not only in Ancient Greece but, as Kawakami and Sada Yakko had demonstrated on their European tour, in the Japanese theatre to this day every movement is dictated by the choreographic rhythm of the action.[10]

For the Japanese there is no part of a production which is not directed towards the enhancement of the overall rhythmical scheme, and this in its turn reflects the inner psychological development of the drama:

The Japanese stage-director makes the colour composition of the costumes and scenery follow the psychical [sic] progress of the play most wonderfully . . . The setting accords with the play, the actors' poses, the figures, groupings and costumes; it is treated as 'beautiful' in line, form and colour, but by itself it is *expressionless*, a rhythmical monotone with no independent significance. However, as a line in the moving spectrum of the whole it has the greatest importance, supplying the final element in the scheme.[11]

The test of the drama Fuchs leaves until last:

The text is nothing but the musical score, from which the re-creative, performing intellects must extract the true embodiment of the work.[12]

Fuchs' advocacy of a theatre based on rhythmical movement is close in spirit to what Meyerhold was attempting in Moscow in 1905, and it is significant that they both took as a paradigm the style of Sada Yakko. But in *The Stage of the Future* Fuchs was more coherent and more radical in his theories than Meyerhold had been in his experiments at the Theatre-Studio. On the other hand, Fuchs' doctrinaire theories had yet to be tempered by the inevitable compromises involved in bringing a production to actual performance: he conducted his first experiments with the relief stage in May 1906 at the Prinzregenten-Theater in Munich, and it was not until 1908 that it was incorporated in modified form in the new Munich Artists' Theatre.[13]

As well as lending weight to Meyerhold's own views, *The Stage of the Future* drew his attention to certain aspects of the theatre which he had previously overlooked. An early opportunity to examine them presented itself in June when he rejoined the Fellowship of the New Drama for a two-week season at Poltava.

For instance, in Schnitzler's *Cry of Life*, Meyerhold consciously modelled the actors' movements on oriental practice, so that their 'moves either preceded or followed their speeches. Every movement was treated like a dance (a Japanese device), even when there was no emotional motivation for it.'[14] But of greatest significance was his utilisation of stage space in a new, more flexible manner:

In *Ghosts* and *Cain* (by Osip Dymov) the unity of place was stressed (in the latter play contrary to the author's stage directions). The plays were performed without a front curtain. This was facilitated by the exceptionally convenient design of the stage of the Poltava theatre . . . it is easy to remove the footlights and cover over the orchestra pit with a floor on a level with the stage; the resultant platform makes a fore-stage* which extends deep into the auditorium.[15]

* Literally 'proscenium' in the Russian. Both here and subsequently I have translated it as 'forestage' in order to avoid possible ambiguity.

A local critic wrote: 'Thanks to the removal of the front curtain, the spectator is confronted throughout with a single setting. In this way the impression conveyed by the drama is better sustained.'[16]

In 1912 Meyerhold wrote in the foreword to his book *On the Theatre*: 'Even though the theme of the forestage is not dealt with comprehensively in any of the articles below, it will be easy for the reader to see that all the threads of the various themes in this book lead towards the question of the forestage.'[17] It was at Poltava in 1906 that he first glimpsed the significance of what was to become a crucial element in his mature style.

II

At the beginning of the twentieth century Vera Komissarzhevskaya was generally recognised as the greatest interpreter in Russia of modern dramatic roles, a reputation she had won by her performance in such parts as Nina in *The Seagull*, Sonya in *Uncle Vanya*, Hilda in *The Master Builder*, and Nora in *A Doll's House*. In 1902, at the height of her fame she left the Imperial Alexandrinsky Theatre, determined to perform in plays of her own choosing in her own theatre. Eventually, after two seasons touring in the provinces, her ambition was realised when she returned to Petersburg and leased the Passage Theatre to house her new permanent company. The season opened on 16 September 1904 with Gutzkow's *Uriel Acosta*. The theatre's repertoire was similar to that of the Moscow Art Theatre, with a strong bias towards Ibsen, Chekhov, and Gorky, and the style of production was very close to the naturalism of Stanislavsky and Nemirovich-Danchenko.

Shortly before the end of the first season Komissarzhevskaya appointed Akim Volynsky, a leading symbolist critic and art historian, as the theatre's literary manager. Clearly thinking along the same lines as Meyerhold was soon to follow in Moscow, Volynsky said to the company before their first rehearsal of *The Master Builder* in March 1905:

I regard this undertaking as most important: sooner or later it will serve as a means of breaking down the theatrical prose in which you have had to work hitherto. Whereas before the actor was both ready and required to surrender to psycho-physiological reflexes, now he must look for gestures and mime capable of symbolising Ibsen's ideas.[18]

However, the transformation apparently heralded by these words failed to materialise. This is hardly surprising, since most of the productions in the following season were the work of Nikolai Arbatov, a former pupil of Stanislavsky and a passionate advocate of naturalism. It is difficult to understand how Arbatov came to join Komissarzhevskaya at the same time as Volynsky, with whom she was clearly in far closer accord. Shortly after her first meeting with Meyerhold in 1906 she wrote:

> For the first time in the existence of our theatre the thought of it does not make me feel like a fish out of water. That feeling came to me first on the evening of the dress rehearsal of *Uriel Acosta*; I failed to admit it and it lived on in the recesses of my soul, preventing it not only from creating but even from breathing as it must in order to live.[19]

Thus Vera Komissarzhevskaya believed – just like Stanislavsky a year earlier – that Meyerhold held the key to the 'New Drama'.

That summer it was decided to move from the Passage to the former Nemetti Theatre on Ofitserskaya Street. Before the start of the new season the auditorium was rebuilt in a style appropriate to the company's lofty ideals and similar to all the other elegant 'art theatres' now opening throughout Europe:

> Everything was unusual about the new theatre and it amazed the spectator, winning the approval of its friends and provoking furious attacks from its enemies. Gay drapery, cheap ornamentation, a frivolous front curtain: all these customary embellishments of the temple of operetta or farce disappeared, and the theatre acquired an austere appearance. It was all white with columns and completely devoid of decoration, with a curtain of dark material which parted slowly to the sides. The only colourful spot was the front curtain designed by Bakst: with its Greek temple and sphinx it reflected the directors' preoccupation with the religious origins of scenic art, with antiquity and the East.[20]

The first season with Komissarzhevskaya put Meyerhold under constant strain. After nearly six months separation from his wife and daughters in Tiflis and Poltava, he soon found himself on the road again. During the rebuilding of the theatre in September he was obliged to join Komissarzhevskaya's company on tour in Lithuania and western Russia in order to rehearse the opening productions for the new season.[21] During his absence the Petersburg press made the most of Arbatov's threatened resignation from Komissarzhevskaya's company, attributing it to 'the decadent elements which she was introducing into the company'.[22] In fact, Arbatov left at Komissarzhevskaya's insistence just before the beginning of the season, by which time the publicity the incident had received was a clear indication of the treatment Meyerhold could expect from the great majority of the Petersburg critics.

Vera Komissarzhevskaya's Dramatic Theatre opened on 10 November 1906 with Meyerhold's production of *Hedda Gabler*, the actress herself playing Hedda. The precise description given by Peter Yartsev, the theatre's newly appointed literary manager, is worth quoting in full:

The theatre has chosen to use a single backdrop as a setting, either representational or simply decorative. The costumes, instead of being naturalistically authentic, are intended to harmonize as colour-masses with the background and present a synthesis of the style of the period and society in question, the subjective view of the designer, and the externally simplified representation of the character's inner nature. For instance, . . . the costume of Tesman corresponds to no definite fashion; although it is somewhat reminiscent of the 1820s, one is reminded equally of the present day. But in giving Tesman a loose jacket with sloping shoulders, an exaggeratedly wide tie, and broad trousers tapering sharply towards the bottoms, the designer, Vassily Milioti, has sought to express the essence of 'Tesmanism', and this has been stressed by the director in the way Tesman is made to move and in the position he occupies in the general composition. To harmonise with the colours of Sapunov's painted back-cloth, Milioti has dressed Tesman in dull grey. The walls, the portières and the sky (seen through a vast ivy-fringed window) are all light blue; the tapestry which covers an entire wall and the openwork screens on either side of the stage are painted in pale gold autumnal tints. The colours of the costumes harmonise amongst themselves and with the background: green (Hedda), brown (Loevborg), pale pink (Thea), dark grey (Brack). The table in the centre, the pouffes and the long narrow divan standing against the wall under the tapestry are all covered in light blue fabric flecked with gold to give it the appearance of brocade. A huge arm-chair stage-left is covered entirely in white fur, the same fur being used to cover part of the divan; a white grand piano projects from behind the screen stage-right and has the same blue and gold fabric hanging from it.

Behind the left-hand screen is glimpsed the silhouette of a huge green vase encircled with ivy and standing on a pedestal also covered with blue and gold fabric. Behind it is supposed to stand the stove for the scene between Hedda and Tesman when Hedda burns Loevborg's manuscript. The stove is suggested by a reddish glow which appears at the appropriate moments.

In front of the divan stands a low square table with a drawer in which Hedda hides the manuscript. On it Loevborg and Brack lay their hats, and on it stands the green box containing the pistols when it is not on the big table.

In small white and green vases on the piano and the table and in the large vase on the pedestal there are flowers, mostly white chrysanthemums. More chrysanthemums rest in the folds of the fur on the back of the armchair. The floor is covered with dark grey cloth, with a fine tracery in blue and gold. The sky is painted on a separate drop behind the cut-out window; there is a day sky, and a night sky with coldly glittering stars (for Act Four).

6. Set design by Nikolai Sapunov for Hedda Gabler.

The stage comprises a broad, shallow strip, 33 feet wide and 12 feet deep, higher than the usual stage level and as close as possible to the footlights. The lighting is from footlights and overhead battens.

This strange room, if indeed it is a room, resembles least of all the old-fashioned villa of [Minister Falk's widow]. What is the significance of this setting which gives the impression of a vast, cold blue, receding expanse, but which actually looks like nothing whatsoever? Why are both sides (where there should be doors – or nothing, if the room is supposed to continue offstage) hung with gold net curtains where the actors make their exits and their entrances? Is life really like this? Is this what Ibsen wrote?

Life is not like this, and it is not what Ibsen wrote. *Hedda Gabler* on the stage of the Dramatic Theatre is *stylised*. Its aim is to reveal Ibsen's play to the spectator by employing unfamiliar new means of scenic presentation, to create an impression (but only an *impression*) of a vast, cold blue, receding expanse. Hedda is visualised in cool blue tones against a golden autumnal background. Instead of autumn being depicted outside the window where the blue sky is seen, it is suggested by the pale golden tints in the tapestry, the upholstery and the curtains. The theatre is attempting to give primitive, purified expression to what it senses behind Ibsen's play: a cold, regal, autumnal Hedda.

Precisely the same aims are adopted in the actual production of the play, in the work of the director with the actors. Rejecting authenticity, the customary 'lifelikeness', the theatre seeks to submit the spectator to its own inspiration by adopting a barely mobile, stylised method of production with a minimum of mime and gesture, with the emotions concealed and manifested externally only by a brief lighting of the eyes or a flickering smile.

The wide stage, its width emphasised by its shallowness, is particularly suited to widely spaced groupings and the director takes full advantage of this by making two characters converse from opposite sides of the stage (the opening of the scene between Hedda and Loevborg in Act Three), by seating Hedda and Loevborg wide apart on the divan in Act Two. Sometimes (particularly in the latter instance) there may seem to be little justification in this, but it arises from the director's attempt to create an overall impression of cold majesty. The huge armchair covered with white fur is meant as a kind of throne for Hedda; she plays the majority of her scenes either on it or near it. The spectator is intended to associate Hedda with her throne and carry away this combined impression in his memory.

Brack is associated with the pedestal bearing the large vase. He sits by it with one leg crossed over the other and clasps his hands round his knee, keeping his eyes fixed on Hedda throughout their keen sparkling battle of wits. He reminds one of a faun. Admittedly, Brack moves about the stage and occupies other positions (as do Hedda and the other characters) but it is the pose of a faun by the pedestal which one associates with him – just as one associates the throne with Hedda.

The table serves as a pedestal for the motionless figures which the theatre seeks to imprint on the spectator's memory. When Loevborg produces the manuscript in Act Two he is standing upstage by the portière near Hedda and Tesman. Brack is by the curtain stage left; the centre of the stage (the table) is empty.

In order to look through the bulky manuscript more comfortably, Loevborg comes forward to rest it on the table and after the words 'This is my real book', he lapses into a thoughtful silence, straightening up and placing his hand on the open manuscript. After a few seconds' pause he starts to turn over the pages, explaining his work to Tesman,

who has now joined him. But in those motionless few seconds Loevborg
and the manuscript have impressed themselves on the spectator and he
has an uneasy presentiment of the words' significance, of what Loevborg is really like, what links him with the manuscript, and what
bearing it has on the tragedy of Hedda.

The first scene between Loevborg and Hedda also takes place at the
table. Throughout the entire scene they sit side by side, tense and
motionless, looking straight ahead. Their quiet, disquieting words fall
rhythmically from lips which seem dry and cold. Before them stand
two glasses and a flame burns beneath the punch bowl (Ibsen stipulates
Norwegian 'cold punch'). Not once throughout the entire long scene
do they alter the direction of their gaze or their pose. Only on the line
'Then you too have a thirst for life!' does Loevborg make a violent
motion towards Hedda, and at this point the scene comes to an abrupt
conclusion.

Realistically speaking, it is inconceivable that Hedda and Loevborg
should play the scene in this manner, that any two real living people
should ever converse like this. The spectator hears the lines as though
they were being addressed directly at him; before him the whole time
he sees the faces of Hedda and Loevborg, observes the slightest change
of expression; behind the monotonous dialogue he senses the concealed
inner dialogue of presentiments and emotions which are incapable of
expression in mere words. The spectator may forget the actual
words exchanged by Hedda and Loevborg, but he cannot possibly
forget the overall impression which the scene creates.[23]

As the critic Alexander Kugel was quick to observe, Meyerhold's
Hedda Gabler owed a great deal to the ideas of Georg Fuchs.[24] Despite the
retention of footlights the broad, shallow stage backed by a decorative
panel seemed an obvious attempt to realise Fuchs' conception of the 'relief
stage'. Furthermore, as we can see from Yartsev's account, Meyerhold
again demonstrated the extent to which, like Fuchs, he had assimilated
the traditions of the Japanese. The form and colour of every visual
element in the production were determined by Meyerhold's subjective
vision of Hedda, with no purely lifelike detail permitted to mar the stage
tableau. Within the limits of this scheme each costume was designed to
synthesise the essence of the type, regardless of inconsistencies in style or
period. Fundamentally speaking, this was the same approach to costume
as that advocated by Fuchs in *The Stage of the Future*, where he cites the
example of the Japanese and draws an analogy between them and the
style of various contemporary painters, notably Anselm Feuerbach, in

whose pictures '. . . the costumes are neither antique nor modern', but 'an extension and a synthesis of our present-day fashions in clothing for the sake of heightened expressiveness'.[25]

Finally, the 'barely mobile, stylised method of production with a minimum of mime and gesture and with the emotions concealed, manifested externally only by a brief lighting of the eyes or the flicker of a smile' was surely influenced by the decorum of eastern stylisation allied to the ideals propagated by Maeterlinck and the French symbolists.

Hedda Gabler was received coldly by the public and even those few critics who admired the elegant beauty of the décor considered that it was hopelessly at odds with Ibsen's intentions. They complained that Sapunov's* sumptuous autumnal vision obscured the point of all Hedda's despairing efforts to escape the trap of the narrow conventions and tawdry bad taste of provincial society. Their objections were directed less against stylisation as such than against what was stylised in this instance: the theme should have been not Hedda's bay mare and liveried footman but George's slippers and Aunt Julie's new hat.[26]

The criticism seems incontestable: *Hedda Gabler* was a classic example of a production subordinated to the director's ruling obsession. In his recent probing analysis of him, the Soviet critic Alexander Matskin refers to 'the tragedy of Meyerhold's one-sidedness' whereby 'at any given moment he had a single ruling idea which forced his more durable preoccupations to retreat into the background'.[27] In this particular instance Matskin suggests that Meyerhold felt overwhelmed by the weight of genius and erudition he had encountered amongst the Petersburg symbolists, and tried to compensate by emphasising the formal aspects of his work, the one area in which he felt truly confident. There may well be some truth in this; certainly the symbolist philosophical debates at this time were of an awesome complexity and abstruseness. But equally Meyerhold's interpretation of *Hedda Gabler* (to say nothing of his subsequent productions with Komissarzhevskaya) was conceived in part at least as a polemic against stage naturalism *and* the whole materialist philosophy from which it sprang. In this aim, certainly, Meyerhold was at one with the symbolists. Konstantin Rudnitsky is making this point when he quotes the philosopher Nikolai Berdyaev:

The vital core of symbolism [is found] in the evocation of the delicate varied nuances of the human soul, in the protest against bourgeois

---

* Sapunov, Sudeikin, and Denisov all worked with Meyerhold in Petersburg after the closure of the Theatre-Studio.

vulgarity and against the total absence of beauty from life. Symbolism justifies itself with an aesthetic which totally rejects the possibility of art as the reflection of reality. An idealistic world-view must recognise the *independent meaning of beauty* and of artistic creativity in the life of mankind. *Beauty is the ideal goal of existence*; it elevates and ennobles man. . . . In bourgeois society and its art there is too little beauty, and in opposing it we must introduce into human existence as much beauty as we can: beauty in human thought, in art, in our whole way of life. To earlier forms of protest is now joined aesthetic protest against bourgeois society.[28]

The doctrine was hardly new: it had been expounded at least twenty years earlier by Mallarmé and the French symbolists; but nobody, with the arguable exception of Craig, had succeeded in bringing it to fruition in the theatre before Meyerhold. It is interesting to note that within a few weeks of Meyerhold's *Hedda Gabler* there were two other major symbolist productions of Ibsen elsewhere in Europe: Reinhardt's *Ghosts* in Berlin (with designs by Edvard Munch), and Craig's *Rosmersholm* with Duse's company in Florence.[29]

III

Meyerhold's production of Maeterlinck's *Sister Beatrice* on 22 November was an even more programmatic statement of symbolist ideas, intended as it was to soothe the audience with a vision of harmony and to induce participation in a corporate mystical experience akin to the medieval miracle play.[30] It proved to be the one generally acknowledged success which Meyerhold enjoyed with Komissarzhevskaya, and for her in the role of Beatrice her sole personal triumph with him.

Maeterlinck's 'petit jeu de scène' tells in simple terms the story of a nun, Beatrice, who elopes from a convent with a knight. A statue of the Virgin comes to life and takes the place of Beatrice in the convent so that her absence is never discovered. After many years during which she sinks to the depths of depravity Beatrice returns in search of retribution. But the Virgin returns to her pedestal and Beatrice dies hallowed by the sisters for her life of selfless devotion.

Maeterlinck sets the play in fourteenth-century Louvain, but again Meyerhold applied the principle of stylisation, seeking to imbue the legend with universality by creating a synthesis based on the style of Pre-Raphaelite and early Renaissance painters.[31] The future director, Alexander Tairov, at that time a member of the company, recalls how

Meyerhold modelled poses and complete groupings on reproductions of the works of Memling, Botticelli, and other masters.[32] In the final act the tableau of the sisters holding the dying Beatrice was a conscious evocation of the traditional descent from the cross.

Dialogue and movement were treated in the style first developed by Meyerhold to render Maeterlinck's 'static tragedy', *The Death of Tintagiles*. 'The melodious style of delivery and movements in slow motion

7. *The last act of* Sister Beatrice *with Komissarzhevskaya as Beatrice.*

were designed to preserve the implicitness of expression, and each phrase was barely more than a whisper, the manifestation of an inner tragic experience.'[33]

Meyerhold succeeded in disciplining his actors' movements by the simple expedient of confining them to a strip of the stage in front of the proscenium arch no more than seven feet in depth. Yevgeny Znosko-Borovsky describes the chorus of nuns:

All dressed as one, with completely identical gestures, with slow restrained movements and following one another precisely, they moved the whole time in profile in order to maintain the repose of a bas-relief; they passed before you like a wonderful design on the grey stone of an ancient cathedral . . . Here was a crowd, a mass in which no individual led a separate life or constituted a separate character which might disrupt the essential idea and impression of the mass. Here was a unity which by its unity, by the rhythm of all its movements, poses and gestures, produced a far deeper impression than a naturalistic crowd split up into separate elements.[34]

The décor by Sergei Sudeikin was executed in contrasting tones of blue, green, and grey. A simple 'gothic' wall stood almost on top of the footlights, a neutral background designed to throw the actors' figures into plastic relief. 'It provides only an accompaniment,' wrote Nikolai Yevreinov; [Sudeikin's] art desires at all costs to remain neutral and quiet – at most a gentle echo of the dialogue.'[35] Although footlights were used it was contrary to Meyerhold's own wishes; financial considerations frustrated his original intention to link the forestage with the auditorium by a flight of polished wooden steps and thereby make the actors stand farther from the flat background.[36] Once again the resemblance to Georg Fuchs' relief stage was unmistakable.

Meyerhold's production drew grudging praise from the previously hostile critics, but the acting (with the exception of Komissarzhevskaya) was condemned as lifeless and uneven. Many blamed Meyerhold's system which, they maintained, reduced the artist to a mere puppet. But probably Peter Yartsev came as close as anybody to the truth when he wrote:

[Komissarzhevskaya's] theatre is seeking to express technically forms which the theatre of the future will have to fill out with content. That is why the new theatre concentrates exclusively on the visual side (settings, costumes, grouping, movements). As yet in the new theatre there is not and cannot be a new actor.[37]

It was the same fault as Stanislavsky had observed at the Theatre-Studio,* and it helps to explain why Meyerhold tended to overstress the inanimate aspects of his productions for all the years until it became possible for him to school actors in his own system and eventually create his own company with them. It was not until his production of *The Magnanimous Cuckold* in 1922 that this ambition was fully realised.

* See p. 50 above.

IV

When Meyerhold was invited in December 1905 to become the artistic director of the proposed 'Torches Theatre', Georgy Chulkov commissioned Alexander Blok to write a play on the theme of his poem *The Fairground Booth* (1905)* which the new company would perform. Although the theatre failed to materialise, Blok completed *The Fairground Booth* within the space of a few days in January 1906 and Chulkov published it in the first number of his journal (also called *Torches*) in April 1906. When Komissarzhevskaya's theatre opened in the autumn it was decided to stage Blok's play and it had its first performance on 30 December 1906 in a double bill with Maeterlinck's *The Miracle of St Antony*.

Like the poem, the play incorporated themes, figures, and images that had disturbed his lyrics intermittently for some years. In the first of the play's 'lyric scenes', an assembly of 'Mystics' awaits the arrival of Death in the person of a beautiful lady. Pierrot, 'in a white smock, dreamy, distraught, pale, with no moustache or eyebrows, like all Pierrots', protests that she is his sweetheart Columbine. She appears, silent and all in white; Pierrot despairs and is on the point of conceding the allegory to the Mystics, when Columbine speaks to reassure him. But at once Harlequin, 'eternally youthful, agile and handsome', his costume decked with silver bells, comes to abduct her, leaving Pierrot and the Mystics confounded. The scene changes quickly to a ball with masked couples gliding back and forth. In the centre sits Pierrot, 'on the bench where Venus and Tannhäuser usually embrace'. He tells how Harlequin carried off Columbine in a sleigh, only for her to turn into a lifeless cardboard doll. Then Pierrot and Harlequin roamed the snow-covered streets together, singing and dancing to console themselves. There appear in turn three pairs of masked lovers. The first pair, in pink and blue, imagine themselves beneath the lofty dome of some church: a vision of sacred love menaced by a dark figure, the man's double, beckoning from behind a column. Dancing figures disclose the second couple, the embodiment of violent passion in red and black; they leave, again pursued by a third, 'a flickering tongue of black flame'. Finally we see courtly love: the knight in cardboard visor and a huge wooden sword, the lady echoing his portentous phrases. Their dignity is rudely shattered by a clown who runs up and pokes out his tongue at the Knight. He strikes him on the head with his sword; the clown collapses over the footlights crying 'Help, I'm bleeding cranberry juice!' and then jumps up and leaves. A

* In Russian '*Balaganchik*'. Sometimes translated as 'the puppet show' or 'farce'.

leaping, jostling torchlight procession of masks makes its entrance.
Harlequin steps from the crowd to greet the world in the springtime:

> Here nobody dares to admit
> That spring is abroad in the air!
> Here nobody knows how to love;
> They all live beset by sad dreams.
> Greetings world! You're with me again!
> So long your soul has been near to me!
> And now once more I will breath your spring
> Through your window of gold!

And he leaps through the window. But the view is only painted on paper,
and he falls headlong through the hole.

Death reappears, a scythe over her back, and all the masks freeze in
terror. But Pierrot recognises her again as his Columbine: the scythe
fades in the morning light and colour floods her cheeks. They are about to
embrace when 'The Author', who throughout has kept appearing to
protest at the misrepresentation of his text, pokes his head between them
to acclaim the happy ending of his simple tale. As he is joining their
hands all the scenery is abruptly whisked aloft and Columbine and
all the masks disappear. The Author withdraws in hurried confusion,
leaving the baffled Pierrot to face the audience alone and play a mournful
tune on his pipe 'about his pale face, his hard life, and his sweetheart
Columbine'.[38]

At the start of his career as a poet Blok was strongly influenced by the
mystical philosophy of Vladimir Solovyov and the like-minded literary
group which included Bely, Bryusov, Balmont, Zinaida Gippius, and
Merezhkovsky. But his work became coloured with a scepticism entirely
inconsistent with their mystical idealism. As early as 1902 in his first
major work, the poetic cycle *On the Beautiful Lady*, Blok had invoked the
traditional figures of Pierrot, Harlequin, and Columbine to convey his
intermittent doubts in the constancy of human relations and even the
coherence of personality itself.[39] The bold sceptic Harlequin and the
childlike, innocent Pierrot came to represent the two conflicting
aspects of the poet's own character, whilst Columbine was both the
'beautiful lady', the ideal of perfect womanhood venerated by the Russian
symbolists, and the very counterfeit of beauty, the deception inherent in
all outward appearances. There is often present in Blok's poems an onlooker (in the poem *Balaganchik*: two children) who registers the transformation of the scene; the situation is virtually dramatic, with audience

and players enacting the pretence of life itself. Now in *The Fairground Booth* he exploited the theatre's irony to give his dualistic vision even greater power. Much of the invention was his own, but in Meyerhold he found an interpreter with the power and insight to extend it still further. The production is described by Meyerhold:

> The entire stage is hung at the sides and rear with blue drapes; this expanse of blue serves as a background as well as reflecting the colour of the settings in the little booth erected on the stage. This booth has its

8. The Fairground Booth (1906). *Nikolai Sapunov's setting for the opening scene with Pierrot and the Mystics.*

> own stage, curtain, prompter's box, and proscenium opening. Instead of being masked with the conventional border, the flies, together with all the ropes and wires, are visible to the audience. When the entire set in the booth is hauled aloft, the audience in the actual theatre sees the whole process. In front of the booth, the stage area adjacent to the footlights is left free. It is here that the 'Author' appears to serve as an intermediary between the public and the events enacted within the booth. The action begins at a signal on the big drum; the music starts and the audience sees the prompter crawl into his box and light a candle. The curtain of the booth rises to reveal a box-set with doors stage-right and centre, and a window stage-left. . . . There is a long table covered with a black cloth reaching to the floor and parallel to the

footlights. Behind the table sit the 'Mystics', the top halves of their bodies visible to the audience. Frightened by some rejoinder they duck their heads, and suddenly all that remains at the table is a row of torsos minus heads and hands. It transpires that the figures are cut out of cardboard with frock-coats, shirt-fronts, collars and cuffs drawn on with soot and chalk. The actors' hands are thrust through openings in the cardboard torsos and their heads simply rest on the cardboard collars. . . . Harlequin makes his first entrance from under the Mystics' table. When the Author runs on to the forestage his tirade is terminated by someone hidden in the wings pulling him off by his coat-tails; it turns out that he is tethered with a rope to prevent him from interrupting the solemn course of events onstage. In Scene Two, 'the dejected Pierrot sits in the middle of the stage on a bench'; behind him is a statue of Eros on a pedestal. When Pierrot finishes his long soliloquy, the bench, the statue and the entire set are whisked aloft, and a traditional colonnaded hall is lowered in their place. When the masked figures appear with cries of 'torches!' the hands of the stage-hands appear from both wings holding flaming Bengal lights on iron rods. As Andrei Bely remarked, 'All the characters are restricted to their own typical gestures; Pierrot, for instance, always sighs and flaps his arms in the same way.'[40]

The part of Pierrot was played by Meyerhold himself; Sergei Auslender describes his portrayal: '. . . he is nothing like those familiar, falsely sugary, whining Pierrots. Everything about him is sharply angular; in a hushed voice he whispers words of strange sadness; somehow he contrives to be caustic, heart-rending, gentle: all these things, yet at the same time impudent. . . .'[41]

Valentina Vergina, who played the second masked lady in the ball scene, writes:

On the stage direction 'Pierrot awakes from his reverie and brightens up' [in Scene One], Meyerhold made an absurd wave with both his sleeves, and in this movement was expressed the suddenly dawning hope of the clown. Further waves of his sleeves conveyed various different things. These stylised gestures were inspired by the musical conception of the characterisation; they were eloquent because, I repeat, they were prompted by the inner rhythm of the role. The gestures always followed the words, complementing them as though bringing a song to its conclusion, saying without words something understood only by Pierrot himself . . . It was as though he was listening to a song being sung by his heart of its own free will. He wore a strange expression, gazing intently into his own soul.[42]*

In the closing scene:

. . . the curtain fell behind Pierrot-Meyerhold and he was left face to face with the audience. He stood staring at them, and it was as though Pierrot was looking into the eyes of every single person. There was

9. *Meyerhold as Pierrot (Nikolai Ulyanov, 1906).*

something irresistible in his gaze. . . . Then Pierrot looked away, took his pipe from his pocket and began to play the tune of a rejected and unappreciated heart. That moment was the most powerful in his whole

* In February 1910, Meyerhold danced the role of Pierrot in the first production of Mikhail Fokine's ballet *Carnival* (to Schumann's music) at a ball organised by the Petersburg journal *Satiricon*. Columbine was danced by Karsavina and Florestan by Nizhinsky. Fokine writes: 'At the first two rehearsals, Meyerhold was like a man from another world: his gestures were out of time with the music, and frequently he misjudged his entrances and exits. But by the third rehearsal our new mime had blossomed forth, and on the night he gave a marvellous portrayal of the sorrowful dreamer, Pierrot.' (M. Fokine, *Protiv techenia*, Leningrad–Moscow, 1962, pp. 219–20). It was Meyerhold's only performance as a dancer.

performance. Behind his lowered eyelids one sensed a gaze, stern and full of reproach.[43]

Rudnitsky senses a deep personal significance in the role: '. . . Meyerhold, who only twice in life (the other time was as Treplev in *The Seagull*) expressed his true self on stage and found lyrical expression through a character, saw and upheld in this vulnerability of Pierrot the ultimate justification for the artist's calling. The theme of Pierrot was interpreted as the theme of the bitter yet splendid isolation of poetry, of art which is doomed to misunderstanding.'[44]*

The opening night and many subsequent performances provoked memorable scenes in the theatre. Sixteen years later Sergei Auslender recalled:

> The auditorium was in an uproar as though it were a real battle. Solid, respectable citizens were ready to come to blows; whistles and roars of anger alternated with piercing howls conveying a mixture of fervour, defiance, anger and despair: 'Blok – Sapunov – Kuzmin – M-e-y-e-r-h-o-l-d, Br-a-v-o-o-o' . . . And there before all the commotion, radiant like some splendid monument, in his severe black frock-coat and holding a bunch of white lilies, stood Alexander Alexandrovich Blok, his deep blue eyes reflecting both sadness and wry amusement. And at his side the white Pierrot ducked and recoiled as though devoid of any bones, disembodied like a spectre, flapping the long sleeves of his loose smock.[45]

Blok clearly revelled in the scandal; three weeks after the opening he wrote to a friend: '. . . at this very moment *The Fairground Booth* is being given its fifth performance at Komissarzhevskaya's theatre, and – I would say – successfully since at the first and second performances I took many curtain-calls and they heartily whistled and catcalled at me. . . .'[46] For his part, Meyerhold regarded the violent demonstrations as conclusive proof of the production's 'true theatricality'.[47] Almost to a man, the critics were nonplussed by *The Fairground Booth* and dismissed it as a joke in very poor taste. Their response is fairly represented by 'Objective', writing in the Petersburg *Theatre Review*: 'Truly what took place at Vera Komissarzhevskaya's theatre on the 30 December must be regarded as an insult, not only to the theatre, but also to literature, poetry, and dramatic writing; it lies beyond the pale no less of art than of common sense.'[48]

Many of Blok's fellow symbolists shared this indignation. Justifiably enough, they saw themselves lampooned in the figures of the Mystics, though equally in a preliminary draft of the play Blok draws attention to their resemblance to the death-fixated characters in the works of

* Cf. pp. 89, 246.

Materlinck and Verhaeren.[49] One does not exclude the other: Blok is clearly ridiculing all idealists who seek to impose a reassuring design on empirical confusion. The production drove a rift between Blok and his bosom companion, Andrei Bely. Bely called it a betrayal of symbolism and 'a bitter mockery of Blok's own past'. He took particular exception to the blasphemy implicit in the depiction of the 'beautiful lady' Columbine.[50] As Blok himself later said, there was essentially nothing new in what he was saying in *The Fairground Booth*; the difference was that he was saying it in public rather than in the personal isolation of the lyric.[51] What had previously been the occasional voicing of self-doubt was now an outright rejection of transcendental reality, a sardonic picture of a spiritually exhausted world devoid of constant values. To no small degree Blok's innate pessimism was greatly exacerbated by the sense of dislocation experienced generally by the Russian intelligentsia in the aftermath of 1905. *The Fairground Booth* in Meyerhold's production captured this mood with acute poetic accuracy, and therein lies the main reason for the violently opposed responses to it. For young and disenchanted radicals it became a rallying point, some going so far as to interpret Columbine as a symbol for the long-awaited, but never-to-appear, Russian constitution.[52] Konstantin Rudnitsky draws attention to the near coincidence of the first production of *The Fairground Booth* and the completion by Picasso of his first great Cubist painting *Les Demoiselles d'Avignon*.[53] The similarity lies in the complete subordination of each work's form to the artist's perception of reality, asserting his primacy as an observer and interpreter in a world totally unamenable to the traditional solutions of faith or logic. Similarly, dramatic parallels readily suggest themselves: in the ten years preceding *The Fairground Booth* – but unknown to Blok – Jarry, Wedekind, Strindberg (notably in *A Dream Play*) had all sought to transform their personal experiences into a theatrical event – like Blok, inviting their audience to share their confusion and identify it with their own. As Roger Shattuck says in *The Banquet Years*: '. . . there are subjects about which one cannot be clear without fraud. Every emotion and conviction has its reverse side, and ambiguity can stand for a profound frankness, an acknowledgment of the essential ambivalence of truth and experience, of life itself.'[54] The essential importance of *The Fairground Booth* was that it proved the means by which Blok and Meyerhold were able to articulate this fundamental truth and in so doing give their art a crucial new direction away from the resigned immobility of Symbolism.

Meyerhold's production of *The Fairground Booth* followed Blok's stage directions almost to the letter: the disappearing Mystics, the Author's intrusions, the clown bleeding cranberry juice, Harlequin's leap through the paper flat, the disappearing settings were all conceived by Blok before his collaboration with Meyerhold, and appear in the first published edition in April 1906. The production introduced one crucial refinement: whereas Blok prescribes 'a normal theatrical room with three walls, a window and a door', Meyerhold and his designer Nikolai Sapunov devised the little show-booth with the prompter and all the scenery exposed, thereby lending a further dimension to the play's irony.

As the descriptions of Meyerhold as Pierrot suggest, the style of acting was far removed from the *tableaux vivants* of his earlier productions. The abrupt changes of mood, the sudden switches of personality, the deliberate disruption of illusion, the asides to the audience, all demanded a mental and physical dexterity, an ability to improvise, a capacity for acting not only the part but also one's attitude to it. These devices were all waiting to be rediscovered in the tradition of the popular theatre stretching back to the *commedia dell'arte* and beyond. It was this theatre, the theatre of masks and improvisation, which the experience of *The Fairground Booth* led Meyerhold to explore. It came to furnish the basis for his entire style, a style which in a word can be called 'grotesque'. In 1912, in his article '*Balagan*', Meyerhold defined his conception of the grotesque:

> It is the style which reveals the most wonderful horizons to the creative artist. 'I', my personal attitude to life, precedes all else. . . .
>   The grotesque does not recognise the *purely* debased or the *purely* exalted. The grotesque mixes opposites, consciously creating harsh incongruity, *playing entirely on its own originality*. . . . The grotesque deepens life's outward appearance to the point where it ceases to appear merely natural. . . . The basis of the grotesque is the artist's constant desire to switch the spectator from the plane he has just reached to another which is totally unforeseen.[55]

But for him the grotesque was no mere stylistic device; it sprang from a recognition of the irrational and an acceptance of it on its own terms. His conviction was that 'Beneath what we see of life there are vast un-fathomed depths. In its search for the supernatural, the grotesque synthesises opposites, creates a picture of the incredible, and encourages the spectator to try to solve the riddle of the inscrutable.'[56] Alexander Matskin writes: 'Once he had met Blok, it became clear that for Meyer-hold the grotesque was not merely *a means of expression*, a way of heighten-ing colours, it was no less than the *content* of that reality, that dislocated world in which he found himself and which formed the subject of his art.'[57]

There were times in the Soviet period when Meyerhold was inclined to play down his affinity with Blok,[58] and certainly their association after 1906 was far from one of unbroken harmony. Nevertheless, *The Fairground Booth* remained a crucial experience for Meyerhold and one which, as we shall see, continued to reverberate through his work long after 1917.

V

Meyerhold's final production of the season on 22 February 1907 was the first performance of *The Life of a Man* by Leonid Andreev. In five episodic scenes the play traces the course of a man's life from the moment of birth through poverty, love, success and disaster to death; the figures involved are allegorical, with little or no characterisation and are called 'The Man', 'The Wife', 'The Neighbours', etc. A prologue is spoken by 'Someone in grey, called He', who then remains on stage throughout, invisible to the protagonists, commenting occasionally on the action, and holding a burning candle to symbolise the gradual ebb of the Man's life and his ultimate return to oblivion.

Although impressionistic rather than naturalistic, Andreev's stage directions are detailed and explicit. But as with *Hedda Gabler* Meyerhold chose once more to exercise his creative autonomy. He devised the settings himself, employing a designer merely as an executant; scenic space was handled with an unprecedented freedom, which demonstrated that the stylised theatre was no longer a slave to painting and no longer confined to the shallow relief-stage. The key to the entire production was light, for the first time exploited by Meyerhold for its sculptural power. The effects achieved are clear from his own account:

> I produced this play *without sets* as they are generally understood. The entire stage was hung with drapes, but not as in *The Fairground Booth* where the drapes were hung in the places usually occupied by scenery. . . . Here the drapes were hung on the walls of the theatre itself and against the back wall of the stage where 'distant views' are normally depicted. We removed all footlights, borders and battens in order to achieve a 'grey, smoky, monochrome expanse. Grey walls, grey ceilings, grey floor.' 'From an unseen source issues a weak, even light which is just as grey, monotonous, monochrome and ghostly, casting no hard shadows, no brilliant spots of light.' [The quotations are from Andreev's stage directions.] In this light the Prologue is read. Then the curtain parts to reveal a deep, gloomy expanse in which everything

stands motionless. After about three seconds the spectator begins to
make out the shapes of furniture in one corner of the stage. 'Dimly
visible are the grey forms of old women huddled together like a group
of grey mice.' They are sitting on a big, old-fashioned divan flanked by
two armchairs. Behind the divan is a screen, in front of it a lamp. The
old women's silhouettes are lit only by the light falling from this lamp.
The effect is the same in every scene; a section of the stage is seen in a
pool of light from a single source, which is sufficient to illuminate only
the furniture and the characters immediately adjacent to it. By
enveloping the stage in grey shadow, using a single light-source to
illuminate one area of it (the lamp behind the divan and the lamp over
the round table in Scene One, the chandelier in the ball scene, the
lamps above the tables in the drunk scene),* we managed to create the
impression of actual walls which were invisible because the light did
not reach them. On a stage free from conventional settings, furniture
and other properties assume a fresh significance; the nature and
atmosphere of a room is determined by them alone. It becomes
necessary to use properties of clearly exaggerated dimensions. And
always very little furniture; a single typical object takes the place of
a host of less typical ones. The spectator is forced to take note of the
unusual contour of a divan, a grandiose column, a gilded armchair, a
bookcase extending across the entire stage, a ponderous sideboard;
given all these separate parts, the imagination fills in the rest. Naturally,
the characters' features had to be modelled as precisely as sculpture,
with make-up sharply accentuated; the actors were obliged to ac-
centuate the figures of the characters they were playing in the same way
as Leonardo da Vinci or Goya.[59]

It is not certain when Meyerhold first encountered Adolphe Appia's
theories on stage lighting, only that when he came to stage *Tristan and
Isolde* in 1909 he was familiar with Appia's book *Die Musik und die
Inscenierung*. In this revolutionary work published in 1899 Appia, at that
time a little-known Swiss artist, rejected traditional painted flats as
incompatible with the three dimensions of scenic space and the actor's
body; instead he advocated, in admirably detailed and practicable terms, a
setting conceived plastically throughout, composed on varying levels to
overcome the unnatural flatness of the stage floor and unified by the
sculptural power of chiaroscuro. As Lee Simonson writes:

The light and shade of Rembrandt, Piranesi, Daumier, and Meryon
was finally brought into the theatre as an interpretative medium, not

* The actual source of light was a spotlight in the flies.

10. *The ball scene in* The Life of a Man.

splashed on a back-drop, as romantic scene-painters had used it, but as an ambient medium actually filling space and possessing actual volume; it was an impalpable bond which fused the actor, whenever and however he moved, with everything around him. The plastic unity of the stage picture was made continuous.[60]

Appia's conception of stage lighting was entirely without precedent in the theatre and attracted little attention before 1912, when his work was first seen on the stage of Jaques-Dalcroze's School of Eurhythmics at Hellerau.[61] Reading Meyerhold's description of *The Life of a Man* it is difficult to believe that he had no knowledge of Appia's theories in 1907.*

Although rehearsed for only twelve days, *The Life of a Man* was a great popular success and played to full houses for the last two weeks of the season; Fyodor Komissarzhevsky, the Head of Design at his sister's theatre, described the production as 'the most fully integrated during the first two seasons at Ofitserskaya Street'.[62] Andreev himself preferred Meyerhold's version to Stanislavsky's at the Moscow Art Theatre soon afterwards, which he said had a refinement akin to Beardsley rather than the Goya-like harshness that he had in mind.[63] Yet so shallow and pretentious does the text seem today, and so far did Meyerhold diverge from Andreev's stage directions,[64] that one feels the production's success must have been due to its visual impact rather than to the intrinsic worth of the play itself.

In his essay *On the History and Technique of the Theatre* (written in 1906–1907),[65] in which he describes the origins and development of the stylised theatre, Meyerhold stresses again and again the role of the spectator:

> In the theatre the spectator's imagination is able to supply that which is left unsaid. It is this mystery and the desire to solve it which draw so many people to the theatre. . . . Bryusov indicates the active role of the spectator in the theatre: '. . . *The stage must supply as much as is necessary to help the spectator picture as easily as possible in his imagination the setting demanded by the plot of the play.*' Ultimately, the stylistic method presupposes the existence of a fourth *creator* in addition to the author, the director and the actor – namely, the spectator. The stylised theatre produces a play in such a way that the spectator is compelled to employ his imagination *creatively* in order to *fill in* the details intimated by the action on the stage.

* For further indication of Meyerhold's debt to Appia see the account of *Tristan and Isolde* (pp. 93–95 below).

This principle is the very foundation of stylisation; it was demonstrated by all Meyerhold's productions for Komissarzhevskaya, but by none so clearly as *The Life of a Man*. It was precisely because the spectator was shown so little that he saw so much, superimposing his own imagined or remembered experiences on the events enacted before him. In this way the dialogue and characters assumed a significance and a profundity which overcame their intrinsic banality. Time and again in the Soviet period Meyerhold exploited this associative power of the spectator's imagination to transform mediocre literature into the most telling theatre.

VI

By the autumn of 1907 Meyerhold's position with Komissarzhevskaya had deteriorated to the point where his impending resignation was being openly discussed in the press. In particular, Meyerhold resented the fact that the company had gone on tour in the summer with a number of their old productions. For her part, Komissarzhevskaya was bitterly disappointed at the rejection of their new work by the Moscow critics, who had ridiculed even her performance in *Sister Beatrice*.

But Meyerhold was far too single-minded to allow the dwindling confidence within the company to curb his experimental zeal. Encouraged by his successes with Blok and Andreev, Meyerhold wanted to explore still further the flexibility of the stage area. He proposed staging Fyodor Sologub's new play *The Gift of the Wise Bees* 'in the round' by building a stage in the centre of the auditorium and seating part of the audience on the permanent stage.[66] Like so many later innovators in this field he was foiled by local theatre regulations, and it was left to Nikolai Okhlopkov a quarter of a century later at the Realistic Theatre in Moscow to present the first modern productions on a stage completely surrounded by the audience.

Even so, Meyerhold's first production in the autumn was hardly less bold – not only in conception but in subject matter too. In April he had gone to Berlin with Fyodor Komissarzhevsky and whilst there they had visited Max Reinhardt's experimental theatre, the Berliner Kammerspiele. Meyerhold was reserved in his opinion of Reinhardt. Whilst admiring his boldness, he was quick to spot the influence of Craig, criticised the indiscriminate use of Art Nouveau, and deplored the traditional manner of most of the acting.[67] One of the productions he saw was Wedekind's tragi-grotesque of adolescent sexuality, *Spring Awakening*, which was being staged for the first time, and he resolved immediately to present it in Petersburg.

Surprisingly enough the play was passed by the Russian censor, albeit extensively cut, and was given its first performance at Ofitserskaya Street on 15 September 1907. Meyerhold describes his interpretation in a production note: 'We have looked for a soft, unemphatic tone. The aim is to tone down the realism of certain scenes, to tone down the physiological aspect of puberty in the children. Sunlight and joyousness in the settings to counteract the chaos and gloom in the souls of the children.' [68] Critics and friends of the theatre alike could find little of merit in Wedekind's text, castigating both its style and theme. Alexander Blok actually doubted that Russian parents ever had such problems with their children, [69] whilst even the ultra-progressive Chulkov wrote that Wedekind 'will please nobody, with the possible exception of Moscow decadents and those German bourgeois who take pride in posing as sated aesthetes'. [70]

Shortly after the opening night the following letter to Vera Komissarzhevskaya appeared in the Petersburg *Theatre Review*:

> We 'advise' you to remove from your repertoire the masonic and yid play *Spring Awakening*. You may put on whatever you like in your flea-pit, but we are not going to let you corrupt children and adolescents. If you persist in staging this filthy piece of work, then fifty of us will come along to hiss it off the stage and pelt you with rotten apples, because it is not theatre but pornographic trash.
>
> (signed) Outraged parents and theatre-lovers. [71]

The one redeeming feature seen in the production was the method of area-lighting which Meyerhold devised to eliminate constant scene changes and to ensure an uninterrupted sequence of the play's eighteen short scenes:

> In accordance with Meyerhold's plan the stage was divided into several levels [by the designer Denisov]. At the bottom left and right were two apartments with part of a room visible in each. Light fell only on the place where the action was taking place, with everything else left in darkness. Above the apartments there was a sloping roof which represented the meadow where Wendla played with her friends. Still higher there was a platform on which Ilse and Moritz met, and finally at the top there was another small platform representing the grave of Moritz visited at the end by Ilse and Martha. [72]

For all its originality, area lighting was a technique accorded little significance by Meyerhold at the time. In fact, *Spring Awakening* seems to have been a production he was anxious to forget, for he makes no mention of it in the survey of his first ten years' work published in 1913. [73]

Nevertheless, the play's episodic structure lent the action both fluency and moments of abrupt contrast of a kind long absent from the theatre. Now that Meyerhold had recognised the limitations of the static drama he was beginning to exploit fully the dimensions of theatrical time and space in a manner which had no precedent on the modern stage. In retrospect, productions such as *The Fairground Booth*, *The Life of a Man*, and *Spring Awakening* appear unmistakably cinematic – cinematic at a time when the cinema itself was little more than filmed theatre. When Meyerhold came to make *The Picture of Dorian Gray* in 1915 he immediately applied his dramatic theories to such telling effect that the result was what Jay Leyda has called '. . . undoubtedly the most important Russian film made previous to the February Revolution'.[74]*

On 10 October 1907 Meyerhold presented Maeterlinck's *Pelléas and Mélisande* in a specially commissioned translation by Valery Bryusov, and with Komissarzhevskaya as Mélisande. Despite the production's imposing credentials, it was a total failure which proved decisive in Meyerhold's career. The principal fault lay in the setting (by Denisov) which consisted of a small raised platform in the centre of the stage; the stage floor was removed to furnish an orchestra pit surrounding the platform. Volkov suggests that this was Meyerhold's attempt to realise within legal limits his frustrated project for a theatre in the round.[75] If this is so, then the whole point was lost by enclosing the platform from behind with walls painted, according to Blok, in the vulgar style of old-fashioned 'cartes postales'.[76] As Meyerhold admitted afterwards, the effect was precisely that of his early productions against decorative panels: the three-dimensional figures of the actors lost all plasticity in their close proximity to the painted background and were so constricted in their movements that they had no choice but to move as automata in obedience to the scheme prescribed by the director.

For Komissarzhevskaya, struggling at the age of forty-three to play the child-like Mélisande, the production was a personal disaster. The critic of *Theatre and Art* wrote:

> In common with the rest of the cast, Miss Komissarzhevskaya, in an attempt to create a primitive, universal character, deliberately moved and gesticulated like a doll; her wonderful voice with its rare tonal range and musical timbre was replaced by something between a bird-like twittering and a child's squeak. . . . It was neither moving nor dramatic.[77]

The only true success that Komissarzhevskaya had enjoyed with Meyer-

* Meyerhold's work in the cinema is discussed on pp. 131–135 below.

hold was in *Sister Beatrice* almost a year earlier, and her total failure as Mélisande was more than she could bear; immediately after the performance she summoned the two other administrative directors of the theatre, Kasimir Bravich and her brother Fyodor, and told them '. . . that the theatre must admit its entire course as a mistake and the artistic director must either abandon his method of production or leave the theatre'.[78]

Two days later Meyerhold was given a chance to justify his policy at a meeting of the company's 'artistic council'. According to the notes of the meeting, Meyerhold eplained that *Pelléas and Mélisande*, far from foreshadowing the future course of his work, represented the close of a cycle of experiments which had begun at the Theatre-Studio with *The Death of Tintagiles*; in future he would pursue the 'sculptural' style of production initiated already in *The Fairground Booth* and *The Life of a Man*.[79] With some justification, Komissarzhevskaya doubted that this signified any greater creative freedom for the actor, whereupon Meyerhold, in Volkov's words '. . . declared categorically that whatever the method of production in the future, he would continue to exert pressure on any actors who failed to grasp his conception in order to realise that conception. Everything he had heard horrified him and he wanted to leave the theatre and go abroad.'[80]

Eventually an uneasy rapprochement was achieved and Meyerhold continued as artistic director. In an atmosphere of confusion previously announced productions were cancelled, but somehow Meyerhold contrived to rehearse Fyodor Sologub's new tragedy, *Death's Victory*, and it was presented for the first time on 6 November 1907. With this production Meyerhold confirmed his repudiation of what he called the 'decorative stylisation' of *Pelléas and Mélisande* and his earlier work.

The settings (devised by Meyerhold) [wrote Chulkov] possessed a stylised simplicity and were most agreeable: a broad flight of steps extended the entire breadth of the stage, massive columns and the muted, severe tones of the overall background facilitated a blend of the visual impressions with the impressions created by the severe and precise style of the tragedy itself . . . At the very end the orgiastic frenzy of the crowd around the magnificent Algista was imbued with the magic of true theatre. Apparently, at this point the author wanted to cross the sacred line, 'to destroy the footlights'. And it would have been possible to do this . . . by extending the steps on the stage into the auditorium,*

* Meyerhold maintained that he was prevented from extending the steps down into the auditorium by the caution of the theatre's management (*Meyerhold I*, p. 252).

thereby enabling the action of the tragedy to culminate amongst the spectators.[81]

Alexander Benois, by no means an uncritical admirer of Meyerhold, called the production 'truly splendid', admiring particularly the effect of the steps in the crowd scenes, in which the face of every extra could be clearly seen. In his review he wrote:

> One wants to take a pencil and sketch those balanced clusters of people, those combinations of gestures and expressions, those beautiful lines – Only a most gifted man could have made a whole mass of people submit in this manner to his will and to his fine inspiration, could have made them memorise such a complex formula within such an incredibly short space of time. This evening has made me believe in Meyerhold.[82]

High praise from so accomplished an artist.

The critical reception of *Death's Victory* was almost unanimously enthusiastic; even Tamarin in the hostile *Theatre and Art* described the production as 'a clear turning-point in style'.[83] However, Komissarzhevskaya (yet again without a part in a successful production) was not re-assured; three days after the premiere she wrote to Meyerhold:

> In recent days, Vsevolod Emilievich, after much thought I have arrived at the firm conviction that you and I do not share the same views on the theatre, and that what you are seeking is not what I am seeking. The path we have been following the whole time is the path which leads to the puppet theatre – if one excepts those productions in which we combined the principles of the 'old' theatre with those of the puppet theatre, for example *Love's Comedy* and *Death's Victory*. . . . In answer to your question at the last meeting of our artistic council 'perhaps I should leave?' I must say: yes, there is no choice for you but to leave.[84]

Meyerhold protested that his summary dismissal in mid-season was a violation of professional ethics and demanded that the affair be submitted to a court of arbitration. However, Komissarzhevskaya's decision was upheld by the court and Meyerhold's place as artistic director was taken by Fyodor Komissarzhevsky.* Only one further production was staged (Remizov's mystery, *The Devil Play*), and the season ended prematurely on 7 January 1908. The following day Komissarzhevskaya left with a section of her company to visit the United States. She never returned to Ofitser-skaya Street; two years later, on tour with her company in Tashkent she contracted smallpox and died at the age of forty-five.

* In 1919 Fyodor Komissarzhevsky (or Theore Komisarjevsky) came to England and established a considerable reputation as a designer and a director.

Eventually Meyerhold and his fellow director Rudolph Ungern (who had resigned with him) assembled a company from those actors who had remained loyal to them and in February 1908 embarked on a three-month tour of western and southern towns, beginning in Vitebsk and ending in Yekaterinoslav. In addition to revivals of most of Meyerhold's successful Petersburg productions, the repertoire included Wedekind's *Earth Spirit*, Ibsen's *The Master Builder*, and Knut Hamsun's *At the Gates of the Kingdom*.

Although Meyerhold's innovations were frequently curbed by the limitations of provincial theatres, he continued to exploit the stage to its limits and even beyond: in *Death's Victory* the spectators were shocked to find the performers in the prologue making their entrances from the rear of the auditorium,[85] whilst *The Fairground Booth* was performed entirely on the forestage with the house lights up throughout, and 'The Author' voicing his protests from the front row of the stalls.[86]

On 7 March 1908 he wrote to his wife: '. . . Just as Poltava resurrected me after the collapse of the Studio, so Minsk has resurrected me now.'[87] All his life he was nothing if not resilient, as he was to prove soon enough to the scornful public back in Petersburg, many of whom doubtless imagined that they had seen the last of him.

4. 1908–1910 Dapertutto Reborn

In November 1907 at the Tenishev Academy in Petersburg Meyerhold delivered a lecture entitled 'On the History and Technique of the Theatre', based on his contribution to an anthology which was published early the following year under the title *Theatre. A Book on the New Theatre*.[1] In this article, begun in the summer of 1906, he gives his personal account of the Moscow Art Theatre's development, traces the origins of the stylised 'New Theatre', and describes his own attempts to realise it, first at the Theatre-Studio and then with Komissarzhevskaya. In the final section, 'The Stylised Theatre', he outlines the conclusions reached after his rejection of the two-dimensional method of staging in favour of the more flexible style of *The Fairground Booth* and subsequent productions. In particular, he emphasises the removal of the footlights and the use of the forestage; the expressive power of rhythm in diction and movement; the director's right to interpret the text freely; the active participation of the spectator in the creative act; and, above all, the dispelling of illusion and the heightening of theatricality.

Recalling Meyerhold's recent dispute with Komissarzhevskaya, it is significant that he now lays particular stress on the actor's role:

> [The director] serves purely as a bridge, linking the soul of the author with the soul of the actor. Having assimilated the author's creation, the actor is left *alone*, face to face with the spectator; and from the friction between these two unadulterated elements, the actor's creativity and the spectator's imagination, a clear flame is kindled.[2]

In conclusion, he considers the kind of auditorium demanded by the new theatre:

> Architecturally, the Greek classical theatre is the very theatre which modern drama needs: it has three-dimensional space, no scenery, and it demands sculptural plasticity. Obviously its design will need to be modified, but with its simplicity, its horseshoe-shaped auditorium, and its orchestra, it is the only theatre capable of accommodating such a varied repertoire as Blok's *The Fairground Booth*, Andreev's *The Life of a*

Man, Maeterlinck's tragedies, Kuzmin's plays, Remizov's mysteries, Sologub's *The Gift of the Wise Bees* and all the other fine new works which have yet to find their theatre.[3]

It is possible that had Meyerhold remained with Komissarzhevskaya he would have continued to stage the symbolist dramatists. But as it was, *A Book on the New Theatre* marked the close of a chapter in the history of the Russian theatre. Fyodor Komissarzhevsky's production of Remizov's *Devil Play* at Ofitserskaya Street was not a success, and after that there were few significant attempts to produce symbolist drama in Russia, so that most of the works of Ivanov, Bely, Kuzmin, Bryusov, and Remizov never reached the stage at all. Nevertheless, as we have seen, it was through seeking solutions to the problems posed by the symbolists that Meyerhold arrived at a new conception of the art of the theatre; it provided a permanent foundation for his own work, and established a tradition of undisguised artifice and conscious theatricality which Yevreinov, Tairov, Vakhtangov, and other directors were later to follow.

The symbolists' dream of a revival of the classical communal ritual which Meyerhold describes in 'The Stylised Theatre' never materialised, but every formal point expounded by him there can be traced throughout his work over the next thirty years. Even the Greek amphitheatre was built in the end after a lifetime spent struggling to burst the bounds of the box-stage and obliterate the picture-frame of the proscenium arch.*

II

The critics' earlier glee at Meyerhold's dismissal by Komissarzhevskaya gave way to consternation when it was confirmed finally in April 1908 that Meyerhold was to be engaged as an actor and stage director at the Petersburg Imperial Theatres. In his statement to the press the Director of the Imperial Theatres, Vladimir Telyakovsky said: 'I consider that Meyerhold with his propensity for rousing people will prove very useful in the state theatres. As regards his extremes, I am confident that he will abandon them with us . . . I am even afraid that his new surroundings might turn him into a conformist.'[4]†

* See pp. 248–249 below.

† In fact, Meyerhold was approached by Telyakovsky a week after his dismissal, and his engagement was agreed in principle in November 1907. But Telyakovsky was careful to conceal it until the excitement over the Komissarzhevskaya scandal had subsided. The official organ of the Imperial Theatres (*The Theatre Review*) went so far as to refute the 'silly gossip', commenting: 'As is well known, the Directorate of the Imperial Theatres is not such an eccentric body as to wish to transform an exemplary theatre into a puppet show.'[5]

The danger of Meyerhold's boldness and originality being stifled was real; at that time the Alexandrinsky Dramatic Theatre was virtually ruled by a small group of august veteran artists, headed by Maria Savina, the redoubtable 'Empress of the Russian stage'. In their eyes all the stage-directors and designers under contract to the Imperial Theatres were no more than craftsmen, of no greater account than stage-managers, carpenters, electricians, and the like, and as such denied any creative pretensions

11. Meyerhold 1907–1908.

of their own.[6] It was under these daunting circumstances that Meyerhold was engaged for an initial twelve months from 1 September 1908 as a stage-director and actor at the Alexandrinsky Theatre and as an occasional director at the Mariinsky Opera. In fact, he remained there for the next ten years and not counting his private studio work, staged over two dozen official productions, eight of them operas.

In anticipation of the hostile reception in store for him, Meyerhold published an article in the summer number of the periodical *The Golden Fleece*, outlining his conception of the future development of the theatre.[7] In it, he divides theatre companies into two broad categories: first, those with an established company and a style and repertoire aimed at a wide audience (these he terms 'big theatres'); second, the theatre-studios whose function it should be to create the 'theatre of the future'.

A theatre-studio – claims Meyerhold – must have a director and a company unhampered by stylistic preconceptions and unharassed by the

commercial considerations of a public theatre. Only from the experiments of such a studio can a completely new form of theatre emerge. This
is the lesson to be derived from the failure of the Moscow Theatre-Studio,
the lesson (he implies) overlooked by Komissarzhevskaya's Theatre,
which sought to embrace the functions both of a 'big theatre' and of a
studio. The big theatres, on the other hand, are the custodians of tradition; the talents of their great veteran actors should be allowed to flourish
in the plays of the dramatists who inspired them: Shakespeare, Schiller,
Goethe, and above all, Ostrovsky, Gogol, and Griboedov. But, continues
Meyerhold, the great works of the traditional repertoire invariably suffer
from inadequate production; either they are staged as they always were
'in the good old days' or the director assembles a host of naturalistic
properties in an attempt to create a perfect illusion of the period in
question. What is the proper approach?

> The underlying idea of a play can be brought out not only through the
> dialogue between the characters created by the actors' skill, but equally
> through the rhythm of the whole picture created on the stage by the
> colours of the designer and by the deployment of practicable scenery,
> the pattern of movement and the interrelationship of groupings, which
> are all determined by the director.[8]

The aim should be a new, more profound realism which '. . . far from
avoiding true life, transcends it by seeking only the *symbol* of the object,
its *mystical essence*'.*

Thus Meyerhold tried to anticipate the protests of his future company;
but as we can see, at the same time he reaffirmed the major principles of
his own artistic credo. Indeed, he went so far as to recommend 'the old
actors' to consult Dmitry Merezhkovsky's recent symbolist reinterpretation of *The Government Inspector*,† thereby implying that their own traditional reading of that immortal work was by no means sacrosanct. We
shall see how far Meyerhold succeeded in overcoming the deep-rooted
prejudices and pre-conceptions of the Imperial stage when we consider
his productions of *Tristan and Isolde*, *Dom Juan*, *The Storm*, and *Masquerade*.

Despite Meyerhold's remarks on the ideal repertoire for the 'big
theatres' his first production at the Alexandrinsky Theatre was of a modern work, *At the Gates of the Kingdom*, by the highly fashionable Norwegian
writer, Knut Hamsun.‡ It had its premiere at the Alexandrinsky Theatre

* Compare Nemirovich-Danchenko's comment on *The Cherry Orchard* (p. 36 above).

† *Gogol and the Devil* (1906).

‡ During the 1908–1909 season *At the Gates of the Kingdom* was also staged at Komissarzhevskaya's Theatre and at the Moscow Art Theatre. Meyerhold himself had already
produced it once before whilst on tour in the spring.

on 30 September 1908. Written in Ibsen's symbolic-realist manner, the play is the first part of a trilogy dealing with the life of a Nietzschean philosopher, Ivar Kareno. As Meyerhold said in an interview at the time, *At the Gates of the Kingdom* belonged to the same cycle of productions as his earlier work on Ibsen.[9]

The visual treatment was strongly reminiscent of *Hedda Gabler*: the single setting depicting Kareno's room was executed in brilliant colours and framed with an ornate false proscenium opening, the intention being to reflect not Kareno's material poverty but rather his spiritual exaltation.[10] The result was like the ante-chamber of some fabulous palace which, as one critic remarked, could as well serve for *Ruslan and Ludmilla* or *La Traviata*.[11] A number of the cast took exception to Meyerhold's innovations and paid little attention to his directions; one of them, Roman Apollonsky, set out deliberately to sabotage the opening performance by treating his part as a burlesque. Inevitably, the outcome was a fiasco and Meyerhold, who himself played Kareno, had difficulty in completing the performance.[12] Most of the company and all the critics, except the sympathetic Lyubov Gurevich in *The Word*, took malicious pleasure in Meyerhold's double failure. In part he had himself to blame: against Telyakovsky's advice he had taken over the part of Kareno from another actor, clearly unable to resist the chance of playing yet another solitary dissident artist-thinker in the line of Hauptmann's Johannes Vockerath, Chekhov's Treplev, and of course Blok's Pierrot.[13]

Meyerhold's next scheduled production was Oscar Wilde's *Salome* at the Mikhailovsky Theatre, a benefit performance sponsored by the wealthy amateur actress Ida Rubinstein with designs by Bakst, music by Glazunov, choreography by Fokine, and with Rubinstein herself as Salome. This extravagant project foundered after lengthy preparation when the cuts demanded by the censor threatened to render it meaningless.[14]

Meyerhold completed no more major productions in his first season and for a time his future at the Imperial Theatres seemed seriously in doubt. However, *At the Gates of the Kingdom* was by no means a total disaster, for it initiated Meyerhold's partnership with Alexander Golovin. Eleven years his senior, Golovin had been a leading member of the 'World of Art' movement since its first exhibition in 1898. Having worked in the Imperial Theatres as a designer for opera and ballet with great success since 1902, he created the settings for Mussorgsky's *Boris Godunov* at Diaghilev's Russian season in the summer of 1908, and again for the premiere of Stravinsky's *Firebird* in 1910. With the exception of *Tristan and Isolde* in 1909, which was the work of Prince Shervashidze, Golovin's designs were a vital and integral part of all Meyerhold's major productions at the Imperial Theatres for the next ten years.

III

No sooner had Meyerhold joined the Alexandrinsky Theatre than he took steps to ensure the furtherance of his experiments into new dramatic forms. At the start of the 1908–1909 season he and the young composer, Mikhail Gnesin, organised a small theatre-studio in Meyerhold's flat in Petersburg. Significantly, the curriculum included courses in 'choral and musical declamation in drama' and 'plastic gymnastics'.[15] It was Meyerhold's first attempt at formal theatrical teaching and reflected his declared ambition to create a new style of theatre with his own pupils. The course ran only one year, but the following season Meyerhold taught acting technique to the second-year students of the well-established Pollak drama school. In the one winter he spent there he paid particular attention to mime and movement, gaining experience which was to prove valuable when eventually he opened a permanent studio of his own in 1913.[16]

At about the same time he was invited to collaborate in the creation of an intimate theatre housed in the Petersburg Theatre Club. Called 'The Strand' ('*Lukomore*'), it was envisaged as the equivalent of the Berlin 'Überbrettl', the original German literary cabaret founded by Ernst von Wolzogen in 1901, and of Nikita Baliev's late-night theatre club 'The Bat' which had opened recently in Moscow. However, 'The Strand' differed from its counterparts to the extent that as well as presenting a late-night programme of parody and satire (called *The Distorting Mirror*), it also staged a programme of one-act plays at normal theatre times. The three main items of the opening programme, all directed by Meyerhold, were *Petrushka*, a 'folk farce' by Peter Potemkin, *Honour and Vengeance*, a buffonade by Count Vladimir Sollogub, and a dramatic adaptation of Edgar Allen Poe's *The Fall of the House of Usher*. Although the costumes and settings for these productions were designed by such accomplished artists as Bilibin and Dobuzhinsky, they were a failure mainly because the programme proved far too long and far too earnest for the informal club atmosphere. Whereas *The Distorting Mirror* survived and continued to flourish right up until 1931, 'The Strand' closed after less than a week.[17] Immediately, Meyerhold announced the intention to create a new intimate theatre, '. . . a haven of rest for the cultured Petersburg theatregoer . . . in an atmosphere unpolluted by the belches of clubmen (pardon the vulgarity)'.[18]

In fact, two years passed before this ambition was realised at 'The Interlude House', but meanwhile Meyerhold continued to pursue a variety of activities outside the Imperial Theatres. In February 1909 Benjamin Kazansky presented a programme of 'Parisian Grand Guignol' at his theatre on Liteiny Prospect in which one of the items was *The Kings of the Air and the Lady from the Box*, a 'sensational melodrama' of circus life based on a short story called *The Four Devils* by the Danish writer Herman Bang. In three short acts without intervals, it was written by Meyerhold in response to a challenge from a friend whilst confined to his home with influenza. The work remained in Kazansky's repertoire for the remainder of the season and was published in Moscow shortly afterwards.[19] Although trivial in content, it reflected Meyerhold's widening interest in all theatrical genres and, in particular, the conventions of popular entertainment. Later in the year he made a translation from German of the Kabuki play *Terakoya*, and that too was staged by Kazansky.

At the same time Meyerhold continued to compose and translate articles on dramatic theory. Following the publication of his long essay 'On the History and Technique of the Theatre', he made translations from the German of two articles by Edward Gordon Craig, 'Über Bühnen-Ausstattung' and 'Etwas über den Regisseur und die Bühnen-Ausstattung', which were published in Petersburg in 1909. The first was prefaced by a short biographical sketch of Craig.[20] Whilst warm in his praise of the Englishman, Meyerhold was careful to point out that his own crucial experiments at the Theatre-Studio were carried out in ignorance of the ideas expressed in Craig's book *The Art of the Theatre*;* it was not until Meyerhold visited Berlin in 1907 that he heard of Craig's stylised productions of Purcell's *Dido and Aeneas* (London, 1900) and Ibsen's *The Vikings* (London, 1903), and identified his influence in the work of Max Reinhardt at the Kammerspiele.

IV

In the space of twelve months with Komissarzhevskaya Meyerhold had staged no fewer than thirteen productions, mostly of formidable complexity; in his ten years at the Imperial Theatres he was seldom called upon to stage more than two major works in a season. Hence, he was left

* Published originally in German as *Die Kunst des Theaters* (Berlin and Leipzig, 1905). A Russian version appeared in 1906. After visiting Moscow in 1935 Craig wrote: 'It is to see Meyerhold's work in its entirety that I want to visit Russia again. . . . I shall enjoy being figuratively tied to my seat for a few weeks, attending rehearsals and performances in the Meyerhold Theatre; and then and only then, undisturbed by having to visit twenty other theatres, I shall be able to watch, learn, and understand this exceptional theatric (sic) genius.'[21]

with time to undertake extensive preliminary research in collaboration with Alexander Golovin. *Tristan and Isolde*, his inaugural production at the Mariinsky Opera was the product of a year's exhaustive study of Wagner and his background.

There could have been no more logical choice for Meyerhold's operatic début than *Tristan and Isolde*.* Summarising the period twenty-four years later, Ivan Sollertinsky wrote:

> Of the whole Wagnerian legacy, *Tristan* with its heady, poisoned atomsphere of buddhist eroticism, with its idea of non-being, of Nirvana, in which the frenzied souls of the medieval lovers find eternal union, with its philosophical meditation verging on Schopenhauer, with its sophisticated harmonic structure initiated by the famous open-ing chords seemingly dissolving in an unhealthy vapour, with its sus-pensions and chromatic effects, *Tristan* of all operas was regarded by the Russian symbolists as peculiarly their own.[22]

Meyerhold's own writings on Wagner reveal a close familiarity with the composer and with the philosophical background of Nietzsche and Schopenhauer. Shortly after the premiere of *Tristan and Isolde* on 30 October 1909 he delivered a lecture on the subject which furnished the text for a long article published shortly afterwards in *The Yearbook of the Imperial Theatres*.[23] In the first section of this article Meyerhold discusses the nature of Wagnerian music-drama and the style of acting appropriate to its realisation on the stage:

> If an opera were produced without words [he begins] it would amount to *a pantomime*. In pantomime every single episode, each movement in each episode (its plastic modulations) – as well as the gestures of every character and the groupings of the ensemble – are determined pre-cisely by the music, by its changes in tempo, its modulations, its overall structure. . . . So why don't operatic artists make their movements and gestures follow the musical tempi, the tonic design of the score, with mathematical precision? Does the addition of the human voice to the art of the pantomime alter the relationship between music and stage action which exists in pantomime? I believe it alters because the opera singer bases his dramatic interpretation on the libretto rather than on the musical score.

Depending on the period of the opera, continues Meyerhold, the gestures

---

* Meyerhold returned to the Tristan theme in March the following year with a pro-duction at the Alexandrinsky Theatre of *Tantris the Fool* by the German neo-romantic dramatist Ernst Hardt.

and movements of the singers will be either conventionally 'operatic' or restrained and life-like. The 'operatic' style is comparatively innocuous, because although it is mechanical and meaningless it does not distract the spectator by contradicting the musical tempi. But the lifelike style not only ignores the music, it exposes the *apparent* absurdity of the operatic convention of people singing in 'real life'. '*Music-drama must be performed in such a way that the spectator never thinks to question why the actors are singing and not speaking.*' [Meyerhold's italics]

In Wagner, unlike the school of Mozart and Bizet, 'the libretto and the music are composed free from mutual enslavement'. The score does not merely provide an accompaniment to the libretto but reveals the world of the soul, gives voice to the inner dialogue of the characters' emotions. Hence, it is not the libretto but the orchestral score which the singer through his acting must manifest in visible, plastic terms. However, it is not from real life that he must draw his inspiration:

Where does the human body possessing the flexibility of expression demanded by the stage attain its highest development? *In the dance.* Because the dance is the movement of the human body in the sphere of rhythm. The dance is to the body what music is to thought: form artificially yet instinctively created.

But at the same time the actor should remember the expressive power of music: his gestures should not duplicate what the orchestra is saying, but rather supply what it fails to say or leaves half-said. Finally, he should understand that he is only one of several means of expression in the opera, neither more nor less important than any other, and he must remain conscious of them throughout his performance.

In the course of this section Meyerhold quotes only once from Adolphe Appia's *Die Musik und die Inscenierung*. But in fact the greater part of what he says here is clearly based on that work, as the following quotations from Appia show:

To understand how music can control the elements of production, let us look briefly at pantomime – that prototype of drama in which, because language has no place, music and the visual elements of theatre are most prominent. In pantomime, music determines the time-durations and the sequence of the action. . . . Obviously, if we now add words to this music, the relationship between the music and the production remains unaltered.

. . . the poet-musician [a composer of the Wagnerian school], thanks to the music, presents us not only with external effects of emotions, the appearance of dramatic life, but with the emotions themselves, the dramatic life in all its reality, as we can know it only in the most profound depths of our being.

The overwhelming power attained by music in our time makes impossible any artistic role for the human body as it functions in daily life. . . .

But there is yet another means of involving the living body in the [poet-musician's] expression: and that is by communicating to the actor the basic proportions of music, without necessarily having recourse to song – in other words, by means of the *dance*. By dance, I do not mean those light parlour entertainments or what passes for dance in the opera, but the *rhythmic* life of the human body in its whole scope.

Dance is to the body what pure music is to our feelings: an imaginative, non-rational form.

. . . for the author of word-tone [Wagnerian] drama, the actor is not the sole or even the most important interpreter of the poet's intention, he is rather but one medium, neither more nor less important than the others, at the poet's disposal.[24]

We have seen already how in 1907 in *The Life of a Man* Meyerhold's exploration of the sculptural power of light resembled the revolutionary lighting plots described by Appia in *Die Musik und die Inscenierung*. Now again his treatment of *Tristan and Isolde* undoubtedly owed much to the same work.

To what extent was Meyerhold influenced by Appia's ideas? Let us consider the opening of Chapter Two of Appia's book:

We have seen that if the *mise en scène* is to be totally expressive of the playwright's intention, the means of controlling it must exist within the text. The *mise en scène*, as a design in space with variations in time, presents essentially a question of proportion and sequence. Its regulating principle must therefore govern its proportions in space and their sequence in time, each dependent on the other.

In drama, the playwright seems to have this power through the quantity and order of his text. However, this is not the case because the text itself has no fixed duration; and the time not filled by the text is impossible to calculate. Even if one were to measure the relative duration of speech and silence with a stop-watch, this duration would be fixed only by the arbitrary will of the author or the director, without *necessarily* having its origins in the original conception.

The quantity and order of the text alone, therefore, are insufficient to govern its staging. Music, on the other hand, determines not only time-duration and continuity in the drama, but, as we have seen, should actually be considered from the visual point of view of dramatic action as being time itself.

It is the word-tone poet, then, who possesses the guiding principle which, springing as it does from the original intention, inexorably and of necessity dictates the *mise en scène* without being filtered through the will of the dramatist – and this principle is an integral part of his drama and shares its organic life.

Thus the production attains the rank of an expressive medium in the drama of the poet-musician; but note that it cannot achieve such rank except in this kind of drama.[25]

It is not clear when Meyerhold first discovered Appia, but from an early stage his anti-naturalistic experiments reveal a conception of the director's role in the dramatic theatre strikingly similar to that of Appia's 'word-tone poet' in Wagnerian opera. One needs only to recall his criticism of the Moscow Art Theatre's production of *The Cherry Orchard* in 1904 when he wrote to Chekhov: 'Your play is abstract, like a Tchaikovsky symphony. Before all else, the director must get the *sound* of it.'* This became the guiding principle of all his work from the Theatre-Studio onwards: having isolated the text's 'inner dialogue', he would 'orchestrate' it in terms of speech rhythms, pauses, gestures, and movements; that is, he used *music* to determine precisely the 'time-duration and continuity in the drama' – occasionally actual music (as in *The Death of Tintagiles* and *Schluck and Jau*), but more often pure rhythm with its discipline reinforced by the purposely contrived spatial restrictions of the stage area (the shallow strip of stage in *Sister Beatrice*, the stage within a stage in *The Fairground Booth*, the flight of steps in *Death's Victory*).

Thus, as early as 1905 Meyerhold had discovered what Appia himself still repudiated: that the production could attain the rank of an expressive medium not only in the opera but also in the dramatic theatre. This he did by seeing what Appia had failed to see: that 'music' is by no means the exclusive property of opera, that rhythm is an expressive quality latent in all the performing arts. Whatever the extent of Meyerhold's debt to Appia, this crucial realisation was his own.

In the second and third sections of his article on *Tristan and Isolde*, Meyerhold considers the kind of stage and stage setting which best complement the plasticity of the actor in the music-drama. He argues that the Bayreuth Festspielhaus, despite its apparently revolutionary design (a concealed orchestra pit, broad proscenium opening, fan-like auditorium with

* See p. 33 above.

no boxes), was really no more than a refinement of the traditional Renaissance box-stage and did little to satisfy Wagner's dream of a stage as a pedestal for human sculpture. The first man, he says, to revive the tradition of the proscenium stage of the Ancient Greek and Shakespearian theatres was Georg Fuchs at the Munich Artists' Theatre.* It is Fuchs' 'relief stage' with its foreground of non-decorative, practicable reliefs and remote painted back-drop which furnishes the ideal setting for Wagnerian music-drama.

As well as the architecture of Bayreuth, Meyerhold rejects its so-called 'historical' treatment of Wagner. The pseudo-period costumes and settings invite the spectator to relate the action to a specific time and place, and in consequence the atmosphere of remote legend conjured up by the orchestral score is lost to his imagination. However, the fault lies not so much with Bayreuth as with Wagner himself: his banal stage directions show that his visual imagination was no match for his musical inspiration and extended no further than the vulgar stereotyped conventions of nineteenth-century opera. Wagner's instructions are best ignored:

> Let the designer and director of *Tristan* take the cue for their stage picture from the orchestra. What extraordinary medieval colouring there is in Kurwenal's song, in the shouts of the sailors' chorus, in the mysterious death *leitmotiv*, in the calls of the hunting horns, and in the fanfares when Mark meets the ship in which Tristan has brought Isolde home to him. Yet Wagner places equal emphasis on the traditional operatic couch where Isolde is supposed to recline in Act One, and where Tristan lies dying in Act Three. In Act Two he stipulates a '*Blumenbank*' where Tristan is supposed to place Isolde during the intermezzo of the love duet; yet the garden with the rustling of leaves blending with the sound of the horns is miraculously evoked by the orchestra. The mere contemplation of real foliage on the stage would be as flagrantly tasteless as illustrating Edgar Allen Poe. In the second act our designer depicts a huge towering castle wall and in front of it, right in the centre of the stage, there burns the mystical torch which plays such an important part in the drama.[26]

Equally Meyerhold might have quoted Appia again:

> A simple indication suffices to place the action in the external world, and once this is done, the setting has only to express what there is *in the place chosen* by the dramatist that corresponds to the inner essence revealed to us by the music – in other words, the eternal aspect with which all transitory forms are endowed.[27]

* See pp. 55–57 above.

12. Shervashidze's setting for Act Three of Tristan and Isolde.

Even though they rejected Bayreuth's conventional 'historical' approach to Wagner, Meyerhold and his designer, Prince Shervashidze, themselves based the settings and costumes for *Tristan and Isolde* on a definite historical period. But their method was not the faithful archaeological reconstruction of the naturalistic school; instead they turned to the age of Gottfried von Strassburg, whose own *Tristan* had been Wagner's original inspiration, and re-created the highly formalised style of his miniaturist contemporaries. In reply to Alexander Benois' criticism that, like the Bayreuth style, this obscured the opera's symbolism, Meyerhold wrote:

> Why, given that the play contains symbols, should the cut of the cloth necessarily be imaginary and why should the ship not resemble a ship of the thirteenth century? The object does not exclude the symbol; on the contrary, as reality becomes more profound, it transcends its own reality. In other words, reality, in becoming supra-natural, is transformed into a symbol.[28]

This argument presumes that the essence of the reality of Tristan and Isolde as perceived by Wagner corresponds to that of von Strassburg and the miniaturist painters, and not to Wagner's own nineteenth-century reinterpretation of it. Furthermore, the success in practice of such an approach would depend on the designer's ability to synthesise that reality, and not merely reproduce it, as Shervashidze's sketches suggest he did. The principle underlying Meyerhold's subsequent work with Golovin was similar, but as we shall see the results were strikingly different.

Faced with the insuperable problem of transforming the conventional stage of the Mariinsky Theatre into a relief stage every night that *Tristan and Isolde* was performed in the repertoire, Meyerhold compromised by constructing the practicable reliefs for the second and third acts immediately behind the setting line, whilst in Act One the ship was built at normal stage level. The distant back-drop showed no more than a bleak expanse of horizon. The forestage in front of the proscenium arch and the curtains to either side (as well as the ship's huge sail) were covered in a traditional medieval lozenge pattern. The lifeless photographs which survive of the settings are perhaps misleading, for they give no indication of their appearance under stage lighting. But they do seem to suggest a degree of lifelike detail which is hardly consistent with Meyerhold's declared approach.

Not surprisingly he encountered considerable difficulties in introducing his revolutionary ideas on mime and movement to the wilful stars of the Mariinsky Opera and their veteran conductor Edward Napravnik.[29]

13 and 14. Shervashidze's costume designs for Tristan and Isolde.

Nevertheless, contemporary accounts suggest that the production possessed a visual, musical, and dramatic coherence in advance of any previous operatic production in Russia. Even the conservative *Theatre Review* commented enthusiastically that 'scarcely a stage in Europe has witnessed such a production of *Tristan and Isolde* as yesterday's premiere at the Mariinsky Theatre',[30] whilst *Theatre and Art* grudgingly acknowledged that 'On the production side there is much that is original. On the operatic stage static poses are entirely appropriate.'[31] The following January the work was conducted by Felix Mottl, the celebrated interpreter of Wagner and conductor of the first Bayreuth performance of *Tristan*. According to Valery Bebutov, Meyerhold's young assistant at that time, Mottl said that he had seen no more accurate interpretation of the score on any stage.[32] Remembering that Appia himself did not succeed in actually staging Wagner until 1923,* *Tristan and Isolde* must be acknowledged as one of the first attempts to free the composer's conception of the '*Gesamtkunstwerk*' from the banal conventions of the nineteenth century and give it credible theatrical form.

* *Tristan and Isolde* at La Scala, Milan.

V

Of the various manifestations of the revolt against naturalism in the Russian theatre before the October Revolution the most fruitful and long-lasting proved to be the resurrection of the plays and stage conventions of the exemplary theatres of the past. This movement, later known as 'Traditionalism', originated with the opening in 1907 of 'The Ancient Theatre' ('*Starinny teatr*') in Petersburg. Created at the initiative of Nikolai Yevreinov, it presented in its first season two programmes devoted to medieval miracles, moralities, farces, and the thirteenth-century pastorale, *Le Jeu de Robin et Marion* by Adam de la Halle. The whole enterprise typified the stand taken by the aesthetic élite against bourgeois bad taste and materialism in the Russia of Tsar Nicholas II.

In collaboration with such leading designers as Benois, Bilibin, Dobuzhinsky, Lanseray, and Roerich, Yevreinov and his fellow directors sought to re-create in precise detail the stages, costumes, settings, and theatrical conventions of the periods in question. Furthermore, an attempt was made to locate each play in its period by building 'a stage within a stage'. In this way the spectator witnessed not only the performance but also the surroundings in which it might once have been presented. Yevgeny Znosko-Borovsky describes Yevreinov's production of *Le Jeu de Robin et Marion*:

> . . . the pastorale was staged as it might have been in some castle in the Age of Chivalry. . . . The setting by Dobuzhinsky represented part of the great hall to either side of which were seated old, grey-haired minstrels with coronets on their heads and instruments in their hands. A master of ceremonies appeared and invited the audience to witness a pastorale, and immediately in full view preparations were begun for the performance. A little cardboard hut represented the peasants' house, imitation lambs served as the flock which was tended by Marion, a drooping cardboard tree was set up to indicate that the action was located in a field, and four attendants with candles placed themselves at each corner. In the same style as all this was the horse on which the knight entered: made also of wood and cardboard, it rolled backwards and forwards on four brightly decorated wheels.[33]

Originally it was Yevreinov's intention to cover the entire history of the theatre, beginning with Attic drama, but after the medieval programme three years elapsed before the second season in 1911–1912. Staged according to the same principles as the earlier programme, this season was devoted to the golden age of Spanish theatre, with works by Lope de Vega, Tirso de Molina, and Calderón.

Despite considerable public interest and critical acclaim, the Ancient Theatre's existence was fraught with internal discord and financial problems. After a further interval, detailed preparations were made for a season of *commedia dell'arte*, but the project was frustrated by the outbreak of war in 1914, and the theatre ceased to exist.[34]

In a short review of the Ancient Theatre's opening season written in 1908 Meyerhold applauded its aims but criticised the means chosen to achieve them.[35] In his opinion, the theatre should either have staged the original works in a precise 'archaeological' reconstruction of the scenic conventions of the period, or have taken plays written in the manner of works of the past and staged them as 'a free composition on the theme of the primitive theatre', like his own production of *Sister Beatrice*. Instead, he maintained, the Ancient Theatre fell between two stools, choosing original medieval texts but staging them as stylised free compositions. The result was a pastiche in which the naïve conventions seemed to be a deliberate parody of the original style.

Meyerhold's own initial venture in the field of 'traditionalism' took place in April 1910, when he assembled an amateur cast of poets and writers and staged a single performance of Calderón's 'religious comedy' *The Adoration of the Cross* at Vyacheslav Ivanov's 'Tower'. Turning the limited space of Ivanov's (admittedly large) dining-room to his own advantage, Meyerhold ignored Calderón's prescribed location of thirteenth-century Siena and tried instead to recreate the spirit of a performance by Spanish strolling players of Calderón's day. Settings and costumes were improvised from Ivanov's abundant collection of rich and exotic fabrics and carpets. The only properties used were wooden crosses and swords; the lighting was by candelabra; and the acting conventions were of the simplest: exits and entrances were made through the auditorium, a character supposed to be concealing himself beneath fallen leaves merely wrapped himself in a curtain. The stage was on a level with the audience, separated by gold brocade curtains which were operated by the two small sons of the hall porter, costumed and made-up to resemble the traditional blackamoors of the eighteenth-century court theatre. Ephemeral and lighthearted as this make-shift production may have been, it marked the beginning of Meyerhold's exhaustive study of the theatres of the past and his extensive application of their techniques to the modern stage.[36]

In autumn 1910 the intimate theatre whose formation Meyerhold had announced after the closure of 'The Strand' finally opened in Petersburg. Called The Interlude House (*Dom intermedii*), it was run by 'The Fellowship of Actors, Writers, Musicians and Artists' and housed in the former Skazka Theatre. With the footlights removed, the tiny stage was joined to the auditorium by a flight of steps and the rows of seats were replaced by restaurant tables and chairs. As well as a late-night cabaret, Meyerhold and his fellow organisers aimed to present a varied repertoire including ancient and modern farces, comedies, pantomimes, and operettas.

The opening programme on 9 October 1910 comprised a musical comedy called *The Reformed Eccentric*, a pastorale, *Liza, the Dutch Girl*, a burlesque, *Black and White – a Negro Tragedy*, and one production by

15. Poster for The Interlude House *by Nikolai Remi (1910).*

Meyerhold, Arthur Schnitzler's pantomime, *The Veil of Pierrette*, with music by Dohnány and settings and costumes by Sapunov. The first three items were greeted with reactions ranging from indifference to derision, but Meyerhold's contribution remained a haunting memory for those present. Freely adapted by himself and with the title altered to *Columbine's Scarf*, the work bore little resemblance to Schnitzler's original. The aim was to eliminate the cloying sweetness so often associated with pantomime and to create a chilling grotesque in the manner of E.T.A. Hoffmann. The three scenes were broken down into fourteen brief episodes, in order that the spectator should be shocked by the constant abrupt switches of mood and have no time to doubt the play's own ghastly logic. It was fitting that Meyerhold should dedicate the production to Blok, for in style, content, and atmosphere it bore a marked resemblance to the 1906 version of *The Fairground Booth*. Here is an eye-witness description of the scenario of *Columbine's Scarf*:

> The frivolous Columbine, betrothed to Harlequin, spends a last evening with her devoted Pierrot. As usual, she deceives him, swearing that she loves him. Pierrot proposes a suicide pact and himself drinks

poison. Columbine lacks the courage to follow him and flees in terror to the wedding ball where the guests await her impatiently. The ball begins; then whilst an old-fashioned quadrille is playing, Pierrot's flapping white sleeve is glimpsed first through the windows, then through the doors. The dances, now fast, now slow, turn into an awful nightmare, with strange Hoffmannesque characters whirling to the time of a huge-headed Kapellmeister, who sits on a high stool and conducts

16. Sapunov's design for the ball scene of Columbine's Scarf *(1910).*

four weird musicians. Columbine's terror reaches such a pitch that she can hide it no longer and she rushes back to Pierrot. Harlequin follows her and when he sees Pierrot's corpse he is convinced of his bride's infidelity. He forces her to dine before the corpse of the love-stricken Pierrot. Then he leaves, bolting the door fast. In vain Columbine tries to escape from her prison, from the ghastly dead body. Gradually, she succumbs to madness; she whirls in a frenzied dance, then finally drains the deadly cup and falls lifeless beside Pierrot.[37]

The rhythm of the entire production was dictated by the hideous Kapellmeister and his sinister band. When the corpses of Pierrot and Columbine were discovered he fled in terror through the auditorium, as though acknowledging his manipulation of the tragedy. Just as in Meyerhold's interpretation of Lermontov's *Masquerade* six years later, when again he devised a sequence of episodes to emphasise the inexorable advance of the tragedy, the luckless victims seemed to have been marked down by some devilish power from which there was no escape.

17. Sapunov's costume design for Harlequin.

In making great play with objects as an aid to mime in *Columbine's Scarf* (a letter, a rose, a glove, the fatal cup) Meyerhold was paying implicit homage to the *commedia dell'arte* from which the principal characters were drawn. Of similar origin were the devices used to involve the audience more closely in the action: the Kapellmeister's flight through the auditorium; the nightmarish polka of the wedding guests weaving amongst the tables; the asides to the audience from the blackamoor 'proscenium servant' (as Meyerhold now termed him). Much of the impact of the production derived from the inspired designs by Nikolai Sapunov. No artist was closer in spirit to Meyerhold's understanding of the grotesque than Sapunov. First in *The Fairground Booth* and now again in *Columbine's Scarf* they both, as Volkov puts it, 'knew how to turn a piercing gaze on the surrounding world, and where others remained blind, they saw clearly into the ugliness of everyday life in Russia'.[38] Sapunov's vision of life as treacherous and two-faced was firmly rooted in a world of tawdry furnishings, assertive bad taste, and small-town claustrophobia; it was unmistakably the world of Gogol.[39] Tragically, the association of Meyerhold and Sapunov came to an untimely end in 1912 when the artist was drowned at the age of thirty-two in a summer boating accident on the

Gulf of Finland. Even so, his influence on Meyerhold's work was an enduring one.

While Meyerhold was working on *Columbine's Scarf* he was asked by Telyakovsky to adopt a pseudonym for his private theatrical activities, as they constituted a breach of contract and might cause mutual embarrassment. At the suggestion of the poet and composer, Mikhail Kuzmin, he took the name of 'Doctor Dapertutto', a character from E.T.A. Hoffmann's *Adventure on New Year's Eve*.[40] Dapertutto was a real-life manifestation of the mask, an ubiquitous Doppelgänger who assumed responsibility for all Meyerhold's unofficial experiments for the rest of his time at the Imperial theatres.

The second programme at the Interlude House on 3 December 1910 included a production by Meyerhold of Znosko-Borovsky's new comedy, *The Transfigured Prince* (designs by Sudeikin, music by Kuzmin). Based loosely on the traditional conventions of the Spanish theatre, it was treated by Meyerhold as 'a free composition on the theme of the primitive theatre'. He describes two of the devices used:

> Here are the kind of horses on which the prince and his entourage managed to complete their long journey. The designer gave the horses' necks deep curves and stuck prancing ostrich feathers into their (papier-mâché) heads, which alone sufficed to make the clumsy frames covered with caparisons look like horses lightly prancing and proudly rearing on their hind legs. . . .
>
> . . . The youthful prince returns from his journey to learn that his father, the king, has died. The courtiers proclaim the prince king, place a grey wig on his head, and attach a long grey beard to his chin. In full view of the audience the youthful prince is transformed into the venerable old man which a king in the realm of fairy-tales is supposed to be.[41]

Znosko-Borovsky himself describes the battle scene in the production:

> Sudeikin's setting in clashing fiery red and gold gave the spectator an impression of raging blood and fire, which was intensified by terrifying rumblings and explosions backstage. An actor dressed as a warrior crawled from underneath the set – thereby emphasising that the theatre was only simulating a battle and dispelling any illusion of a real battle that the audience might have – and began to give a graphic picture of a violent conflict between two vast armies. As he spoke, shots rang out and bullets and cannonballs flew; eventually he took flight, tumbled down the steps and hid under the first available table. Recovering his breath, he said: 'I should imagine I'll be safer here.'

18. Portrait by Boris Grigoriev showing Meyerhold with his double, Doctor Dapertutto (1916).

However, the continuing gunfire drove him from that refuge as well and finally he fled from the theatre, crying: 'Every man for himself.'[42]

The second programme at the Interlude House proved to be its last, but for Meyerhold the insight gained through those two short-lived productions in that modest little theatre was priceless. He realised the full significance of those aspects of the traditional popular theatre which he had glimpsed already through his productions of *The Fairground Booth* and, to a lesser extent, *The Adoration of the Cross*. Behind the familiar masks and knockabout tricks of the *commedia dell'arte* he discovered a fund of theatrical wisdom and drew on it to create a style which in its essentials remained unaltered for the rest of his creative life.

VI

On 9 November 1910, a month after the opening of the Interlude House, Meyerhold presented Molière's *Dom Juan* at the Alexandrinsky Theatre in a production which exactly reflected the revivalist mood then prevailing in the Russian theatre. As he himself admitted, his treatment of Molière's comedy contradicted the rules governing the recreation of the exemplary ages of drama which he had formulated in his criticism of the Ancient Theatre.[43] It was neither an exact reconstruction of the theatre in question nor a new work conceived in the spirit of a former age; instead, like Yevreinov's productions, it was an original text staged as a free composition designed to evoke the atmosphere of the theatre for which it was written. The crucial difference, claimed Meyerhold, was that in *Dom Juan* he avoided any impression of pastiche by preserving only those stylistic features which he considered vital to the spirit of Molière's comedy. In saying this he had one particular feature in mind:

> If we go to the heart of Molière's works [he writes] we find that he was trying to remove the footlights from the contemporary stage, since they were better suited to the heroic drama of Corneille than to plays with their origins in the popular theatre.
> The academic theatre of the Renaissance failed to take advantage of the projecting forestage, keeping actor and audience at a mutually respectful distance. Sometimes, the front rows of the orchestra stalls were moved right back to the middle of the parterre, sometimes even further.
> How could Molière accept this segregation of actor and public? How could his overflowing humour have its proper effect under such conditions? How could the whole range of his bold, undisguisedly authentic

characterisation be accommodated within such a space? How could the waves of accusatory monologue of an author outraged by the banning of *Tartuffe* reach the spectator from such a distance? Surely the actor's ability and freedom of gesture were hemmed in by the wings?

Molière was the first amongst the stage-masters of the Roi-Soleil to attempt to shift the action from the back and centre of the stage forward to the very edge of the forestage.[44]

Meyerhold, usually the most scholarly of apologists for his own productions, seems here to have read into accounts of Molière's theatre what he himself wished to find. Despite Molière's long apprenticeship on improvised platform stages in the provinces and his love of the intimate cut-and-thrust of the popular theatre, there is no evidence that when he became established in Paris he attempted to halt the retreat of the French theatre behind the Italianate proscenium arch and out of the range of the unruly parterre. On the contrary, it seems likely that out of necessity he came to prefer a less intimate relationship with his audience, for at that time it had become the custom for young noblemen to demand seats on the stage itself whence they frequently caused obstruction, bodily as well as vocal, to the performers. Molière voices his distaste for this practice through the person of Eraste (one of his own parts) at the opening of *Les Fâcheux*.[45]

But historically justifiable or not, the forestage was used to telling effect by Meyerhold in his production at the Alexandrinsky. The footlights were removed and the normal stage area was augmented by a deep semi-circular apron which extended over the orchestra pit up to the first row of the stalls. The sense of intimacy thus achieved was enhanced by Golovin's permanent setting, which was designed to obliterate the division between stage and auditorium and thus engulf the spectator in all the grandiose splendour of Louis XIV's Versailles. To this end the front curtain was discarded and the theatre left fully illuminated throughout the performance except at such dramatic moments as the final encounter with the Commander. Valery Bebutov describes the initial impact of the spectacle on the opening night:

> I enter the auditorium long before the start of the performance and stop short, amazed at the spectacle revealed before me. The oval of red velvet loges is joined to the stage in a harmonious ensemble by the huge false proscenium designed for the production. My enraptured gaze is lost in the splendour of the wings, screens, lambrequins and the tapestry curtain in the background which for the present conceals the secrets of Golovin's artistic wonders. The forestage covering the deep orchestra pit makes the spectacle seem like a ship entering the harbour

19. A scene from Dom Juan *showing ten 'proscenium servants' with the prompters' screens and stools for Varlamov's Sganarelle to either side.*

which is the auditorium. Above the forestage hang three big chandeliers with wax candles. . . . To either side of the forestage there are big candelabra on pedestals which also bear real candles.[46]

Very few properties were used and no scenery at all in the conventional sense. Behind the false proscenium arch a series of ornate borders decreasing progressively in aperture led back to the tapestry mentioned by Bebutov, placed just beyond the actual proscenium opening. The scene was set by a series of painted flats, revealed when teh tapestry was drawn aside.

Some critics, notably Kugel and Benois, objected that Meyerhold and Golovin's *Dom Juan* was mere spectacle for spectacle's sake which blunted the satire of Molière's text.[47] But Meyerhold maintained that his intention was precisely the reverse:

. . . When a director sets about staging *Dom Juan*, his first task is to fill the stage and the auditorium with such a compelling atmosphere that the audience is bound to view the action through the prism of that atmosphere.

When one reads Griboedov's *Woe from Wit*, every page seems to reflect some aspect of modern life, and it is this which makes the play so meaningful to the modern public. But if Molière's *Dom Juan* is read without any knowledge of the age that shaped the genius of its author, what a dull play it seems! How tedious is the exposition of its plot compared with even Byron's *Don Juan*, to say nothing of Tirso de Molina's *El Burlador de Sevilla*. If one reads Elvira's great speeches in Act One, or Juan's long attack on hypocrisy in Act Five, one soon gets bored. If the spectator is not to get bored too, and if whole passages are not to strike

20. *Two of the 'proscenium servants' from* Dom Juan.

him as simply obscure, it is essential somehow to remind him constantly of the thousands of Lyonnais weavers manufacturing silk for the monstrously teeming court of Louis XIV, the 'Hôtel des Gobelins', the whole town of painters, sculptors, jewellers and carpenters under the supervision of the celebrated Le Brun, all the craftsmen producing Venetian glass and lace, English hosiery, Dutch mercery, German tin and bronze. . . .

The more grandiose and colourful the costumes and properties – only remember to keep the design of the stage itself as simple as possible! – the more clearly the *comédien* in Molière stands out in contrast to the stiff formality of Versailles.[48]

One of the most potent means employed by Meyerhold to evoke the required atmosphere was a whole crew of the now-familiar liveried proscenium servants, inspired, as he says, by the '*kurogo*', the black-clad stage-hands of the Japanese theatre. He describes their ubiquitous role in the production:

> . . . little blackamoors floating about the stage sprinkling intoxicating perfumes from crystal bottles on to red-hot platinum; little blacka-moors darting about the stage picking up a lace handkerchief dropped by Dom Juan, offering a stool to a tired actor; little blackamoors fasten-ing Dom Juan's shoelaces as he argues with Sganarelle; little blacka-moors appearing with lanterns for the actors when the stage is plunged into semi-darkness; little blackamoors removing cloaks and rapiers from the stage after Dom Juan's desperate fight with the brigands; little blackamoors crawling under the table at the appearance of the Com-mander's statue; little blackamoors summoning the public with tink-ling silver bells and announcing the intervals (in the absence of a cur-tain): all these are not merely tricks designed for the delectation of snobs, but serve the central purpose of enveloping the action in a mist redolent of the perfumed, gilded monarchy of Versailles.[49]

It was with good reason that Benois' review of the production was entitled 'Ballet at the Alexandrinka', for *Dom Juan* was a deliberate attempt to recreate a 'comédie-ballet' of the kind so popular at the court of Versailles. Seemingly oblivious to the intended satirical overtones Znosko-Borovsky writes:

> . . . what most amazed the public and what caused greatest disagree-ment was the dance rhythm to which all the characters were subordin-ated. The actors were not actually transformed into dancers, and Sganarelle in the rich interpretation of Varlamov moved as he always did; but the majority of them (in particular Dom Juan, played with superb grace and beauty by Yuriev, one of the most decorative artists in the Russian theatre) assumed an ease, an elegance, a lightness and a melodiousness of gait and movement. It was as though every character was played to the constant accompaniment of Lully's music,* for it echoed in the floating cadences of their speech and movements. The spectator was reminded irresistibly of that happy age when the whole world danced, when the Sun-King himself opened the festive ballet which concluded the performance.[50]

The mountainous Sganarelle of Konstantin Varlamov was the one stationary figure in the entire production; not only did his bulk and a severe heart condition seriously limit his mobility, but with his incor-rigibly bad memory he was left helpless by the removal of the downstage

---

* The actual music for the production was taken from Rameau's *Hippolyte et Aricie* and *Les Indes galantes*.

prompter's box which the construction of the forestage necessitated. Rather than sacrifice his unique comic genius, Meyerhold and Golovin devised two ornate prompters' screens which were placed to either side of the stage. Before the performance two bewigged prompters entered bearing large folios and lighted candles and seated themselves behind apertures in the screens. Varlamov was permitted to spend most of the play happily ensconced on a stool adjacent to one screen or the other and

21 and 22. Golovin's costume designs for Dom Juan and Sganarelle.

the entire mise-en-scène was adapted to accommodate him. Furthermore, he was allowed a freedom to improvise which delighted the audience and was wholly in keeping with the mood of the production.[51] Nikolai Khoddotov describes his perambulation with Dom Juan around the forestage:

> Lantern in hand, Varlamov's vast Sganarelle appears on the proscenium behind Yuriev's Dom Juan. Raising the lantern to eye-level, he looks for his friends in the auditorium; then his gaze halts: 'Ah! Nikolai Platonovich! (the well-known lawyer, Karabchevsky) How do you like our play? I don't know about you, but it suits me fine! By the way, don't forget that you're having a bite with me on Tuesday, will you, old chap?' He spots the Director in his box: 'My dear Vladimir Arkadievich, I'll be along at twelve to talk over that business of mine with you. . . . Mind you don't let anyone in before me. . . .' He spots a friend sitting with a young lady: 'Ah! So that's your better half. You

take her out to the theatre, but hide her away from me. . . . Tut, tut! Ivan
Ivanovich, you should be ashamed of treating an old man like that!'[52]

Varlamov's lovable Sganarelle drew a warm response from every critic,
but the real point of Yuriev's Dom Juan seems to have been missed by even
the most discerning of them. In reply to Benois' criticism that the production amounted to no more than 'an elegant fairground show' ('*nary-
adny balagan*') Meyerhold said that this was the greatest compliment that
he and Golovin could wish for: their *Dom Juan* was indeed inspired by the
popular travelling show, 'based on the apotheosis of the mask, gesture,
and movement'.[53] Earlier in the same article* he explains the implications of the mask:

> If you examine the dog-eared pages of old scenarios such as Flaminio
> Scala's anthology of 1611, you will discover the magical power of the
> mask.
>   Arlecchino, a native of Bergamo and the servant of the miserly
> Doctor, is forced to wear a coat with multicoloured patches because
> of his master's meanness. Arlecchino is a foolish buffoon, a roguish ser-
> vant who seems always to wear a cheerful grin. But look closer! What
> is hidden behind the mask? Arlecchino, the all-powerful wizard, the en-
> chanter, the magician; Arlecchino, the emissary of the infernal powers.
>   The mask may conceal more than just two aspects of a character. The
> two aspects of Arlecchino represent two opposite poles. Between them
> lies an infinite range of shades and variations. How does one reveal this ex-
> treme diversity of character to the spectator? With the aid of the mask.
>   The actor who has mastered the art of gesture and movement (herein
> lies his power!) manipulates his masks in such a way that the spectator
> is never in any doubt as to the character he is watching: whether he is
> the foolish buffoon from Bergamo or the Devil.
>   This chameleonic power, concealed beneath the expressionless visage
> of the comedian, invests the theatre with all the enchantment of chiaro-
> scuro. Is it not the mask which helps the spectator fly away to the land
> of make-believe?
>   The mask enables the spectator to see not only the actual Arlecchino
> before him but all the Arlecchinos who live in his memory. Through
> the mask the spectator sees every person who bears the merest resemb-
> lance to the character.[54]

What Meyerhold means here is not the traditional half-mask of the
commedia dell'arte (which he never used in his productions), but rather the
style of acting which the mask signifies: the emotional detachment and

* 'Balagan' (1912) – see pp. 122–124 below.

physical dexterity that enable the actor to assume the various aspects of his part ('to manipulate his masks') and at the same time to comment – both implicitly and explicitly – on the actions of himself and his fellow-characters, thereby affording the spectator a montage of images, a multi-faceted portrait of every role. It was in such a manner that Meyerhold conceived the figure of Dom Juan:

> For Molière, Dom Juan is no more than a wearer of masks. At one moment we see on his face a mask which embodies all the dissoluteness, unbelief, cynicism and pretentions of a gallant of the court of Le Roi-Soleil; then we see the mask of the author-accuser; then the nightmarish mask which stifled the author himself, the agonising mask he was forced to wear at court performances and in front of his perfidious wife. Not until the very end does he hand his puppet the mask of El Burlador de Sevilla, which he borrowed from the touring Italians.[55]

As we have seen, it was *The Fairground Booth* that revealed to Meyerhold the powerful magic of the mask, but only now through his studies of the *commedia dell'arte* did he grasp its full complexity. Yet, although this is made eloquently clear by Meyerhold in his writings, it seems likely that in *Dom Juan* his complex reinterpretation of the central character was obscured by the opulence of the production as a whole, even supposing that Yury Yuriev himself had fully grasped it.[56] Alexander Benois ended his review by asking: 'How is it possible to establish a new order of theatre whilst ignoring human thoughts, human emotions, and human beings in general?'[57] And Sergei Volkonsky lamented: 'Where is the word here, where is the thought, where is the soul, where is man?'[58]

But however justified these criticisms may have been, they do not invalidate what Meyerhold was *attempting* to do in *Dom Juan*: not only is that explained in convincing detail by himself but it is corroborated by all his major productions in later years. *Masquerade*, *The Forest*, *The Government Inspector*, *The Bed Bug*, *The Queen of Spades*: in each one of these the treatment of character is based on the principle of the mask, as it was first explored in *Dom Juan*. As we shall see, once Meyerhold was in a position to school his own actors, the principle of the mask became a reality: a fact convincingly demonstrated by descriptions of the performances of Igor Ilinsky, Erast Garin, and others in the 'twenties.

Even if the full complexity of Meyerhold's conception never fully emerged, *Dom Juan* enjoyed an immediate and vast popular success. The first of a series of 'festive spectacles' mounted by himself and Golovin, it was performed many times, and after the Revolution was revived first in 1922 and then again ten years later.

5. 1911–1917   A Double Life

Following the success of *Tristan and Isolde* in 1909 Meyerhold was entrusted with a production at the Mariinsky Opera in each of the three succeeding seasons. The first, *Boris Godunov*, is noteworthy only because it was the one occasion on which Meyerhold worked with Fyodor Chaliapin, who appeared as Boris in the first two performances. The settings and costumes were those which Golovin had designed for Alexander Sanin's production during Diaghilev's 1908 Russian season in Paris. With much of his time taken up until December by his work on *Dom Juan* and *The Transfigured Prince*, Meyerhold was able to devote barely a month to the rehearsals of *Boris Godunov*. The first night fixed for 6 January 1911 was immovable, since that was the date when Nicholas II and the entire royal household were expected to attend. In consequence, Meyerhold did no more than revise Sanin's production, concentrating on more concerted effects in the major ensemble scenes. He made no attempt to improve on Chaliapin's unique portrayal of Boris, preferring to accommodate his idiosyncrasies rather than risk a major scandal which might jeopardise the whole production.[1] Despite Chaliapin's hypnotic presence, the critics recognised the performance for what it was: a routine piece of revival work executed by a staff director. In the context of Meyerhold's artistic development it represented an opportunity lost, all the more tantalising given the unique regard he felt for Chaliapin's theatrical genius.[2]

By contrast, Gluck's *Orpheus and Eurydice* staged at the Mariinsky the following December was the most completely realised as well as the most widely acclaimed of all Meyerhold's operatic work. First performed in 1762, *Orpheus* was the earliest significant attempt to expose the absurdities of the 'concerts in costume' of the Neapolitan school and to restore opera to the dramatic heights first attained by Monteverdi. With this in mind, Meyerhold set out to stage *Orpheus* not as the conventional sequence of arias and ballet interludes but as total drama in the manner of his *Tristan* two years earlier. Faced this time with a considerably more complicated scenario, in addition to Golovin as designer and Napravnik as musical-director, he enlisted the aid of Mikhail Fokine as choreographer. Six years younger than Meyerhold, Fokine had already established himself as the foremost innovator in modern ballet with his choreography for *Carnival*,* *Les Sylphides*, *The Firebird*, *Petrushka*, and other works performed during Diaghilev's Russian seasons.

23 and 23A. *Golovin's costume designs for Orpheus and Eurydice.*

This time Golovin's settings incorporated a richly embroidered pink and silver front curtain and act-drop to facilitate scene changes, but otherwise the production bore a distinct external resemblance to *Dom Juan* at the Alexandrinsky: the forestage was covered with an ornamental carpet, the proscenium opening was reduced in size by using decorative borders, the blue and white auditorium was illuminated throughout by means of specially designed blue lanterns, and the costumes were conceived in the style of antiquity as an artist in Gluck's time might have seen it – that is, like *Dom Juan*, 'the work was viewed, so to speak, through the prism of the age in which the author lived and worked',[3] with no attempt made to create an illusion of classical antiquity or to reconstruct in precise detail a production by Gluck himself.

* His first association with Meyerhold (see footnote to p. 71 above).

But at the same time Meyerhold retained one outstanding feature of the settings for *Tristan and Isolde*, namely the 'relief stage'. He describes its use in *Orpheus*:

Technically speaking, the stage was divided into two planes, the fore-stage, which remained devoid of painted scenery and was decorated exclusively with embroidered hangings; and the main stage, which was given over entirely to painted sets. Particular attention was paid to the so-called 'planes of action': practicable rostra deployed in such a way as to dictate the groupings and movements of the characters. For example, in Scene Two the descent of Orpheus into Hades takes place on a path descending steeply across the stage from a considerable height with two sheer cliffs falling away to either side and downstage of it. This arrangement of the places of action ensures that the figure of Orpheus dominates the chorus of Furies and does not become confused with them. With these cliffs on either side of the stage, the only possibility is to have the chorus and the corps de ballet in two groups straining upwards from the wings towards Orpheus. In this way, the scene at the Threshold of Hades is not chopped up into a number of episodes but becomes a synthesis of two directly opposed movements: Orpheus descending, and the Furies first meeting him menacingly, then retreating before him.[4]

In scenes such as this, Golovin's settings became more than mere backdrops. There was absolute continuity between the painted setting, the lines of the three-dimensional practicable rostra and the precisely choreographed movements of the living figures. Thus, Golovin's sketches were not mere artist's impressions, but specific indications of the colour and rhythm of the eventual scene. This is nowhere more apparent than in his sketch of Scene One at the tomb of Eurydice where the very sky and trees seem to be sharing the grief of the mourners.[5]

The size of the chorus and corps de ballet, the complex rhythmical patterns dictated by the plot, and the use of practicable settings together created problems of choreography beyond the scope of any dramatic stage-director, even one with Meyerhold's appreciation of the role of movement in the theatre. For this reason Fokine's contribution was vital to the success of the production. Treating the chorus and corps de ballet (together some two hundred strong) as a single homogeneous mass, he created effects as spectacular as those he had achieved with Golovin in Stravinsky's *Firebird* for Diaghilev a year earlier. Here is his description of the scene in Hades:

24. Sketch by Golovin for the opening scene of Orpheus.

. . . when the curtain rose the entire stage was covered with motionless bodies. Groups in the most unnatural poses, as though frozen in the
midst of convulsions, clung to the lofty cliffs and hung suspended over
the abyss (open traps in the stage floor) wracked by the ghastly torments
of hell. As the chorus sang 'He who strays here, knowing no fear . . .',
the entire mass made a single slow movement, one awful concerted
gesture. It was as though some monster of unimaginable size had been
disturbed and was ominously raising itself up. A single gesture throughout the duration of the chorus' long phrase. Then after freezing for a
few minutes in a new pose, the mass began slowly to curl up and then
to crawl about the stage. All those who represented the Shades – the
whole corps de ballet, the whole chorus of male and female voices, all
the students of the theatre school, plus hundreds of extras – were all
crawling, changing places. Some climbed from the traps up onto the
cliffs, others slid into the traps. The mass of performers was crawling
all over the stage. They were all exhausted from finding no place to
rest.[6]

This scene and the descent into Hades described by Meyerhold illustrate
the extent to which all the elements of the production were synthesised
and subordinated to the rhythm of the musical score. In Fokine's demand-

ing scheme the chorus was spared no more than the corps de ballet. Fundamentally, the conception was the same as that of *Tristan and Isolde*, the one difference being that Fokine frequently moved the chorus in *Orpheus* in counterpoint to the orchestra rather than in strict unison as Meyerhold had done in *Tristan*. But in both cases it was the music rather than any consideration of 'realism' or operatic convention which dictated every movement and gesture.[7]

The collaboration between Meyerhold and Fokine was far from harmonious: Fokine complained that Meyerhold belittled his contribution, and years later in his memoirs went so far as to claim that with the exception of a few scenes involving only the principal characters he staged the entire opera.[8] Fokine's claim seems extravagant: firstly, the original conception of the production and the plan to use the relief settings which dictated the whole pattern of the choreography belonged to Meyerhold and Golovin; secondly, the crucial factor in a work of such complexity is the coordinating of every element to produce a coherent whole – and this was indisputably Meyerhold's achievement. At the same time, however, it is significant that Meyerhold and Fokine's dispute in no way concerned the actual style of choreography in *Orpheus*: over this they were in full accord, which is some measure of the affinity between what Meyerhold and the ballet-masters and stage-designers of Diaghilev's company were pursuing through their respective media at that time.

On 18 February 1913 Meyerhold staged Richard Strauss' *Elektra* at the Mariinsky, the first opera by the German composer to be performed in Russia. The approach to the work adopted by Meyerhold and Golovin was in complete contrast to their previous productions: three years earlier during a study visit to Greece Meyerhold had visited the legendary palace and tombs of the House of Atreus at Mycenae; inspired by the memory of this and by the Minoan treasures recently excavated by Sir Arthur Evans in Crete, he resolved with Golovin, as Volkov puts it, 'not to modernise but to archaise the production'.[9] Enlisting the aid of Professor Bogaevsky, a Russian archaeologist who had worked with Evans, they set about creating an historical reconstruction which, for all its stylisation, differed little in appearance from the Meiningen manner of early Moscow Art Theatre productions, even the characters' movements being modelled on the poses depicted on relics of the period. Telyakovsky was uneasy at the first dress-rehearsal, noting in his diary: 'Golovin's designs are splendidly executed and very interesting, based on the recent excavations in Crete. Meyerhold's production interesting, but in places *style moderne* creeps in, which I pointed out to him afterwards. Some of the singers' movements are most comical.'[10] In any case, as Meyerhold later admitted,[11] his interpretation took no account of the demands of Strauss' savagely atonal score, which was far closer in spirit to the morbid visions of the German Expressionist painters than to the formalised tableaux on the frescoes and ceramics of Mycenae and Knossos. The critics were quick to seize on this contradiction; for instance, Vyacheslav Karatygin wrote:

> In itself most interesting and ingenious, the production . . . consistently evoked the spirit of the Mycenaean age and transported the spectator's imagination into an historically authentic antiquity. But should this have been attempted? Whilst the stage spoke of archaeology, the orchestra emitted howls, cries, and groans, giving voice to the writhing, tormented soul of the neurasthenic composer – an Impressionist of the very latest mode! The contrast was most striking![12]

After three poorly attended performances the opera was taken off, due not so much to Meyerhold's misconceived production as to the failure of critics and public alike to comprehend Strauss' score (even Blok dismissed it out of hand as 'worthless ballyhoo').[13] What finally sealed the production's fate was the reaction of the conservative press, which pronounced that it was 'absolutely impermissible at the time of the three-hundredth anniversary of the Romanov dynasty to put on an opera in which members of a royal house are beheaded'.[14]

As Rudnitsky rightly stresses, such productions as *Orpheus*, *Elektra*, and D'Annunzio's *La Pisanelle* in Paris in June 1913* demonstrated Meyerhold's involvement in the general mood of escapism which overtook Petersburg in the last pre-revolutionary decade. It was an escapism that took many paths: to the exotic, the archaic, the mystical, the supernatural, even the coyly pornographic. Its predominant decorative mode was art nouveau, or '*style moderne*' as it was termed in Russia. As a movement in the theatre it embraced the Ancient Theatre, the *commedia* revival, the early work of Tairov at the Kamerny Theatre in Moscow, the numerous ornate productions of Molière – and pre-eminently the dazzling Paris seasons of Diaghilev. So dominant was it, that it completely overshadowed psychological realism, even at the Moscow Art Theatre itself. Nor did it encounter much resistance, save the occasional skirmish like *Columbine's Scarf* or the two isolated forays into the theatre by the Futurists, Mayakovsky's *Vladimir Mayakovsky* and Kruchenykh's *Victory over the Sun*, staged in Petersburg in December 1913.[15] Overwhelmingly, it was a period of rarefied taste and social disengagement. There is no denying that much of Meyerhold's work served only to further these tendencies.

* See pp. 124–125 below.

II

Despite his dual role as a director of drama and opera at the Imperial Theatres, Meyerhold continued to make time for the activities of his alter ego, Doctor Dapertutto. Immediately following an unsuccessful Moscow season in the summer of 1911 the Interlude House disbanded, but Meyerhold and the young director and theatre critic, Vladimir Solovyov, assembled another small group of actors to pursue their interest in the *commedia dell'arte* and pantomime in general. During the next year they gave occasional performances in public halls, private houses, and in the summer at the seaside resort of Terioki just over the Finnish border. The most frequently performed item was a one-act harlequinade devised by Solovyov himself and called *Harlequin, the Marriage Broker*.* It is described here by Meyerhold:

This harlequinade, written with the specific aim of reviving the theatre of masks, was staged according to traditional principles and based on our studies of the scenarios of the *commedia dell'arte*. Rehearsals were conducted jointly by the author and the director; the author, in accordance with his aim of reviving the traditional theatre, would outline the mise-en-scène, moves, poses and gestures as he had found them described in the scenarios of improvised comedies – the director would add new tricks in the style of these traditional devices, blending the traditional with the new to produce a coherent whole. The harlequinade was written in the form of a pantomime because, more than any dramatic form, the pantomime is conducive to the revival of the art of improvisation. In the pantomime the actor is given the general outline of the plot and in the intervals between the various key moments he is free to act *ex improviso*. However, the actor's freedom is only relative, because he is subject to the discipline of the musical score. The actor in a harlequinade needs to possess an acute sense of rhythm, plus great agility and self-control. He must develop the equilibrist skills of an acrobat, because only an acrobat can master the problems posed by the grotesque style inherent in the fundamental conception of the harlequinade.

Instead of conventional sets there are two decorated screens, placed some distance apart to represent the houses of Pantalone and the Dottore (standing on stools, they appear above these screens and motion to one another in a mimed discussion of the Dottore's marriage to Aurelia). The stage groupings are invariably symmetrical and the actors'

* First performed at the Assembly Hall of the Nobility, Petersburg, 8 November 1911.

movements acrobatic. All the jokes (whether prescribed or improvised) conform to the style of a traditional buffonade: striking one's rival across the face with a glove; a character transformed into a magician with the aid of the traditional pointed cap and false beard; one character carrying off another pick-a-back; fights, blows with clubs, cutting-off noses with wooden swords; actors jumping into the auditorium; dances, acrobatic numbers, Harlequin somersaulting; thumbing of noses from the wings; leaps and kisses; the final curtain with the actors forming up in a line and bowing comically to the audience; masks; shouts and whistles at the final exit; the introduction of short spoken phrases at moments of dramatic tension.[16]

June 1912 saw the creation of a new Fellowship of Actors, Writers, Musicians, and Artists at Terioki. Under the artistic directorship of Meyerhold, the young company lived communally in a large dacha with extensive grounds, and gave occasional performances at the Casino Theatre from a repertoire which included Strindberg's *Crimes and Crimes*, comic interludes by Cervantes, and new productions of *The Adoration of the Cross* and *Harlequin the Marriage Broker*. The easy regimen at Terioki enabled Meyerhold to complete his essay 'The Fairground Booth' (*Balagan*) which was published together with his other theatrical writings under the collective title *On the Theatre* in 1913.

Apart from the article 'On the History and Technique of the Theatre' and those on the productions of *Tristan and Isolde* and *Dom Juan*, 'The Fairground Booth' forms the major part of *On The Theatre*. It is an erudite disquisition on the theatrical traditions which Meyerhold had been exploring since he left Komissarzhevskaya: the theatre of the grotesque, the theatre of the *cabotin*, the theatre of mime, the theatre of the juggler and the acrobat, the theatre of improvisation, the theatre of the *mask*.* He begins by quoting a recent article by Benois which hailed the Moscow Art Theatre's adaptation of *The Brothers Karamazov* (first staged in October 1910) as a revival of the tradition of the mystery-play and saw in it the means of arresting the decline in the theatre which had been brought about by 'the deception and *cabotinage*' of such theatres and directors as the Comédie Française, Max Reinhardt, and Meyerhold.[17] But, argues Meyerhold, the reverse is the case:

> . . . it is the 'mystery' (in Benois' sense) which is ruining the theatre, and *cabotinage* which can bring about its revival. In order to rescue the Russian theatre from its own desire to become the servant of literature,

---

* For earlier references to this article see pp. 74, 113–114 above.

we must spare nothing to restore to the stage the cult of *cabotinage* in its broadest sense. . . .

In the contemporary theatre the comedian has been replaced by the 'educated reader'. 'The play will be read in costume and make-up' might as well be the announcement on playbills today. The new actor manages without the mask and the technique of the juggler. The mask has been replaced by make-up which facilitates the exact representation of every feature of the face as it is observed in real life. The actor has no need of the juggler's art, because he no longer 'plays' but simply 'lives' on the stage. 'Play-acting', that magic word of the theatre, means nothing to him, because as an imitator he is incapable of rising to the level of improvisation which depends on infinite combinations and variations of all the tricks at the actor's command.

The cult of *cabotinage*, which I am sure will reappear with the restoration of the theatre of the past, will help the modern actor to rediscover the basic laws of theatricality. Those who are restoring the old theatre by delving into long-forgotten theories of dramatic art, old theatrical records and iconography, are already forcing actors to believe in the power and the importance of the art of acting.

In the same way as the stylistic novelist resurrects the past by embellishing the works of ancient chroniclers with his own imagination, the actor is able to re-create the technique of forgotten comedians by consulting material collected by scholars. Overjoyed at the simplicity, the refined grace, the extreme artistry of the old yet eternally new trick of the histrions, mimi, atellanae, scurrae, jaculatores and ministrelli, the actor of the future should or, if he wishes to remain an actor, *must* coordinate his emotional responses with his technique, subjecting both to the traditional precepts of the old theatre.

Meyerhold calls upon the dramatist to assist the actor in the renaissance of the theatre of improvisation by composing scenarios after the manner of the *fiabe* which Carlo Gozzi wrote for Sacchi's troupe during the eighteenth-century revival of the *commedia dell'arte* in Venice. This is a point of profound significance: Meyerhold had always insisted on the right of the director and the actor to interpret the written text as they saw fit; now he demands that the author merely provide the actor with material on which to base his improvisations. For, he argues, 'drama in reading is primarily dialogue, argument and taut dialectic. Drama on the stage is primarily action, a taut struggle. The words are, so to speak, the mere overtones of the action. They should burst spontaneously from the actor gripped in the elemental movement of the dramatic struggle.'[18]

But whilst the actor is gripped in the dramatic struggle, continues Meyerhold, he remains in full control of his actions by virtue of the physical dexterity and self-control which he has inherited from the *cabotin*; at the tensest moments of the drama he continues to 'manipulate his masks'. thereby conveying without ambiguity the most subtle shades of irony and the most complex patterns of emotion.*

From this point Meyerhold proceeds to a discussion of the grotesque, not only as a stylistic approach but as the expression of a comprehensive view of existence. We have already seen in the accounts of *The Fairground Booth* and *Columbine's Scarf* the significance which Meyerhold attached to the grotesque. Now he saw that the dexterity and flexibility available to the actor through improvisation and all the varied skills of popular theatre contained the power to break the deadly grip of institutionalised drama.

In writing 'The Fairground Booth' Meyerhold undoubtedly took pleasure in flaunting his recondite erudition under Alexander Benois' sophisticated nose. Similarly, in his practical research with Solovyov he was probably motivated by a kind of archaeological zeal which paid little heed to the relevance of *commedia* for a modern audience. Then again, with his inveterate capacity for self-dramatisation, he must have enjoyed casting himself in the role of a latter-day Gozzi charged with the mission of routing the Goldonis of the established stage. All this said, the fact remains that the theatre which Meyerhold presented to a truly wide audience from 1920 onwards had its stylistic origins in the experiments initiated with Vladimir Solovyov some ten years earlier.

III

In March 1913, shortly after the failure of *Elektra* at the Mariinsky, Meyerhold went to Paris to work abroad for the first and only time in his career. He had accepted the invitation of Ida Rubinstein to direct her in *La Pisanelle, ou la mort parfumée*, a verse drama of some absurdity by Gabriele d'Annunzio devised especially to show off her talents. Lavishly staged at the huge Théâtre du Châtelet with settings by Bakst, choreography by Fokine, music by Pizzetti (under the pseudonym 'Ildebrando di Parma'), and a cast of almost two hundred dancers and actors, the production drew attendances surpassed only – as Meyerhold proudly noted – by those at the Grand Opera.[19] However, apart from affording Meyerhold valuable experience in the handling of large-scale crowd scenes, *La Pisanelle* marked no particular advance in his technique. Like *Elektra*, it was a lavish indulgence of the exotic and the spectacular. Meyerhold's letters to

* Compare the discussion of *Dom Juan* on pp. 113–114 above.

his wife suggest that he was pleased enough with the production,[20] but many critics were uneasy. Lunacharsky concluded his review in *Theatre and Art*: 'I left *La Pisanelle* not only exhausted by the frantic whirl of colour, but also with a disagreeable sense of extravagance of every kind which turned the head but left the mind unnourished, and which infected the heart with a sense of aesthetic protest against a spectacle which seemed to put one in mind of certain kinds of fun-fair.'[21]

Meyerhold's alliance with his fellow collaborators was uneasy (particularly with Ida Rubinstein, whom he considered 'weak-willed, unprincipled, and prepared to betray true art'), and although he personally gained the respect of many prominent artists, men of the theatre, and writers – notably Guillaume Apollinaire – it was seventeen years before his work was seen in Paris again.[22]

In September 1913 Meyerhold achieved a long-cherished ambition when he opened his own permanent theatre-studio at 18 Troitskaya Street in Petersburg.* It functioned throughout the theatre season on four afternoons a week. Initially the curriculum was made up of three subjects: 'musical reading in the drama' (taught by Mikhail Gnesin); 'the history and technique of the *commedia dell'arte*' (Vladimir Solovyov); and 'stage movement' (Meyerhold).

Gnesin's class was concerned with the principles of rhythm and melody and their application to verse speaking, practising on choruses from Greek tragedy.

Solovyov delivered a course of lectures devoted to the origins, development, and influence of the *commedia*, and also instructed the students in the traditional tricks or *lazzi* of the genre. Initially, the scenarios of existing works by Gozzi, Marivaux, Cervantes, and Solovyov himself were used for practice, but later the students composed their own pieces as well. From 1914 onwards Solovyov's programme was expanded to include the French, Spanish, and Italian theatres of the seventeenth and eighteenth centuries.

In Meyerhold's classes the students were instructed in the basic skills which previously he had always been obliged to impart during the course of his productions – often to unwilling or incorrigible pupils. The student was taught:

1 spontaneous control of the body in space, with the whole body involved in every gesture.
2 to adapt his movements to the area available for the performance.

* The following year the Studio moved to 6 Borodinskaya Street where it functioned until 1917 in a small concert hall belonging to the Petersburg Municipal Transport Engineers.

3 to distinguish between the various kinds of movement to music: in melodrama, circus and variety theatre; in the Chinese and Japanese theatres; the style of Isadora Duncan and Loie Fuller.

4 to imbue every action on the stage with joy – the tragic as well as the comic.

5 the power of the grotesque ('the grotesque helps the actor to portray the real as symbolic and to replace caricature with exaggerated parody').

6 the self-sufficiency of the form of the actor's performance (his movements and gestures) in the absence of the conventional plot from an improvised mime, and the significance of this lesson for acting as a whole.[23]

These were the principles on which Meyerhold's classes were based throughout the four years of the Studio's existence. At the start of the second year he and Solovyov introduced an additional joint course devoted to 'the practical study of the material elements of the performance: the construction, decoration and lighting of the stage area; the actor's costume and hand properties'.[24]

In February 1914 the Studio published the first number of its own periodical, *The Love of Three Oranges – The Journal of Doctor Dapertutto*. The publication took its name from Carlo Gozzi's 'fiaba teatrale', *The Love of Three Oranges*, of which a free adaptation by Meyerhold, Solovyov, and Konstantin Vogak appeared in the inaugural edition.* Gozzi was adopted as the Studio's exemplar, since it was he who had revived the declining *commedia dell'arte* in the eighteenth century with fairy-tale plays which combined the conventions of the literary and improvised theatres. In addition to chronicling the Studio's activities, the Journal included articles on the history and theory of the theatre, texts of plays (including *The Transfigured Prince*, *Harlequin the Marriage Broker*, and new translations of Gozzi, Plautus, and Tieck), reviews of contemporary productions and books on the theatre, and a poetry section which contained the works of modern Russian poets. The poetry section was edited by Alexander Blok, and as well as his own verses† it introduced a number of the works of Anna

---

* Prokofiev used this version for his opera which he wrote in 1919. Meyerhold recalls: 'I gave Prokofiev the first number of our journal . . . just before he left for America (it must have been at the very end of 1918). I urged him to write an opera based on our *Love of Three Oranges*, and he replied that he would read it on the ship.' Apparently, as early as 1913 Meyerhold had considered approaching Richard Strauss with the proposal, but decided against it because of Strauss' 'lack of taste'.[25] This was shortly after his production of *Elektra*.

† *To Anna Akhmatova* (1914, No. 1); *Carmen* (1914, No. 4–5); *A Voice from the Chorus* (1916, No. 1).

Akhmatova, Konstantin Balmont, Zinaida Gippius, Fyodor Sologub, and others. As well as being editor, Meyerhold himself contributed occasional critical and theoretical articles. Following the outbreak of war in August 1914 the journal was published at irregular intervals, the ninth and last number appearing late in 1916.

The editorial board of *The Love of Three Oranges* was responsible for the staging of Blok's two plays *The Unknown Woman* and *The Fairground Booth*, which were performed together seven times at the Tenishev Academy in Petersburg between 7 and 11 April 1914. Although officially not Studio productions, the cast was composed largely of Studio pupils and staff,* whilst the scenery and costumes, designed by Yury Bondi, were executed by them. The Academy amphitheatre was specially converted to resemble a Greek classical theatre with a semi-circular *orchestra* and shallow raised *skena*. Blok had completed *The Unknown Woman* in November 1906, a few weeks before the premiere of *The Fairground Booth*. Meyerhold planned to stage it the following season, but it was rejected by the censor on the suspicion that the character of the Unknown Woman was meant to represent the Virgin Mary – although, as he admitted, he didn't pretend to understand 'such decadent obscurity'.[26] It was given its first performance in 1913 by drama students in Moscow. Znosko-Borovsky describes the Petersburg production:

> The opening scene takes place in a tavern. A number of actors with no parts in the play acted as 'proscenium servants' and performed the task of scene-shifting. Dressed in special unobtrusive costumes and moving rhythmically, they brought on tables, stools, a bar, and to the rear raised a green curtain on bamboo poles. Then in half-darkness the actors appeared, carrying bottles and glasses which they tried to place unobtrusively on the tables; they took their seats and after a momentary silence began to laugh softly, creating a buzz of conversation to draw the public into the atmosphere of a tavern. One of the servants sat down on the floor close at hand, ready to act as prompter if need be, but only if someone really forgot his lines. When the scene ended there was a roll of drums and the servants who had been holding up the curtain walked forward, stretching the curtain above the actors and then lowering it to hide them from the audience whilst they removed all the properties from the stage. Then the proscenium servants behind the curtain climbed on to stools and raised their end of it to expose the white, reverse side to the audience. Meanwhile, directly in front of

---

* Meyerhold acted as one of the proscenium servants and Solovyov played the Author in *The Fairground Booth*. Yury Bondi was named as co-director.

the platform other servants rolled on from either side the two component parts of a wooden bridge, and on the platform a further group erected a new curtain of blue gauze with gold stars. So finally, when the white curtain was lowered, the audience saw a hump-backed bridge against a sky sprinkled with stars. As the actors mounted the bridge, the servants waved tarlatan veils in front of them to represent a snowy, starlit night. When a star was supposed to fall, all the chandeliers in the hall were extinguished and one of the servants lit a simple sparkler on a long pole which another raised right to the ceiling and then lowered for the first to extinguish in water; then the chandeliers came on again.

The last scene, a 'grotesque' representation of a drawing room in varying shades of yellow, was enacted on the platform itself. In front of it knelt the proscenium servants, holding candles to parody footlights. On a table were exaggeratedly artificial fruits and flowers which the actor-guests themselves removed as they went off. There was also a door onstage leading nowhere (to an entrance hall?), through which the guests entered, throwing off their overcoats and joining in a conversation in which some were audible, others not.

When the time came for the Unknown Woman to disappear, she simply went off between the wing curtains whilst a proscenium servant lit a blue star on a pole and held it in the window. To a roll of drums, the curtain fell once more on the furniture and it was borne away like the sailing ships mentioned in the text. The play was over.[27]

In the tavern scene the characters were dressed naturalistically, but the men wore false red noses (some had gaudy wigs as well) and the women's cheeks were daubed bright red like wooden dolls. The Unknown Woman had huge lashes painted round her eyes. Even more clearly than in Meyerhold's *Dom Juan* the role of the proscenium servants recalled the '*kurogo*' of traditional Japanese theatre: apart from their tasks of scene-shifting, prompting, and scenic effects, one of them constantly rearranged the voluminous cloak of the Man in Blue.

For *The Fairground Booth* the little theatre was represented by blue canvas screens behind the platform and paper-covered lanterns were suspended above the acting area. Meyerhold retained the device of the cardboard cut-out mystics on the platform from the 1906 production, but the rest of the action was performed on the semi-circular *orchestra* in front. Apparently, this greatly detracted from the play's original impact: it proved impossible to sustain the necessary aura of mystery in a space hemmed in by a largely sceptical audience.[28] In order to heighten the impression of contrived theatricality Meyerhold persuaded a troupe of

itinerant Chinese jugglers to perform during the interval, and the proscen-
·ium servants threw real oranges to the audience – designed to advertise
the sale of the Studio's journal in the foyer. By all accounts, the point of
both these attractions was lost on those present.

How far did Meyerhold succeed in conveying Blok's peculiar blend of
visionary lyricism and sardonic burlesque? In his review of the production, Znosko-Borovsky, one of the most balanced and perceptive of

25. An artist's impression of the Mystics scene at the Tenishev Academy.

Meyerhold's admirers, suggests that so enamoured was he with all the
tricks of the grotesque he had discovered through his researches and
studio experiments, that he neglected the tragic aspect of the plays which
had been such a poignant feature of the original *Fairground Booth*.[29] But on
that occasion so much had depended on Meyerhold's own haunting portrayal of Pierrot, whereas in 1914 the performers were almost entirely
students who could hardly be expected to possess Meyerhold's own in-
tuitive understanding of the poet or his exceptional powers of expression
as an actor. Blok himself did not share Meyerhold's enthusiasm for the
popular theatre; indeed it was often the cause of violent disagreement
between them. Initially he was exasperated by the productions at the

Tenishev Academy; but by the end of the run he conceded the point of Meyerhold's interpretation of his work and regretted not seeing every performance.[30]

In 1926 Meyerhold wrote: 'The first attempt at a stage setting in the Constructivist manner was the erection of the bridge in the second part of Blok's *The Unknown Woman* on the empty platform of the Tenishev Auditorium. . . . In that part of the production there were no theatrical elements whatsoever: the stage was cleared even of stylised objects.'[31] Even if Meyerhold does use the term 'Constructivism' loosely and chooses to ignore the depictive aspect of the scene in question, what he says lends further weight to the contention that his style in the 'twenties had its roots far back in his studio experiments in Petersburg before 1917.

The coming of the war did not halt the activities of the Studio, but its impact was reflected in the increasingly irregular appearances of *The Love of Three Oranges*. The combined sixth and seventh issue for 1914 (published in February 1915) contained a patriotic play by Meyerhold, Solovyov, and Yury Bondi entitled *Fire*. Based on actual events on the Belgian front, the work is a scenario in eight scenes with an apotheosis, and is designed to leave full scope for improvisation. Although never performed, it bears a close resemblance to another agitatory work, *Earth Rampant** staged by Meyerhold in 1923. In particular, the stage directions for *Fire* ('a series of iron girders and beams, with the centre occupied by an observation platform joined by a system of catwalks to the invisible foundations of the whole structure. On the platform a series of levers for controlling a complex system of dykes. . . .') strikingly if coincidentally anticipate Lyubov Popova's gantry construction for the later production.†

The studio's patriotic fervour was short-lived and Meyerhold and his colleagues continued their experiments uninterrupted by the effects of mobilisation. Their official public début took place on 12 February 1915. For this occasion the Borodinskaya Street auditorium was arranged to resemble in miniature the amphitheatre used for the Blok plays. The thirty-one Studio 'comédiens', as they were called, who took part were dressed in two uniform styles of costume, one for the actors and one for the actresses. The programme included Cervantes' interlude *The Cave of Salamanca* (directed by Solovyov), a mimed version of the play within the play from *Hamlet*, scenes in the manner of the *commedia dell'arte*, an interlude with circus clowns and a fragment from a Chinese play *The Lady, the Cat, The Bird and the Snake*, performed in the manner of Gozzi's *Turandot*. The programme was repeated twice more before the season closed.[32]

* Translated in *Meyerhold on Theatre* as 'The Earth in Turmoil'.
† See pp. 179–183 below.

War forced the curtailment of the 1915–1916 season and the Studio gave no further public performances. Meyerhold's plan to stage a full-length production of *Hamlet* with his pupils never materialised,[33] and after one further season the Studio closed in 1917. Although it never yielded the permanent theatre which Meyerhold had hoped for, the four seasons there gave him the chance to consolidate his ideas in practice and to lay the foundations for the style which he perfected in Moscow after the Civil War.

In 1915 Boris Pronin, the impresario of the old Interlude House, opened a new intimate cellar theatre in Petersburg called 'The Comedians' Rest' ('*Prival komediantov*'), with Meyerhold as artistic director. It was there in April 1916 that Meyerhold presented a new version of *Columbine's Scarf*. However, the designs by Sudeikin were poor by comparison with Sapunov's for the original production, and the work was not a success. One feature worthy of note was a rudimentary flying ballet performed by Harlequin on a wire from the flies. A planned production of Tieck's *Puss in Boots* failed to materialise, and Meyerhold soon became disenchanted with the whole venture. On this muted note the public career of Doctor Dapertutto closed.[34]

IV

Before returning to the Imperial Theatres, mention should be made of Meyerhold's work in the cinema. In 1912 he wrote:

> There is no place for the cinematograph in the world of art, even in a purely auxiliary capacity. . . . The cinema, that dream come true of those who strive for the photographic representation of life, is a shining example of the obsession with quasi-verisimilitude.[35]

The following year, when he was in Paris for the production of D'Annunzio's *La Pisanelle*, he made the acquaintance of D'Annunzio himself, Guillaume Apollinaire, and the actor Edouard de Max.* As Jay Leyda suggests, it may well have been they who persuaded Meyerhold to reconsider the artistic possibilities of the cinema.[36] In any case, when in May 1915 he was invited by Pavel Thiemann to make a film for the Moscow company of Thiemann and Reinhardt, he accepted, albeit cautiously. In an interview he said:

> First of all I must say that the technical aspect of cinematography is far more advanced than the artistic. My task is perhaps to discover unex-

---

* De Max, as well as the young Abel Gance, played in *La Pisanelle*.

plored techniques. First of all I want to study, to analyse the element of movement in the cinematograph.

The screen demands its own actors. So often we have seen artists who are splendid in the theatre or opera prove themselves totally unsuited to the cinematograph. Their movements are either too free or too cramped, their gestures far too weighty. . . .

In my opinion, it is a grave mistake to try to transfer dramatic or operatic works to the cinematograph. . . .

My opinion of existing cinematography is totally negative. . . .

It is still too early to say whether the cinematograph will become an art form in its own right or simply an adjunct to the theatre.[37]

At Meyerhold's suggestion, it was decided to make a film of Oscar Wilde's novel, *The Picture of Dorian Gray*. Meyerhold himself composed the scenario and the shooting was completed in rather less than three months. In order to enhance the effect of Dorian's unsullied youthful beauty, the part of Dorian was played by the actress Yanova, whilst Meyerhold himself played Lord Henry Wotton.

Alexander Levitsky, the foremost cameraman in Russia before the Revolution, worked on the film with Meyerhold, and, as both later admitted, their collaboration was fraught with discord.[38] The main trouble seems to have been Meyerhold's initial reluctance to concede the creative role of the cameraman, and his own slight appreciation of the practical difficulties of photography. For his part, Levitsky was astonished to be confronted for the first time with a series of sketches (prepared by Meyerhold and his designer, Yegorov) specifying the pictorial composition of each sequence, in which particular attention was paid to the disposition of colour masses and chiaroscuro effects. At that time, the normal practice in Russia was first to design a complete setting and then to shoot the whole scene against it from varying angles. Levitsky claims that much of what Meyerhold specified was impracticable, and indicates that it was himself who suggested the use of dissolves, close-ups, brief takes, even rudimentary montage, to make Meyerhold's inspiration viable cinematically.

Certainly Meyerhold was avid to utilise every means of expression the cinema had to offer, and in return he brought to it his own unique understanding of the dramatic power of rhythm and gesture. As Jay Leyda writes:

Meyerhold's theories of actors' movement seem from today's perspective ready-made for an adolescent cinema, and were indeed later adapted by Kuleshov to film use.[39]

. . . *The Picture of Dorian Gray* was original and daring as few films before it or since have dared to be. Russian artists who saw it and then *The Cabinet of Doctor Caligari* a few years later in Europe tell me that if it had been shown abroad it would have surpassed *Caligari*'s reputation as a heightening of film art. It was undoubtedly the most important Russian film made previous to the February revolution.[40]

In his authoritative account of the pre-revolutionary Russian cinema, Semyon Ginsburg goes so far as to say that 'Meyerhold was the very first

26. *Dorian and Lord Henry at the performance of* Romeo *and* Juliet, *with Meyerhold (right) as Lord Henry. (Still from film.)*

in the history of the cinema to put forward the idea of the silent cinematograph as, above all, a pictorial art'.[41] One scene in particular serves to illustrate this point. In the story, Dorian takes Lord Henry to the theatre to see Sybil play Juliet; as Sergei Yutkevich recalls:

On the screen one saw neither the auditorium nor the stage, but only the box which Dorian Gray and his companion entered in darkness. At first, when they sat down you didn't realise what was happening. But on the rear wall of the box there was a tall mirror and in it you saw the reflection of the stage-curtain opening and then a part of the balcony with a rope ladder suspended for the famous scene between Romeo and Juliet. The entire scene from Shakespeare was seen in the mirror, whilst the reactions on the faces of the seated onlookers could be observed in close-up.[42]

Keen to pursue his experiment, Meyerhold agreed the following summer to make a second film for Thiemann and Reinhardt, this time of Przybyszewski's novel, *The Strong Man*, in which Meyerhold himself was to play the supporting role of Gursky. He chose a new cameraman, complaining that previously he had been held back by Levitsky's 'conservative ways'.[43] On this occasion the collaboration seems to have been far more harmonious and the film was finished by the end of August 1916. However, it was not shown publicly until October the following year.

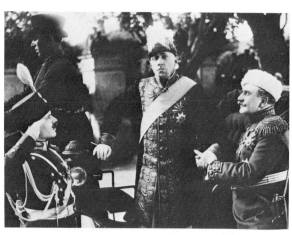

27. *Still from* The White Eagle *with Meyerhold as the Senator (centre) and Kachalov as the Governor (right).*

Understandably enough at that time, it attracted little attention and no substantial critical accounts appeared. In April 1917 there was talk of a film version of Blok's play *The Rose and the Cross*, which came to nothing. That summer Meyerhold started shooting a version of Fyodor Sologub's novel *The Spectre's Charms*, but the revolution forced the studio to suspend work and the film was never finished. The designer for the project was Vladimir Tatlin, soon to become a leading figure in the Constructivist movement.

Meyerhold never directed another film, although various projects were mooted. At the end of 1925 it was announced that he had agreed to film John Reed's *Ten Days that Shook the World* for Proletkino,[44] but work was never started by him and three years later it appeared under the title *October*, directed by his former pupil, Eisenstein. Finally, in 1929 Meyerhold began work on a version of Turgenev's *Fathers and Sons*. Initially, it was suggested that the part of Bazarov might be played by Mayakovsky, but eventually it was offered to the actor and director Nikolai Okhlopkov, with Meyerhold's second wife, Zinaida Raikh, playing Mme Odintsova.

However, the start of shooting was delayed by the Meyerhold Theatre's departure on its foreign tour in March 1930 and by the time Meyerhold and Raikh returned in September the project had been dropped.[45]

Unfortunately, no trace of either of Meyerhold's completed films survives. However, in 1928 he played the role of the Senator in Protazanov's *The White Eagle*. A copy is still preserved in the Soviet State Film Archive, and although as a film highly derivative, it remains an intriguing record of acting styles, with Meyerhold's precise angularity contrasting sharply with the highly emotional playing of the celebrated Kachalov from the Moscow Art Theatre in the role of the Governor. It was Meyerhold's only appearance on stage or screen after the Revolution.[46]

V

In the years following his productions of *Orpheus* and *Elektra* Meyerhold's various unofficial activities did not prevent him from extending his repertoire at the Imperial Theatres. Between 1914 and 1917 he was responsible

28. Design by Golovin for Act Two of The Storm.

for the staging of such widely differing works as Pinero's *Mid-Channel*, Lermontov's *Two Brothers*, Calderón's *The Constant Prince* (utilising the basic setting of *Dom Juan*), Zinaida Gippius' *The Green Ring*, and Dargomyzhsky's opera *The Stone Guest*. However, his productions were seldom distinguished by the adroit manipulation of theatrical conventions which continued to enhance his reputation elsewhere; he remained true to his word and kept his studio and 'big theatre' activities strictly segregated.

One production which questioned accepted practice and which fore-shadowed a vital line in Meyerhold's development after the Revolution was Ostrovsky's *The Storm* (9 January 1916). In his opinion, the true nature of Ostrovsky had been distorted by the naturalistic school which saw him as a mere genre dramatist of scant modern interest. Stressing Ostrovsky's affinity with Pushkin, Lermontov, and traditional Spanish tragedy, Meyerhold reinterpreted *The Storm* as a Russian romantic tragedy. He rejected the conventional emphasis on the vernacular in Ostrovsky's dialogue and sought to reveal its underlying poetry. In an attempt to bring out the predominant national character of the drama, Golovin based the settings and costumes on the strong colours and ornamentations of tradi-tional weaving and carving. Although restrained by comparison with later productions of nineteenth-century works such as *Tarelkin's Death*, *The Forest*, and *The Government Inspector*, *The Storm* was a bold challenge to tradition and the first of Meyerhold's many invigorating reinterpretations of the Russian classics.[47]

In 1917 the monumental production of Lermontov's *Masquerade* was revealed to the public. Although put on finally at eighteen days' notice, it had been in preparation and intermittently rehearsed for almost six years. Planned originally for autumn 1912, it was put back to November 1914 to coincide with the centenary of Lermontov's birth, but then postponed owing to the outbreak of war. Now in 1917 Meyerhold was warned that any further delays would mean the abandonment of the whole costly enterprise. The cast of over two hundred comprised the permanent Alex-andrinsky company augmented by students from various drama schools, including Meyerhold's own Studio. His 'comédiens' were particularly suited to the production by virtue of their familiarity with the grotesque, which was so vital to the realisation of the work as he conceived it.

Lermontov's verse drama tells of the cynical and dissolute Petersburg nobleman, Arbenin, who has become reformed by the love of his young wife, Nina. They attend a masked ball and through the intrigue of the society which he despises, Arbenin is persuaded that Nina has been un-faithful to him. Enraged with jealousy, he poisons her and on discovering her innocence, goes mad himself. Written in 1835–1836, the play was repeatedly rejected by the censor largely on account of the embittered trenchancy of its satire. Despite the many modifications that Lermontov made to the text (including even the substitution of a happy ending), it had yet to be performed when he died in 1841. Finally, a number of scenes from the work were staged at the Alexandrinsky Theatre in 1852 with Karatygin as Arbenin. From this and from the first complete stage version at the Maly Theatre ten years later there grew the tradition of interpreting *Masquerade* as a romantic melodrama in which Arbenin was driven to destroy his wife and himself by some demonic force within him.

Meyerhold, however, set out to restore the satirical emphasis of Lermontov's original version. One of his early notes reads '. . . whatever Arbenin might be, whatever horrors he might perpetrate, we shall castigate not him but the society which has made him what he is'.[48] He saw

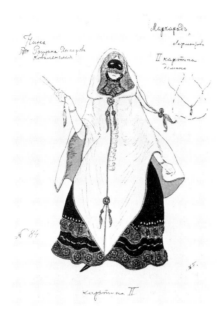

29. *Costume design by Golovin for Nina in the opening ball scene.*

Arbenin's murder of Nina and his subsequent loss of reason not as the outcome of mistrust and jealousy but as the price exacted by a malign society from one who had sought to reject and discredit its corrupt way of life, having himself long pursued it. The figure of 'The Stranger' was made the principal agent of this vengeance, with Shprikh and Kazarin his henchmen to weave the deadly intrigue round Arbenin. In his preliminary notes on the characters Meyerhold writes:

> The Stranger is a hired assassin. Society has engaged the Stranger to take vengeance on Arbenin for 'his bitter disdain for everything in which once he took such pride'.
>
> The death of Pushkin and the death of Lermontov – one should remember the evil machinations of society in the 1830s – two deaths: the best sources for an explanation of the importance and the air of mystery surrounding the Stranger.

Martynov* stands behind Lermontov like a shadow, simply waiting for an order from 'his side'. . . .[49]

Before he appears in the last act to reveal to Arbenin his ghastly mistake, the Stranger is glimpsed only fleetingly at the masked ball (Act One, Scene Two), when he warns Arbenin of the disaster that is shortly to befall him. In the text he is identified merely as 'A Mask,' one amongst many at

30. Costume designs by Golovin for Shprikh.

the ball, but Meyerhold left no doubt as to his menacing significance in the drama. Yury Yuriev, who on this occasion played Arbenin describes his entrance:

> Finally the mysterious figure of the Stranger appears, clad in a black domino cloak and a weirdly terrifying white Italian mask. He enters through the door in the proscenium arch to the left of the audience, and moves silently in an arc around the very edge of the forestage towards the opposite door. Behind him, as though in a current drawn by his hypnotic power, there floods onto the stage a long, broad ribbon of masked figures; suddenly he turns to face them, halts, and stares fixedly at them through his strange mask; they all freeze as one, riveted by his gaze.[50]

* Nikolai Martynov killed Lermontov in a duel in 1841, four years after the death of Pushkin in the same manner.

31. Illarion Pevtsov in the rôle of 'The Stranger'.

This vision of the supernatural is confirmed by Yakov Malyutin who played the Stranger in a later revival of the production:

He seemed to be the embodiment of an implacable tragic fate ruling and pursuing the life and future of man. In the interpretation of the director, the designer and the composer, the Stranger was a symbolic figure in every sense of the word: there was menace in his external appearance, menace in the musical theme which accompanied his appearance on stage, there was meant to be menace even in his voice, the stern, prophetic voice of a merciless, wrathful judge. The black cloak and the hideous mask in which he appeared at Engelhardt's masquerade, the tall hat and tightly buttoned frock-coat which he wore for his final appearance in the drama made the Stranger not so much a man as a devil in disguise, coldly inciting Arbenin to commit his crime and just as coldly punishing him for it.[51]

The Stranger's costume closely resembles a figure in the Venetian Pietro Longhi's painting 'Cavadenti'. This was no coincidence: in the summer of 1911 Meyerhold and Golovin read the recently published *Italian Images* by the art historian Pavel Muratov, in particular the chapter on eighteenth-century Venice.[52] Not long afterwards Meyerhold made the following note:

> In my opinion the romanticism which colours *Masquerade* should be looked for in the surroundings which Lermontov discovered when he read Byron from cover to cover as a student in Moscow. Isn't it eighteenth-century Venice which appears between the lines of Byron's poetry and which revealed to Lermontov that world of fantasy and magic dreams which envelops *Masquerade*? 'The mask, the candle, and the mirror – that is the image of eighteenth-century Venice', writes Muratov. Isn't it masks, candles and mirrors, the passions of the gaming tables where the cards are scattered with gold . . . those intrigues born of tricks played at masked-balls, those halls 'gloomy despite the glitter of candles in the many chandeliers' – isn't it all this that we find in Lermontov's *Masquerade*? Isn't it this very Venetian life 'imbued with the magic which always lies hidden in cards and in gold' which shows through the images of *Masquerade*, 'hovering *on the borderline of delirium and hallucination*'.[53]

Thus, in Meyerhold and Golovin's interpretation, Lermontov's Petersburg setting took on these imagined attributes, and so became a true 'Venice of the North', sharing its atmosphere of outward show and inner corruption.

In the 1917 production the atmosphere of the supernatural, dominated by the Stranger as the emissary of infernal powers, tended to obscure the satirical aspect of the drama.* But this vision of man at the mercy of a malevolent capricious fate was familiar in Meyerhold's work: it appeared first in Blok's *Fairground Booth*, it inspired the phantasmagoria of *Columbine's Scarf*, it was embodied in his own portrayal of the satanic Lord Henry in his film of *The Picture of Dorian Gray*, and above all it was germane to the sinister ambiguity of the mask as he interpreted it in his crucial essay, 'The Fairground Booth'. Even in the Soviet period Meyerhold did not suppress it entirely: there was the spectral aspect of Khlestakov and his strange double in *The Government Inspector*, and the unexplained figure of 'The Stranger' who suddenly materialised to take up Hermann's fatal challenge in *The Queen of Spades*.†

From start to finish Meyerhold worked on *Masquerade* in closest collaboration with Golovin. In order to emphasise the remorseless advance

---

* Discussing the second revival of *Masquerade*, Meyerhold said in 1939: 'The elements of mysticism have been removed from the figure of the Stranger. I am breaking free of Blok's influence, which I can now see in my production. Now I have emphasised that the actions of the Stranger are dictated by human feelings (revenge).'[54]

† See pp. 214–217, 257–259 below.

of the tragedy, Lermontov's cumbersome five acts were treated as ten
episodes; each had its own lavish setting, but the forestage and a series of
five exquisitely figured act-drops were used to ensure no pause in the
action, the concluding lines of one scene being spoken before the curtain
as the scene behind was swiftly prepared for the next. Critical scenes were
played at the edge of the semi-circular forestage and a series of borders
and screens was devised to reduce the stage area and frame the characters

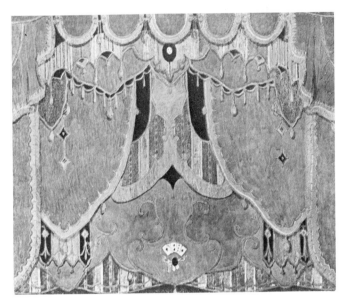

32. *Golovin's front-curtain design for* Masquerade.

for the more intimate episodes. The full stage area was used only for the
two ball scenes. As well as the many settings and costumes, Golovin designed all the furniture, china, glass-ware, candelabra, swords, walking-
canes, fans – everything down to the last playing card, yielding a total of
some four thousand design sketches. Not a single item was taken from
stock and everything of significance was made slightly over life-size in
order to ensure the required effect on the spectator.[55] As with *Dom Juan*
the auditorium was illuminated throughout, whilst tall mirrors flanking
the proscenium opening helped to break down the barrier between stage
and audience; not only did the reflected images emphasise the affinity between Golovin's settings and the 'Empire' style of Rossi's auditorium so
redolent of Lermontov's own period, but they also served to heighten the
all-prevailing atmosphere of illusion. Much of the action was accompanied by music specially composed by Glazunov and based on themes

33. *The second ball scene (Scene Eight).*

from Glinka. On this occasion the entire choreography was arranged by Meyerhold, including the masked ball in which over a hundred and fifty guests took part.

The premiere on 25 February 1917 was the theatrical event of the decade, but on that day the tsarist régime was forced to a final confrontation with the Petrograd proletariat, and the first shots of the Revolution

34. Portrait of Meyerhold by Golovin (1917).

were exchanged. Not entirely without justification, critics hostile to Meyerhold seized on this ironic coincidence and condemned the profligacy of this, the richest spectacle the Russian theatre had ever seen, representing it as typical of Meyerhold's own decadence and megalomaniac extravagance. With his usual asperity Alexander Kugel commented:

> At the entrance to the theatre stood tight black lines of automobiles. All the rich, all the aristocratic, all the prosperous Petrograd pluto-, bureau-, and 'homefrontocrats' (*tylokratia*) were present in force . . . and when that Babylon of absurd extravagance was unveiled before us with all the artistic obscenity of a Semiramis, I was horrified. I knew – everybody knew – that two or three miles away crowds of people were crying 'bread' and Protopopov's policemen were getting seventy roubles a day for spraying those bread-starved people with bullets from their machine-guns. What is this – Rome after the Caesars? Should we

go on afterwards to Lucullus and feast on swallows' tongues, leaving those starving wretches to go on shouting for bread and freedom?[56]

Rudnitsky refutes Kugel's condemnation; rather, he says, 'Meyerhold's production echoed like a grim requiem for the empire, like the stern, solemn, tragic, fatal funeral rites of the world which was perishing in those very days .[57] Whether one regards the premiere as a masterpiece of instinctive timing or as a monumental gesture of social indifference, the fact remains that *Masquerade* survived all criticism to be performed over five hundred times after the October Revolution right up to 1941. The settings and costumes were destroyed by bombing during the Siege of Leningrad, but Meyerhold's legacy survived even that, for after the war *Masquerade* was revived for the last time as a production without décor at the Leningrad Philharmonic with Yuriev, then over 70, still in his original part of Arbenin.*

Although Meyerhold retained his posts at the Imperial Theatres for a further season after the October Revolution and completed several more productions, it is *Masquerade* which must be regarded as the culmination of his Petersburg period. Before the year was out he had declared his support for the Bolshevik cause and pledged himself to the democratisation of the new, Soviet theatre.[59]

---

* According to Yuriev, *Masquerade* was performed only fifteen or sixteen times in 1917 but over five hundred times after the Revolution plus at least two hundred concert performances.[58] The production was restored to the repertoire in 1923, and then revised twice by Meyerhold, first in 1933 and finally in December 1938. The second revival was Meyerhold's last completed work in the theatre.

6.   1917–1921
Revolution and Civil War

———————◆———————

When Meyerhold left Moscow in 1902 to form his own company he was
deeply concerned with the role of the theatre as a reforming influence in
society. Indeed, the failure of the Moscow Art Theatre to discharge this
function to his satisfaction was a major factor in his dispute with its
directors. But although the repertoire of the Fellowship of the New
Drama was based on the works of such 'progressive' dramatists as
Chekhov, Gorky, Ibsen, and Hauptmann, it never made any attempt to
exploit the theatre for overtly propagandist ends. Whatever Meyerhold's
convictions, this was never a practical possibility, since any attempt at
political involvement would have been instantly suppressed by the
nervous local authorities.* After the events of 1905 they became more
vigilant still, but in any case by that time Meyerhold was preoccupied
exclusively with symbolist drama, which had no true bearing on the
urgent problems of the day, whatever metaphorical significance might be
attached to it.† In 1906 the Marxist Lunacharsky stigmatised the 'New
Theatre' as counter-revolutionary: in striving for a drama purged of all
external action, in depicting the 'inner dialogue' of the spirit through the
means of static poses and rhythmical movements, the New Theatre – he
maintained – fostered a passive acceptance of life with all its imperfections.
Its aesthetic could be compared to that of Schiller, of whom Karl Marx
said: 'Schiller's retreat from life to the ideal amounts to the rejection of
everyday misery for the sake of grandiloquent misery.'[3]

* In the winter of 1904–1905 during the period of unrest which followed the disastrous
Russo-Japanese war, Ibsen's *An Enemy of the People*, Gorky's *Summer Folk*, and Kosorotov's
Torrent of Spring were all removed from the Fellowship's programme on the orders of the
local police. In 1906 Chirikov's *The Jews*, which contained a vivid representation of a
pogrom, was banned by the Tiflis authorities after three highly successful performances.[1]

† Thus, when Meyerhold staged *The Death of Tintagiles* in Tiflis in March 1906, he
sought to relate the suffering of Tintagiles to the suffering of the Russian people in the
recent abortive Revolution.[2]

The main objective of Lunacharsky's attack was the 'static theatre' of Meyerhold's initial years as a director. But Meyerhold's rejection of that style after *Pelléas and Mélisande* in 1907 was largely for aesthetic reasons, and his subsequent work continued to have little or no direct bearing on contemporary events. In 1913, shortly after he had opened his Studio in Petersburg, he said in an interview:

> A theatre which presents plays saturated in 'psychologism' with the motivation of every single event underlined, or which forces the spectator to rack his brains over the solution of all manner of social and philosophical problems – such a theatre destroys its own theatricality. . . . The stage is a world of marvels and enchantment; it is breathless joy and strange magic.[4]

It took the outbreak of war to open Meyerhold's eyes to an alternative role for the theatre. As well as collaborating in the composition of *Fire*,* he was responsible in the autumn of 1914 for the staging of a number of propagandist pieces. One of them was a free adaption of Maupassant's story *Mademoiselle Fifi*, which was presented at the Suvorin Theatre on 15 August 1914. Meyerhold transformed it into 'a patriotic manifestation' in which 'All the performers spoke their parts clearly and precisely, like orators at a political meeting'; the play culminated with the entry of victorious French troops singing *La Marseillaise*.[5] Strictly speaking, this was Meyerhold's first acquaintance with agitatory theatre.

The demand for this kind of jingoism passed quickly enough once the true horror of war was grasped, and current events encroached no further on Meyerhold's theatrical activities. However, this is not to say that the social awareness of his youth had declined with the passage of time: in common with many other Russian intellectuals he shared a disdain for tsarist obscurantism, a disdain which in his case was greatly exacerbated by the languid indifference of the Alexandrinsky stalls patrons and his own failure ever to disturb it. During the War the rehearsals at his Studio were frequently attended by wounded soldiers from the hospital housed in the same building, and after one rehearsal he was moved to write '. . . in the way they responded to the performance of the comedians, they constituted the very audience for which the new theatre, the truly popular theatre, is intended'.[6] In April 1917, at a debate entitled *Revolution, Art, War*, Meyerhold castigated 'the silent, passionless parterre where people come for a rest', and asked 'Why don't the soldiers come to the theatre and liberate it from the parterre public?'[7] By this time he had become recognised as a member of the 'left bloc' which had emerged in the newly-

* See p. 130 above.

formed Arts Union and was agitating for a more democratic system of administration in the theatre.

In November 1917 the Bolsheviks transferred all theatres to state control and Lunacharsky, the first People's Commissar of Enlightenment, invited a hundred and twenty leading artists to a conference to discuss the reorganisation of the arts. Only five accepted the invitation, and they included Blok, Mayakovsky, and Meyerhold.[8] In January 1918 the Petrograd paper *Our Gazette* reported sarcastically that 'The ranks of the Bolsheviks have been joined by the ultra-modernistic Mr Meyerhold, who for some unknown reason has acquired the title of "Red Guard".'[9] It has been suggested that Meyerhold was merely exploiting the Revolution in order to propagate his own reforms.* However, the caution displayed by the majority is significant: Bolshevik power was still far from secure and a declaration of solidarity amounted to a hazardous act of faith. This act Meyerhold committed and soon affirmed it in August 1918 by joining the Bolshevik Party.[10] Alexander Matskin speaks with justification of the 'saving clarity' which the Revolution brought to Meyerhold's relationship with the external world, and continues:

> No doubt Meyerhold linked his fate with the Revolution because he expected it to give him greater creative freedom, and there was no harm in that. After all, many Russian intellectuals, Pavlov and Stanislavsky among them, did just the same. But to Meyerhold . . . it brought an inner freedom as well; it broke the circle of alienation and at one stroke cut all the knots which he had struggled for so long to unravel. That was why he followed the Revolution to the very limit.[11]

Whilst retaining his posts at the former Imperial Theatres, Meyerhold organised courses in production technique in Petrograd. These courses, the first of their kind in Russia, were held under the auspices of the newly established Theatre Department of the Commissariat of Enlightenment, of which Meyerhold was deputy head in Petrograd. The first, which ran from June to August 1918, was attended by nearly a hundred students with ages ranging from fourteen to fifty-three, and consisted of evening lectures designed to give a 'polytechnical education in the theatre arts'. There was a certain resemblance to Meyerhold's earlier Studio, with instruction in movement and mime; but equally, considerable stress was laid on the need for cooperation between the stage-director and the designer. Meyerhold continued with this work until ill health forced him to move south in May 1919. After a further term, the courses were discontinued.[12]

* Notably by the Russian artist Yury Annenkov in his autobiography *Dnevnik moikh vstrech* (New York, 1966), Vol. II, p. 46.

II

In September 1918 plans were made to stage the first Soviet play, Mayakovsky's newly completed *Mystery-Bouffe*, to mark the first anniversary of the October Revolution. Meyerhold was present at Mayakovsky's first informal reading of the play and was immediately enthusiastic.* Shortly afterwards, he invited Mayakovsky to read it again to the Alexandrinsky company with a view to staging it with them, but the absurdity of this idea was demonstrated by the shocked reactions to the play's futuristic form, its overtly Bolshevik sympathies, and its outrageous blasphemy.[13] Meyerhold's career at the Imperial Theatres had run its course; it remained only for him to discharge his obligation to stage Auber's opera *La Muette de Portici* at the Mariinsky, which he did with the very minimum of effort and enthusiasm. This was all too evident in the production, and it was dropped after a single performance, which ironically enough also took place on the anniversary of the Revolution.[14]

With barely a month left for rehearsal Meyerhold was commissioned by the Narkompros (Commissariat of Enlightenment) to stage *Mystery-Bouffe* at the theatre of the Petrograd Conservatoire. Vladimir Solovyov and Mayakovsky himself were to be his assistants, and the suprematist painter, Kasimir Malevich, was responsible for the settings and costumes. There remained the problem of casting: at that time all the Petrograd theatres were maintaining a position of cautious neutrality towards the Bolshevik government, and the production was boycotted by the vast majority of professional actors. Consequently, on 12 October the organisers were forced to make an appeal through the press for actors. Eventually all but a few main parts were played by students, and Mayakovsky himself filled three roles, including 'Simply Man'.

The Bolshevik government was more than a little embarrassed by the enthusiatic support it was receiving from the futurists,† fearing that their uncompromising brutalist vision of the new mechanised age might prove insufficiently beguiling for the masses. Lunacharsky, himself a critic of considerable liberality and perception, published an article in *Petrograd Pravda*, championing *Mystery-Bouffe* and excusing in advance the worst aberrations of the production:

---

* This was Meyerhold's first professional association with Mayakovsky. Their acquaintance originated in the winter of 1915–1916 when Mayakovsky came to Meyerhold's Studio and gave an impromptu reading of a number of his poems.

† 'Futurism' was a term applied to no specific group in Russia, but to the so-called 'left' avant-garde in general.

35. *Poster for Meyerhold's production of* Mystery-Bouffe *(1918).*

As a work of literature, it is most original, powerful and beautiful. But what it will turn out like in production I don't yet know. I fear very much that the futurist artists have made millions of mistakes. . . . But even if the child turns out deformed, it will still be dear to us, because it is born of that same Revolution which we all look upon as our own great mother.[15]

As David Zolotnitsky remarks, the style of the play is what Lenin defined not unapprovingly some years later as 'hooligan communism'.[16] The play parodies the biblical story of the Ark, with the flood representing world revolution, the seven 'clean' couples who survive – the exploiters, and the seven 'unclean' couples – the international proletariat. Having overthrown the 'clean', the 'unclean' are led by 'Simply Man' through an innocuous hell and a tedious paradise to the promised land which is revealed as the utopian mechanised state of Socialism where the only servants are 'things' (tools, machines, etc.). Meyerhold and his collaborators treated this allegory with all the rigid schematisation of the propaganda poster. In order to stress their solidarity, the 'unclean' spoke in the uniform elevated style of political oratory. The 'clean' were played in the broad, knockabout manner of the popular travelling show, a direct application of the skills explored in recent years by Meyerhold and Solovyov at their Studio, and an early demonstration of the style soon to be called 'eccentricism'.* Now added to the commedia *lazzi* and other tricks was the new element of circus acrobatics, to become even more prominent when Meyerhold and Mayakovsky staged the second version of the play in May 1921. In 1918, Mayakovsky himself as 'Simply Man' brought off one of the more spectacular effects:

> Hidden from the audience's view, he climbed four or five metres up an iron fire-escape behind the left-hand side of the proscenium arch. Then a broad leather strap was fixed to his waist, and at the appropriate moment he seemed to hurtle into view, soaring over the 'Unclean' crowded on the deck of the ark. . . . In that position he hammered out the lines of his speech.[17]

No pictures of Malevich's designs survive, but years later he talked about them to Alexander Fevralsky:

> My approach to the production was cubist. I saw the box-stage as the frame of a picture and the actors as contrasting elements (in cubism every object is a contrasting element in relation to another object). Planning the action on three or four levels, I tried to deploy the actors in space predominantly in vertical compositions in the manner of the latest style of painting; the actors' movements were meant to accord rhythmically with the elements of the settings. I depicted a number of planes on a single canvas, I treated space not as illusionary but as cubist. I saw my task not as the creation of associations with the reality existing beyond the limits of the stage, but as the creation of a new reality.[18]

Fevralsky describes the effects produced:

> In Act One there was a three-dimensional ultramarine hemisphere (five metres in diameter) representing 'the Earth' in vertical cross-section against a skyline background and giving the spectator the impression of a globe. On the reverse, open side of the globe, and hidden from the public, there were steps which the actors playing the Eskimos could mount to appear on the 'Pole'. The hemisphere was

* See p. 178 below.

made of light materials so that it was impossible to stand on it. Most of the action took place in front of 'the Earth'.

The Ark in Act Two took the form of a three-dimensional ship-like construction with its prow pointing at the audience. The artist employed a variety of colour combinations which clashed rather than harmonised with each other.

'Hell' was represented by a red and green gothic hall resembling a cave with stalactites. 'Paradise' was depicted in grey tones with clouds like aniline pink, blue, and raspberry-coloured round cakes – to quote Malevich, the colour scheme was 'nauseating'.

In the 'Promised Land' scene the audience saw a suprematist canvas and something like a big machine. The colours resembled iron and steel. The forestage lighting was slightly dimmed and the area upstage brightly illuminated. The 'Unclean' entered the 'City of the Future' through an arch.

The costumes of the 'clean' bourgeoisie and the 'unclean' pro-letariat were realistic. The 'Devils' were clad half in red, half in black. The costumes of the 'Things' were particularly unusual, being made from sacks.[19]

Clearly Malevich adopted a painter's approach to the production, which led to his collaboration with Meyerhold and Mayakovsky being less than harmonious. But in any case the play was put on in such a hurry that confusion and misunderstandings were inevitable: the final cast, speaking and non-speaking, seemed to vary in number between seventy and eighty; the Conservatoire refused to sell copies of the play-text on its bookstall and, according to Mayakovsky, even nailed up the doors into the theatre to prevent rehearsals; the posters had to be finished off by Mayakovsky himself on the day of the performance. There was no question of giving more than the scheduled three performances since the Conservatoire was due to follow them immediately with a programme of opera.

The reaction of the public to *Mystery-Bouffe* is difficult to establish since few critics deemed the production worthy of report. Andrei Levinson in the magazine *Life of Art* vilified the futurists for their calculated opportun-ism; yet wondered at the production's 'noisy success.'[20] But some years later Vladimir Solovyov recalled: 'The production had a rather cool reception; to be frank, it didn't get across to the audience. The witty satirical passages . . . which had us doubled up with laughter at rehearsals were greeted in performance with stony silence.[21] However, the unassailable fact remains that Mayakovsky had created a new dramatic style which was soon to influence the course of the whole agitprop

movement in Russia. The true vitality of *Mystery-Bouffe* was revealed in
Meyerhold's production of the revised version in Moscow three years
later, and thereafter the play was staged throughout the Soviet Union.[22]

III

In May 1919, weakened by illness and over-work, Meyerhold was forced
to leave Petrograd for convalescence in the Crimea. He entered a
sanatorium in Yalta, where he spent the summer receiving treatment for
tuberculosis. The Civil War was at its height, and when the Whites
captured the town he fled by sea to join his family in Novorossiisk, but
there his Bolshevik sympathies were revealed by an informer and in
September 1919 he was arrested. He spent four months in prison and
narrowly escaped execution for alleged subversive activities. Still
suffering from tuberculosis, Meyerhold was released on parole. When
Novorossiisk was reoccupied by the Red Army in March 1920, he
immediately joined its political section. For the remainder of his stay in
the south he participated in regular military training and spoke at both
political and theatrical debates, as well as producing *A Doll's House* at the
local Lenin Theatre.[23]

As soon as Lunacharsky learnt of Meyerhold's vicissitudes, he summoned
him to Moscow to take charge of the Narkompros Theatre Department
for the entire Soviet Republic. The actor Igor Ilinsky describes Meyerhold's appearance on his arrival in Moscow in September 1920:

> He was wearing a soldier's greatcoat and on his cap there was a badge
> with Lenin's picture. . . . In spite of its apparent simplicity, his
> appearance was somewhat theatrical, because although he was dressed
> modestly and without any superfluous 'Bolshevik' attributes, the style
> was still *à la Bolshevik*; the carelessly thrown-on greatcoat, the boots
> and puttees, the cap, the dark red woollen scarf – it was all quite
> unpretentious, but at the same time effective enough.[24]

Meyerhold's actions were no less dramatic than his appearance: he
transformed the bureaucratic and ineffectual Theatre Department into a
military headquarters and proclaimed the advent of the October Revolution in the theatre. Taking control of the Department's organ, *The
Theatre Herald* ('*Vestnik teatra*'), he initiated a violent polemic on behalf of
the proletarian, provincial, non-professional, and Red Army theatres, and
demanded a ruthless redeployment of the manpower and material
resources concentrated in the small group of 'Academic Theatres' in
Moscow. This group comprised the Bolshoi, the Maly, the Moscow Art

36. Meyerhold in 1922–1923.

Theatre with its First and Second Studios, Tairov's Kamerny Theatre, and the Moscow Children's Theatre. These the State considered the most worthy custodians of Russian theatrical traditions and rewarded them with its financial support. They were the true objective of Meyerhold's offensive, and his tirades soon resolved into an undisguised assault on their anachronistic styles and repertoires.

His hostility was not altogether objective: as Zolotnitsky records, certain well-known opera singers and members of the Art Theatre on tour in Novorossiisk had made no effort to secure his release from prison.[25] Then again, there were his bitter memories of the haughty eminences of the Imperial stage and their languid public. But perhaps most influential was the desire to purge certain aspects of his own extravagant and over-refined artistic past by attacking similar tendencies in the work of others.[26] The targets were not hard to find; by 1920 the Revolution had left little impression on the Russian professional stage and not one Academic Theatre had attempted to present a Soviet play. Whilst the repertoire abounded in such works as Byron's *Cain* (Moscow Art Theatre), Wilde's *Salome*, and Claudel's *The Tidings brought to Mary* (Kamerny Theatre), and Lecocq's operetta, *The Daughter of Madame Angot* (Moscow Art Theatre Musical Studio), not one serious attempt had been made to exploit the professional theatre for propaganda purposes since the three performances of *Mystery-Bouffe* in 1918. Tairov summed up the prevailing attitude in December 1920: 'A propagandist theatre after a revolution is like mustard after a meal.'[27]*

Not content with mere exhortation, Meyerhold took control of the Free Theatre company, renamed it the 'R.S.F.S.R. Theatre No. 1', and augmented it with his own young and inexperienced nominees. In his opening speech to the company Meyerhold outlined his programme and policy:

> The Artistic Soviet of the R.S.F.S.R. Theatre has compiled a pro-visional repertoire which includes *The Dawn* (Verhaeren), *Mystery-Bouffe* (Mayakovsky), *Hamlet* (Shakespeare), *Great Catherine* (Bernard Shaw), *Golden Head* (Claudel) and *Women in Parliament* (Aristophanes). But since all this is merely literature, let it lie undisturbed in the libraries. We shall need scenarios and we shall often utilise even the classics as a basis for our theatrical creations. We shall tackle the task of adaptation without fear, and fully confident of its necessity. It is possible that we shall adapt texts in cooperation with the actors of the company, and it is a great pity that they were not able to help Valery Bebutov and me with *The Dawn*. Joint work on texts by the company is envisaged as an integral part of the theatre's function. It is possible that such team-work will help us to realise the principle of improvisation, about which there is so much talk at the moment and which promises to prove most valuable.
>
> The psychological make-up of the actor will need to undergo a number of changes. There must be no pauses, no psychology, no 'authentic emotions' either on the stage or whilst building a role. Here is our theatrical programme: plenty of light, plenty of high spirits, plenty of grandeur, plenty of infectious enthusiasm, unlaboured creativity, the participation of the audience in the corporate creative act of the performance.[29]

* In 1917–1918 Meyerhold and Tairov had jointly directed Claudel's play *The Exchange* at the Kamerny Theatre (premiere 20 February, designs by Yakulov). At the same time, the two directors, together with Yevreinov, were contemplating the formation of a new 'left theatre' in Moscow to be directed by the three of them.[28] The project came to nothing and by 1920 Meyerhold and Tairov could find little in common; their hostility then flared in the many public debates of the time.

The play chosen to inaugurate the new theatre was *The Dawn* (*'Les Aubes'*) an epic verse drama written in 1898 by the Belgian symbolist poet Emile Verhaeren, depicting the transformation of a capitalist war into an international proletarian uprising by the opposing soldiers in the mythical town of Oppidomagne. It was translated by Georgy Chulkov and hurriedly adapted by Meyerhold and his assistant Valery Bebutov in an attempt to bring out its relevance to recent political events.

The first performance, timed to coincide with the third anniversary of the October Revolution, took place on 7 November 1920 at the former Sohn Theatre on what is now called Mayakovsky Square. The derelict, unheated auditorium with its flaking plaster and broken seats was more like a meeting-hall; this was wholly appropriate, for it was in the spirit of a political meeting that Meyerhold conceived the production. Admission was free, the walls were hung with hortatory placards, and the audience was showered at intervals during the play with leaflets. Also derived from the meeting was the declamatory style of the actors, who mostly remained motionless and addressed their speeches straight at the audience. Critics rightly compared the production with Greek tragedy, which furnished the precedent for the static manner of delivery and for the chorus in the orchestra pit commenting on the peripeteia of the drama. The chorus was assisted in the task of guiding and stimulating audience reaction by a claque of actors concealed throughout the auditorium.

A fortnight after the production had opened, the actor playing the Herald interrupted his performance to deliver the news received the day before that the Red Army had made the decisive breakthrough into the Crimea at the Battle of Perekop. As the applause died down, a solo voice began to sing the Revolutionary funeral march 'As Martyrs You Fell' and the audience stood in silence. The action on stage then resumed its course.* Meyerhold felt that his highest aspirations were gratified, and the practice of inserting bulletins on the progress of the war continued. However, such unanimity of response did not occur every night, but usually only when military detachments attended *en bloc* – as they sometimes did, complete with banners flying and bands ready to strike up.

Whilst the more sophisticated spectator was likely to find the conventions crude and the acting maladroit – not to mention the political message oversimplified or even repugnant – the new audience at whom ostensibly the production was aimed could not help but be puzzled by its appearance. The young designer, Vladimir Dmitriev, who had attended Meyerhold's theatre arts course in Petrograd, favoured the geometrical

* Various myths have grown up around this event. The version given here seems to be the most reliable.[30]

37. The Dawn, Scene Seven, showing the merging of the chorus in the orchestra pit with the crowd onstage.

schematisation of the Cubo-Futurist school of artists. His assembly of red, gold, and silver cubes, discs and cylinders, cut-out tin triangles, and intersecting ropes blended uneasily with the occasional recognisable object such as a graveyard cross or the gates of a city, to say nothing of the soldiers' spears and shields, or the curious 'timeless' costumes of daubed canvas. Furthermore, the overall picture was made to look tawdry in the harsh white light with which Meyerhold sought to dispel all illusion. Defending his choice of Dmitriev as a designer, Meyerhold said:

> We have only to talk to the latest followers of Picasso and Tatlin to know at once that we are dealing with kindred spirits . . . We are building just as they are building . . . For us the art of manufacture is more important than any tediously pretty patterns and colours. What do we want with pleasing pictorial effects? What the *modern* spectator wants is the placard, the juxtaposing of the surfaces and shapes of *tangible materials*! . . . We are right to invite the Cubists to work with us, because we need settings which resemble those which we shall be performing against tomorrow. The modern theatre wants to move out into the open air. We want our setting to be an iron pipe or the open sea or something constructed by the new man. I don't intend to engage in an appraisal of such settings; suffice it to say that for us they have the advantage of getting us out of the old theatre.[31]

His enthusiasm was not shared by Lunacharsky, who remarked drily: 'I was very much against that piano-lid flying through the sky of Oppidomagne.'[32]

As with the *Mystery-Bouffe*, the Party was discomforted by this manifestation of the style of its Futurist supporters. Lenin's wife, Nadezhda Krupskaya, writing in *Pravda* had no complaint against the 'timelessness' of the production, but she objected violently to the ill-considered adaptation which related the action to a Soviet context and transformed the hero, Hérénien, into a traitor to his class who comes to terms with a capitalist power. Above all, she objected that it was a sheer insult 'to cast the Russian proletariat as a Shakespearian crowd which any self-opinionated fool can lead wherever the urge takes him'.[33]

As a direct consequence of Krupskaya's criticism the work was re-written to render it dialectically more orthodox, but all the original theatrical devices were retained.

With all its imperfections, *The Dawn* depended very much on the mood of the audience on the night for its success, but even so it ran for well over a hundred performances to packed houses. It proclaimed an epoch in the

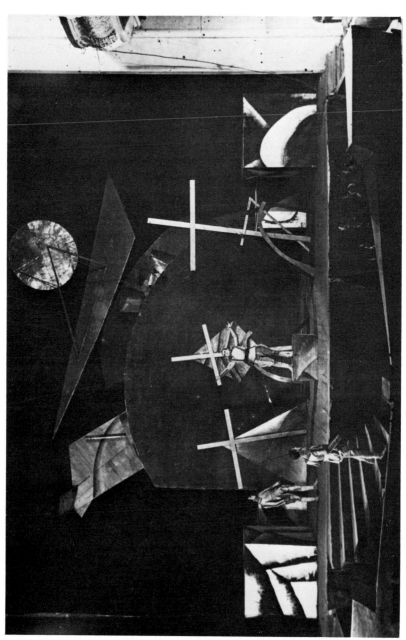

38. The Dawn, *Scene Four (the cemetery).*

Soviet theatre and is rightly considered a *locus classicus* in the history of the political theatre.

Whilst criticising the 'pretentiousness of the Futurist elements' in *The Dawn*, Lunacharsky considered it was a reasonable price to pay for the production's revolutionary fervour.[34] However, he refused point-blank to surrender the Academic Theatres to Meyerhold's demolition squad, saying:

> I am prepared to entrust Comrade Meyerhold with the destruction of the old and bad and the creation of the new and good. But I am not prepared to entrust him with the preservation of the old and good, the vital and strong, which must be allowed to develop in its own way in a revolutionary atmosphere.[35]

All Academic Theatres in Moscow and Petrograd were brought under the direct aegis of Narkompras, thereby rendering Meyerhold's Theatre Department innocuous in the one sector it truly coveted. His ambitions were realised to the extent that the Academic Theatres began now to stage Soviet works, but it was in their own good time and in their own well-tried manner.* The Nezlobin Theatre, the Korsh Theatre, and the Chaliapin Drama Studio rallied to Meyerhold and were renamed R.S.F.S.R. Theatres Nos. 2, 3, and 4 respectively, but they enjoyed only a brief existence in this guise and achieved no productions of note. On 26 February 1921 Meyerhold resigned as Head of the Theatre Department, and in May he severed his last effective connection with it.[36]

May Day 1921 saw the second production at the R.S.F.S.R. Theatre No. 1. It was *Mystery-Bouffe*, completely rewritten to make it relevant to the course of events since 1917. As a playwright Mayakovsky was accorded unique status by Meyerhold. In 1933 he said:

> In his work with me, Mayakovsky showed himself to be not only a remarkable dramatist but a remarkable director as well. In all my years as a director I have never permitted myself the luxury of an author's cooperation when producing his work. I have always tried to keep the author as far from the theatre as possible during the period of actual production, because any truly creative director is bound to be hampered by the playwright's interference. In Mayakovsky's case I not only permitted him to attend, I simply couldn't begin to produce his plays without him.[37]

Mayakovsky was present from the first read-through of *Mystery-Bouffe* and added numerous topical couplets right up to the final rehearsal. The

---

* The first production of a Soviet play at the Moscow Art Theatre was in September 1925 (*The Pugachov Rising* by Trenyov).

published text of this revised version is prefaced by the following exhortation:

Henceforth everyone who performs, stages, reads or prints *Mystery-Bouffe* should alter the contents in order to make it modern, up to date, up to the minute.[38]

Among his amendments were the inclusion in the ranks of 'The Clean' of Lloyd George and Clemenceau, and the creation of a new central character

39. Ilinsky as the Menshevik (sketch by Victor Kiselyov).

'The Conciliator', or Menshevik, who was brilliantly portrayed by the nineteen-year-old Igor Ilinsky in red wig, steel gig-lamps, and flapping coat-tails, with an open umbrella to symbolise his readiness for flight. He was a figure derived from the traditional red-haired circus clown. His performance set the key for the whole production: an hilarious, dynamic, caricaturist rough-and-tumble, a carnival celebration of victory in the Civil War in total contrast to the still, hieratic solemnity of *The Dawn*. 'The Clean' wore costumes designed by Victor Kiselyov with much of the pith and vigour which made the ROSTA satirical 'windows'* the most telling political posters of the early Soviet period. They were close in spirit to the sketches which Mayakovsky himself had made for the play in

---

* A series of strip cartoons ('Okna ROSTA') on social and political themes issued by the Russian Telegraph Agency (ROSTA). Mayakovsky was a regular contributor.

reaction against Malevich's original designs. As Fevralsky observes, these costumes were not unlike Picasso's cubist paintings in style, with pieces of newspaper and cardboard placards attached to them.[39] However, 'The Unclean', clad this time in blue overalls,* were of a uniform dullness which not even Mayakovsky's rhetoric could hide. Meyerhold was quick to realise that the portrayal of virtue – even Socialist virtue – untarnished and triumphant is inherently tedious and, as we shall see, his avoidance of it at all costs was to cause him unending trouble in the years to come.

40. Model reconstruction of the setting for Mystery-Bouffe.

The proscenium which had been bridged by the placing of the chorus in the orchestra pit in *The Dawn* was demolished once and for all in *Mystery-Bouffe*.† The stage proper was taken up by a series of platforms of differing levels, inter-connected by steps and vaguely suggestive of the various locations in the action. In front a broad ramp sloped right down to the first row of seats, bearing a huge hemisphere over which the cast clambered and which revolved to expose the exit from 'Hell'. In this scene, one of the devils was played by a circus clown, Vitaly Lazarenko, who entered by sliding down a wire and performed acrobatic tricks. In the final act, set in the new *electrified* promised land, the action spilled into the boxes adjacent to the stage, and at the conclusion the audience was invited to mingle with the actors on stage.

* Soon to serve as the prototype for the uniforms of the 'Blue Blouse' agitprop theatre groups which were to appear in the Soviet Union from 1923 onwards.

† The settings were by Anton Lavinsky and Vladimir Khrakovsky.

In this production Meyerhold dispensed finally with a front curtain and flown scenery. The theatre was bursting at the seams, unable to accommodate the kind of popular spectacle which he was striving to achieve, and it was now that the questions arose whose answers he was shortly to seek in Constructivism.

Meyerhold and Mayakovsky were accused once again of futurist obscurity and the production was boycotted by all but three Moscow newspaper critics. One of the few to subject it to constructive analysis was the Bolshevik writer Dmitry Furmanov, the future author of *Chapaev*. Reporting in a provincial paper, he found the play's form confused and its humour crude, but in conclusion he wrote: 'This new theatre is the theatre of the stormy age of the Revolution; it was born not of the tranquillity of the Cherry Orchard, but of the tempests and whirlwinds of the Civil War. . . . This new theatre of storm and stress undoubtedly has a great future. It can't be dismissed as a mere aberration: it has its roots deep in our heroic, proletarian struggle.'[40] Despite all opposition, *Mystery-Bouffe* was a far greater popular success than *The Dawn*, and was performed daily until the close of the season on 7 July. In the five months up to the end of May 1921, one hundred and fifty-four performances of the two plays in the thousand-seat Sohn Theatre were watched by roughly 120,000 spectators.[41]

In Spring 1921, when Soviet Russia was on the verge of bankruptcy as a consequence of the privations and chaos wrought by the Civil War, Lenin introduced his New Economic Policy in order to restore the economy. Under its provisions, certain sectors of the economic system reverted to private control and the ban on the investment of foreign capital was lifted. Its effects were quickly felt in the theatre, where some companies reverted to private ownership and were required once more to yield their investors a realistic profit, whilst those run by collectives or state organisations such as the unions or the Red Army were subjected to more stringent controls, and many were forced to close.

The R.S.F.S.R. Theatre No. 1 depended for its survival on ad hoc subsidy, and in June 1921 the Moscow Soviet ordered its closure, implausibly accusing it of overspending. Thanks largely to Lunacharsky's intervention, the theatre continued to live a precarious existence throughout the summer, managing to stage one more production, Ibsen's *The League of Youth*, in August. But a 'revolutionised' version of Wagner's *Rienzi* was abandoned after the second run-through, and on 6 September 1921 the theatre closed for good. Thus Meyerhold, the first Bolshevik director, was left with nowhere to work.[42]

7. 1921–1926 People's Artist

In the autumn of 1921 Meyerhold was appointed director of the newly formed State Higher Theatre Workshops in Moscow.* He was joined on the staff by Valery Bebutov, his assistant director at the R.S.F.S.R Theatre, and Ivan Aksyonov – Civil War commissar, leading member of the 'Centrifuge' group of poets, authority on Elizabethan drama, and polyglot translator.[1] Aksyonov was Principal and gave courses in playwriting, the English theatre, and mathematics. His polymath skills typified the depth of intellectual enquiry which accompanied Meyerhold's work.

In the first year the Workshops' courses in theatre history, theory and practice were attended by some eighty students; some had been with Meyerhold at the R.S.F.S.R. Theatre, but most were newcomers, no more than seventeen or eighteen years old. Henceforth, Meyerhold's company was composed exclusively of actors who had grown up during the Civil War period; many were of working-class origin or had seen military service, and were violently opposed to the traditions of pre-revolutionary art. Understandably, their devotion to the 'Master', as Meyerhold was now commonly known to his students, bordered on the fanatical.

Amongst those who enrolled for the first course were the future film-directors Sergei Eisenstein, Sergei Yutkevich, and Nikolai Ekk, together with many others who were to become leading actors and directors in the Soviet theatre and cinema. One student was Zinaida Raikh, the ex-wife of the poet Sergei Yesenin and soon to marry Meyerhold when he and

* Called initially the State Higher Director's Workshops. In 1922 it was incorporated in the State Institute of Theatrical Art ('GITIS'), but shortly broke away to form the 'Meyerhold Workshop'. In 1923 this was given the new title of 'Meyerhold State Experimental Theatre Workshops' ('GEKTEMAS') and continued to function as such under various further names until 1938. It remained throughout an integral part of Meyerhold's theatre. (See also p. 175 below.)

Olga Munt were divorced. Beginning with Aksyusha in *The Forest*, Raikh
played many leading roles in Meyerhold's productions. Meyerhold's
biographer Nikolai Volkov writes:

> Vsevolod Emilievich made an actress out of her. After the theatre's
> visit to Berlin* the Germans called Raikh 'die grosse Schauspielerin';
> but she wasn't a great actress, or even a particularly outstanding one.
> The Moscow critics were positively and sharply opposed to her. But

41. Meyerhold and Zinaida Raikh in 1923.

the fault for this unjustified rejection was largely Meyerhold's. His
promotion of her as an actress was pursued aggressively. At times he
neglected the interests of the other actors in his company by surrounding her with untalented actresses. . . . He entrusted Raikh with the
best parts, beginning with Anna Andreevna in *The Government Inspector*
and ending with Marguerite in *The Lady of the Camellias*.[2]

As early as January 1921 Meyerhold had made plans to open a 'theatrical
technical school' attached to his theatre. It was designed to give actors
methodical practical instruction in speech and movement 'based on the

* In 1930 – see p. 242 below.

general physical laws of technology, as expressed most clearly in physics, mechanics, music and architecture'.[3] With Meyerhold's resignation from Narkompros the school failed to materialise but now at the Higher Theatre Workshops the curriculum was very similar, including a course given by himself in 'biomechanics'. Meyerhold envisaged biomechanics as the theatrical equivalent of industrial time-and-motion study. He compared it on the one hand to the experiments in the scientific organisation of labour by the American Frederick Winslow Taylor and his Russian follower Gastev, and on the other to the theories of 'reflexology' developed by the 'objective psychologist' William James and the Russians Bekhterev and Pavlov.[4] The first public demonstration of his biomechanics exercises or 'études' was given by Meyerhold and his students on 12 June 1922. Here are the main points from his introductory lecture:

> In the past the actor has always conformed to the society for which his art was intended. In future the actor must go even further in relating his technique to the industrial situation. For he will be working in a society where labour is no longer regarded as a curse but as a joyful, vital necessity. In these conditions of ideal labour art clearly requires a new foundation. . . .
>
> In art our constant concern is the organisation of raw material. Constructivism* has forced the artist to become both artist and engineer. Art should be based on scientific principles; the entire creative act should be a conscious process. The art of the actor consists in organising his material: that is, in his capacity to utilise correctly his body's means of expression.
>
> The actor embodies in himself both the organiser and that which is organised (i.e. the artist and his material). The formula for acting may be expressed as follows: $N = A_1 + A_2$ (where N = the actor; A_1 = the artist who conceives the idea and issues the instructions necessary for its execution; A_2 = the executant who executes the conception of A_1).
>
> The actor must train his material (the body), so that it is capable of executing instantaneously those tasks which are dictated externally (by the actor, the director). . . .
>
> Since the art of the actor is the art of plastic forms in space, he must study the mechanics of his body. This is essential because any manifestations of a force (including the living organism) is subject to constant laws of mechanics (and obviously the creation by the actor of plastic forms in the space of the stage is a manifestation of the force of the human organism). . . .

* See pp. 170 ff. below.

All psychological states are determined by specific physiological processes. By correctly resolving the nature of his state physically, the actor reaches the point where he experiences the *excitation* which communicates itself to the spectator and induces him to share in the actor's performance: what we used to call 'gripping' the spectator. It is this excitation which is the very essence of the actor's art. From a sequence of physical positions and situations there arise 'points of excitation' which are informed with some particular emotion. Throughout this process of 'rousing the emotions' the actor observes a rigid framework of physical prerequisites.[5]

The series of individual and group exercises had such titles as 'Dagger thrust', 'Leap onto the chest', 'Lowering a weight', and 'Shooting a bow'. One of the students, Erast Garin, describes 'Shooting a bow':

An imaginary bow is held in the left hand. The student advances with the left shoulder forward. When he spots the target he stops, balanced equally on both feet. The right hand describes an arc in order to reach an arrow in an imaginary belt behind his back. The movement of the hand affects the whole body, causing the balance to shift to the back foot. The hand draws the arrow and loads the bow. The balance is transferred to the front foot. He aims. The bow is drawn with the balance shifting again to the back foot. The arrow is fired and the exercise completed with a leap and a cry.

Through this, one of the earliest exercises, the pupil begins to comprehend himself in spatial terms, acquires physical self-control, develops elasticity and balance, realises that the merest gesture – say with the hand – resounds throughout the entire body, and gains practice in the so-called 'refusal' [or 'reaction' – EB]. In this exercise the 'pre-gesture', the 'refusal', is the hand reaching back for the arrow. The étude is an example of the 'acting sequence', which comprises intention, realisation and reaction.[6]

Meyerhold describes the 'acting sequence' or cycle referred to by Garin:

Each *acting cycle* comprises three invariable stages:

1. INTENTION 2. REALISATION 3. REACTION.

The Intention is the intellectual assimilation of a task prescribed externally by the dramatist, the director or the initiative of the performer.

The realisation is the cycle of volitional, mimetic and vocal reflexes.

The reaction is the attenuation of the volitional reflex after its realisation mimetically and vocally, preparatory to the reception of a new intention (the transition to a new acting cycle).[7]

In October 1922 Meyerhold and his students gave a further display of his system. Shortly afterwards, in an article entitled 'Biomechanics according to Meyerhold' Ippolit Sokolov dismissed Meyerhold's claim to the invention of biomechanics, referring to 'over 100 major works on the

42. *'The Leap onto the Chest' in Meyerhold's production of* The Magnanimous Cuckold (*1922*).

subject', most notably Jules Amar's *Le Moteur humain et les bases scientifiques du travail professionel* (Paris, 1914). Furthermore, he claimed that Meyerhold's exercises were either physiologically unsound and 'downright anti-Taylorist' or simply rehashed circus clowning.[8]

Meyerhold answered his critic in a lecture entitled 'Tartuffes of Communism and Cuckolds of Morality'. Judging from the one brief résumé published, he made little attempt to refute Sokolov's charges, saying that his system had no scientific basis and that its underlying theory rested on 'one brochure by Coquelin'.[9] He doubtless meant either Constant Benoît Coquelin's *L'art et le comedien* (1880) or his *L'art du comedien* (1886), in which the remarks on the dual personality of the actor are strikingly similar to Meyerhold's formulation $N = A_1 + A_2$.[10] In his memoirs Meyerhold's pupil Erast Garin confirms that great emphasis was placed on Coquelin's theories in the early days of the Theatre Workshops.[11]

As we have seen, from 1905 when Meyerhold became director of the Theatre-Studio in Moscow his production methods were shaped by a preoccupation with mime and movement. With the opening of his Petersburg Studio in 1913 came the opportunity to explore the formal discipline of the *commedia dell'arte* and the conventions of the Oriental theatres. It was then that he laid the basis for what later became codified as biomechanics. One of the Studio's 'comédiens', Alexander Gripich, recalls that '. . . . from the exercise "Shooting a bow" there developed the étude "The Hunt", and then a whole pantomime which was used to train every "generation" in the Studio. A whole series of exercises and études became "classics" and were used later in the teaching of bio-mechanics.'[12] Similarly, Valery Bebutov says that Meyerhold got the idea for 'The Leap onto the Chest' from the Sicilian actor, Giovanni Grasso, who visited Petersburg before the First World War.[13]

Thus Meyerhold derived his exercises from various sources, refining them and adding new ones during the first year of the Theatre Workshops until they numbered more than twenty. As he said to Harold Clurman when he visited Moscow in 1935, 'each exercise is a melodrama. Each movement gives the actor a sense of performing on the stage.'[14]

There seems little doubt that Meyerhold, spurred on by the polemical mood of the times, exaggerated the scientific aspect of biomechanics in order to show that his system was devised in response to the demands of the new machine age, in contrast to those of Stanislavsky and Tairov, which were unscientific and anachronistic. But even though his initial claims were quickly seen to be specious, biomechanics became accepted as a thoroughly viable system of theatrical training which he employed to school his actors for all his subsequent productions. Eventually, its practical success was largely responsible for the introduction of some form of systematised physical training into the curriculum of every Soviet drama school.[15] A final comment on Meyerhold's conception of the actor's art is supplied by something he said in 1913:

It is well known that the celebrated Coquelin began with externals when working on his roles, but does that mean he did not experience them? The difference here lies only in the method, in the way that one studies a role. What it boils down to is this: talent always experiences a role deeply, whereas mediocrity merely enacts it.[16]

II

In February 1922 the former Sohn Theatre reopened under the new title of 'The Actor's Theatre'. Initially the repertoire was composed entirely of revivals of productions by the former Nezlobin Theatre, but on 22 April Meyerhold presented Ibsen's *A Doll's House* as a joint production with the Nezlobin Company and his own students. It was rushed on after only five rehearsals in order to establish Meyerhold's claim to the now empty theatre. It bore the sub-title 'The Tragedy of Nora Helmer, or how a woman of bourgeois upbringing came to prefer independence and labour'. On the day of the performance Meyerhold and his students moved into the Sohn Theatre and cleared the stage of all the ancient scenery which cluttered it. Then they constructed a setting for *A Doll's House* by taking flats from stock and propping them back to front against the stage walls in order to symbolise – or so Meyerhold claimed – 'the bourgeois milieu against which Nora rebels'.[17] Reviewing the production in *Theatrical Moscow*, Mikhail Zagorsky wrote: '. . . clearly it is a joke, a stroke of irony, a parody of itself, a long tongue poked out at NEP, but least of all a performance connected in any way with the name of Meyerhold. . . .'[18] But he was not altogether right; insofar as it was a carefully calculated outrage against the tenets of illusionistic theatre, it had a most definite connection with the name of Meyerhold. And in one vital respect it was spectacularly successful: the scandal it caused was more than the 'Nezlobintsy' could stand and they fled after the one production. Thus Meyerhold and his young company were left in sole occupation of the dilapidated theatre, which remained theirs until it closed for renovation in 1932.

The first production cast exclusively from the students of Meyerhold's Workshop was Fernand Crommelynck's *The Magnanimous Cuckold*, staged five days after *A Doll's House*. As Meyerhold himself said, circumstances forced him to seek a setting which could be erected anywhere, without resort to conventional stage machinery.* It was a chance to realise the desire he had expressed a year earlier after his production of *The Dawn* 'to move out into the open air'. He came close to doing precisely that in April 1921 when he planned to stage a mass spectacle *Struggle and Victory*, devised by Aksyonov and involving some 2,500 performers including artillery, aeroplanes, military bands, choirs, and gymnasts. Due to lack of funds the project had to be abandoned, but a design was completed by two

* Describing the setting for *The Magnanimous Cuckold*, Meyerhold wrote: 'After the closure of the R.S.F.S.R. Theatre No. 1 we were left without a theatre and began to explore the possibility of non-stage productions.'[19]

young artists, Alexander Vesnin and Lyubov Popova, both of whom participated in the first exhibition of the Constructivists which opened under the title '$5 \times 5 = 25$'* in Moscow later that year. In their constructions Meyerhold saw the possibility of a utilitarian, multi-purpose scaffolding which could be easily dismantled and erected in any surroundings. Furthermore, this industrial 'anti-art' which recognised practicability as its sole criterion and condemned all that was merely depictive, decorative, or atmospheric, seemed to Meyerhold a natural ally in his repudiation of naturalism and aestheticism.

43. Design collage by Popova for The Magnanimous Cuckold.

At his invitation Popova joined the teaching staff of the Theatre Workshop and agreed to build a construction for *The Magnanimous Cuckold*. It consisted of the frames of conventional theatre flats and platforms joined by steps, chutes, and catwalks; there were two wheels, a large disc bearing the letters 'CR-ML-NCK', and vestigial windmill sails, which all revolved at varying speeds as a kinetic accompaniment to the fluctuating passions of the characters. Blank panels hinged to the framework served as doors and windows. As Rudnitsky says, the aim was simply 'to organise scenic space in the way most convenient for the actors, to create for them a "working area" '.[20] But despite the skeletal

* It consisted of five works by each of five artists, Vesnin, Popova, Rodchenko, Stepanova, Exter.

44. *Scene from* The Magnanimous Cuckold (*1922*).

austerity, the grimy damp-stained brickwork of the exposed back wall, and the absence of wings to hide either stage-crew or cast, Popova's contraption evoked inevitable associations with the windmill in which the play was supposed to be set, suggesting now a bedroom, now a balcony, now the grinding mechanism, now a chute for the discharging of the sacks of flour.[21] Only in the isolated moments when it enhanced the synchronised movements of the complete ensemble did it work simply as a functional machine. In the theatre, whose whole allure depends on the associative power of the imagination, every venture by the Constructivists led to an unavoidable compromise of their utilitarian dogma and each time demonstrated the inherent contradiction in the term 'Theatrical Constructivism'. As Nikolai Tarabukin wrote:

> Lyubov Popova's work reflects the traditions of painting, albeit non-figurative painting. One is struck by the deliberate frontal emphasis of the *Cuckold* construction. The wheels of the windmill, the white letters on a black background, the combination of red with yellow and black – they are all decorative elements derived from painting. The 'installation' shows a predominance of flat surfaces and suprematism. Its lightness and elegance are entirely in keeping with the style of Crommelynck's farce, but as a utilitarian construction it does not stand close scrutiny of all its components. One needs only to mention the door on the second level and the difficulty the actors have in making exits onto the landing behind it.[22]

But for all the solecisms of Popova's setting in the eyes of the Constructivists, it proved the ideal platform for a display of biomechanical agility, 'a spring-board for the actor which quite rightly was compared to the apparatus of a circus acrobat'.

Written in 1920, Crommelynck's tragi-farce tells of Bruno, a village scribe and poet who is so infatuated with his beautiful and innocent young wife, Stella, that he convinces himself that no man could conceivably resist her. Deranged with jealousy, he forces her to share her bed with every man in the village in the hope of unmasking her true lover. Although still in love with Bruno, Stella eventually flees with a man who at least is sure to trust her, leaving Bruno convinced that this is yet another trick to conceal 'the only one'. Some critics, notably Lunacharsky in *Izvestia*,[24] were scandalised by what they regarded as little more than a salacious bedroom farce, but the majority were agreed that the risqué plot was completely redeemed by the brio, the style, and the good humour of Meyerhold's production. Erast Garin describes the opening scene:

. . . You heard an exultant voice ring out offstage, full of joyful strength, love and happiness; and then up the side ladder to the very top of the construction flew – and 'flew' is the word – Ilinsky as Bruno. His wife Stella (played by Babanova) ran to meet him and stood, indescribably youthful, lithe and athletic, with her straight legs planted wide apart like a pair of compasses. Without pausing, Bruno hoisted her onto his shoulder, then slid down the highly-polished chute

45. Maria Babanova as Stella.

and gently lowered his weightless load to the ground. Continuing this childishly innocent love-play, Stella ran from him and he caught her by the bench, where they remained face to face, excited and happy at the thought of being together again and full of the whole joy of living.[25]

Meyerhold transformed the play into a universal parable on the theme of jealousy, with the style of the performance furnishing a constant implicit commentary on the dialogue and situations.* The characters all wore loose-fitting overalls with only the odd distinguishing mark such as a pair of red pom-poms, an eye-glass, a riding-crop, or a pair of button-boots. The actor's attitude to his part was conveyed through an eloquent succession of poses, gestures, and acrobatic tricks, many of them derived from the biomechanical études and all accomplished with the casual dexterity of a circus clown. Thus, 'as he is leaving, the Bourgmestre

* The question of the production's implicit meaning is developed by Nick Worrall in his extended semiological analysis in *The Drama Review*, Vol. 17, No. 1 (T-57), pp. 14–34.

46. The Magnanimous Cuckold (*Act Three*) *with Ilinsky as Bruno and Baba-nova as Stella (right and extreme right).*

strikes the right-hand half of the revolving door with his behind, causing the left-hand half to hit Petrus who flies forward onto the bench. The Bourgmestre ("pardon me") accidentally leans on the right-hand half of the door, thereby causing the other half to hit his own nose. Finally he steps round the door and exits via the space between it and the left-hand corner of the set.'[26] Boris Alpers describes Igor Ilinsky's performance:

> Bruno . . . stood before the audience, his face pale and motionless, and with unvarying intonation, monotonous declamatory style and identical sweeping gestures he uttered his grandiloquent monologues. But at the same time this Bruno was being ridiculed by the actor performing acrobatic stunts at the most impassioned moments of his speeches, belching, and comically rolling his eyes whilst enduring the most dramatic anguish.[27]

One needs only to compare this with Meyerhold's disquisition on the comedy of masks in his essay *The Fairground Booth** to see that *The Magnanimous Cuckold*, for all its modernist exterior, was a revival of the spirit, and in good measure, the letter too of the *commedia dell'arte*. It was the culmination and the vindication of all the explorations into the traditions of the popular theatre which Meyerhold had been pursuing for the past fifteen years; at last he had realised his ambition of creating a new theatre with his own actors. Igor Ilinsky writes in his memoirs:

> Many of those who saw *The Magnanimous Cuckold* and many of the young actors (including myself) who worked with Meyerhold regard it as the most complete and the most significant of all his productions during the entire period of his theatre's existence – because of the way it demonstrated his method of working with the actor, the way it revealed the fundamental purity of his style of acting, and the way it displayed most eloquently his system of biomechanics.[28]

Despite the spectacular success of *The Magnanimous Cuckold*, in June 1922 Meyerhold was faced once more with the possible loss of the Sohn Theatre. This was averted only after violent protests from the theatrical Left and the Constructivists,[29] and an open letter from himself in which he threatened 'to cease work in the Republic altogether'.[30] Eventually, Meyerhold not only retained the use of the Actor's Theatre, but he became Artistic Director of the newly formed 'Theatre of the Revolution' as well. At the same time he assumed overall control of the State Institute of Theatrical Art (GITIS), which was formed by an amalgamation of the former Theatre Workshop, the State Institute of Musical Drama and nine smaller autonomous theatre-studios. So disparate were the various factions that violent friction was bound to be generated, and this quickly led to the formation of an unofficial, quite separate Meyerhold Workshop within the Institute. Without official recognition and with only the box-office to support it, this Workshop ran the Actor's Theatre, with its young students discharging every function from door-keeper to scene-shifter. On 24 November 1922 *The Magnanimous Cuckold* was joined in the repertoire by Alexander Sukhovo-Kobylin's *Tarelkin's Death*.

This 'comedy-jest', completed in 1869, is a barely concealed satire on tsarist police methods. Sukhovo-Kobylin had to wait until 1900 when he was eighty-three to see it performed, and then only after he had been obliged to blunt its edge with numerous amendments. It was Meyerhold who first staged the original uncut version on the eve of the Revolution in October 1917 at the Alexandrinsky Theatre. Conceived in the phantasma-

* See pp. 122 ff. above.

gorical, Hoffmanesque style of much of Meyerhold's earlier work, it was a great popular success, although as a production it was relatively straightforward.

In a note on the play, Sukhovo-Kobylin writes: 'In keeping with the play's humorous nature, it must be played briskly, merrily, loudly – *avec entrain.*'[31] Meyerhold's response was to employ once again the

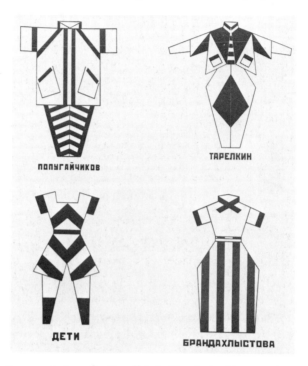

ПОПУГАЙЧИКОВ

ТАРЕЛКИН

ДЕТИ

БРАНДАХЛЫСТОВА

47. Costume designs for Tarelkin's Death *by Varvara Stepanova.*

knockabout tricks of circus clowns and strolling players. Varvara Stepanova designed a series of drab, baggy costumes decorated with stripes, patches, and chevrons which looked like nothing so much as convicts' uniforms. On the empty stage there was an assortment of white-painted 'acting instruments' ready to be shifted and used by the actors as required. Each one concealed a trap: the table's legs gave way, the seat deposited its occupant onto the floor, the stool detonated a blank cartridge. Most spectacular of all was the cage used to simulate a prison cell into which the prisoner was propelled head-first through something resembling a giant meat-mincer. As though all this was not enough to tax the spectator's nerves and the actor's courage, an assistant director (or 'laboratory assistant', as they were called) seated in the front

48. Tarelkin's Death (*Act Three*), showing the '*meat-mincer*' in use as a prison cell.

row announced the intervals by firing a pistol at the audience and shouting 'Entrrr-acte!'; there were helter-skelter chases with the pursuers brandishing inflated bladders on sticks; at the end Tarelkin escaped by swinging across the stage on a trapeze. Illusion was never given a chance to intrude: Ludmilla Brandakhlystova, 'a colossal washerwoman of about forty', was played by the slender, youthful Mikhail Zharov with no make-up and ridiculous padding under his skirts;* Tarelkin, bound hand and foot in prison and frantic with thirst, tried in vain to reach a cup of water held by a warder – then suddenly he winked broadly at the audience and took a long draught from a bottle of wine he had concealed in his pocket. The overall intention, as Eisenstein and Vasily Fyodorov described it, was 'to circumvent the most "dangerous" parts of the play which in a naturalistic treatment would inevitably produce a distressing, almost pathological effect'.[32]

For all the production's vigour and invention it failed to share the success of *The Magnanimous Cuckold*. This was partly because Sukhovo-Kobylin's grim satire was hardly amenable to burlesque. But mainly it was due to practical deficiencies: Stepanova's 'acting instruments' functioned so capriciously that the young performers soon lost all confidence in them; the shapeless costumes tended to camouflage rather than enhance their movements; and frequently they had to perform in half-darkness when the erratic military searchlights which served as stage lighting fluctuated in power. Worst of all, throughout the Moscow winter it was necessary to leave the draughty auditorium unheated due to the company's desperate financial position, and the sparse audiences were often augmented by the large brown rats which inhabited the theatre.[33] Nevertheless, *Tarelkin's Death* remains one of the most celebrated pro-ducts of the movement known as 'Eccentrism' which flourished in Russia in the early 'twenties.†

One of Meyerhold's two 'laboratory assistants' for the production was Sergei Eisenstein. Since joining the Theatre Workshop in 1921 Eisenstein had emerged as its most gifted student and had worked on a number of

---

* In fact the playing of Brandakhlystova by a man is authorised by Sukhovo-Kobylin himself in his prefatory note.

† The term 'Eccentrism' was coined by Grigory Kozintsev, Georgy Kryzhitsky, and Leonid Trauberg to describe their experiments at the theatre-studio which they opened in Petrograd in 1921 and called the 'Factory of Eccentricism' or 'FEKS'.[34] The style may be said to have originated with Yury Annenkov's production of Tolstoy's comedy, *The First Distiller* in Petrograd (1919), when he staged a scene in hell with the aid of circus acrobats performing a flying ballet – that is, if one discounts the occasional use of circus devices by Meyerhold's *The Unknown Woman* and *The Fairground Booth* in 1914, and *Columbine's Scarf* in 1916, to say nothing of the 1918 production of *Mystery-Bouffe*.

highly original projects, including the designs for Meyerhold's un-completed production of Shaw's *Heartbreak House*, in which he proposed to augment his settings with cages of wild animals.[35] Shortly after *Tarelkin's Death* he left Meyerhold to return to the Moscow Proletkult Theatre where two years earlier he had worked as a designer. It was there that in April 1923 he staged Sergei Tretyakov's free adaptation of Ostrovsky's *Enough Simplicity in Every Wise Man* as a 'montage of attractions' on an arena stage and complete with a tightrope act by one of the characters.[36] In 1936 Meyerhold said:

> All Eisenstein's work had its origins in the laboratory where we once worked together as teacher and pupil. But our relationship was not so much of teacher and pupil as of two artists in revolt, up to our necks and afraid to swallow for fear of the disgusting slime in which we found the theatre wallowing in 1917.[37]

III

On 28 March 1923 it was announced in *Izvestia* that on his completion of twenty years as a director and twenty-five in the theatre altogether, Meyerhold had been awarded the title of 'People's Artist of the Republic'. He was the first theatre director and only the sixth Soviet artist overall to be so honoured. On 2 April his jubilee was celebrated with a programme of extracts presented by his own theatre, the Theatre of the Revolution, the Foregger Theatre Workshop, and the Proletkult Theatre together with a display of biomechanics in the ornate and totally inappropriate setting of the Bolshoi Theatre. Yet on the very same day the Sohn Theatre's electricity was cut off because they could not pay the bills, and Meyerhold was obliged to appeal yet again for a state subsidy.[38]

Fortunately, the theatre's position was soon eased by the great popular success of its latest production, Sergei Tretyakov's *Earth Rampant*, (otherwise translated as '*The Earth in Turmoil*'), which had its premiere on 4 March and was performed forty-four times in the remaining eleven weeks of the season. The text was freely adapted by Tretyakov from a translation of Marcel Martinet's verse drama *La Nuit* which had already been staged the previous October as the opening production at the Theatre of the Revolution. Originally published in 1921, the play concerns an abortive mutiny of troops engaged in an imperialist war. As with *The Dawn*, the aim of the adaptation was to transform the play's vague universality into a direct commentary on recent Soviet history. Tretyakov sought to strengthen the dialogue by giving it the laconicism of the agitatory placard and by schooling the

49. Scene from Earth Rampant, *showing the two screens for projected titles and slogans.*

actors in an appropriately aggressive style of declamation.* The action's relevance to historical events was underlined by familiar Civil War slogans projected onto a screen above the stage during the performance; they also performed a formal function, replacing the long-discarded front curtain as a means of dividing the play up and announcing the theme of each episode. Both in its form and objectives, Tretyakov's treatment closely resembled what Brecht was later to call 'Epic'.†

In *The Dawn* and *Mystery-Bouffe* both characters and events were synthesised through the medium of costumes and settings, but arbitrary aestheticism rather than universality was the overriding impression created by the Futurist abstractions, and the topical relevance of the

* As a leading spokesman of the 'Left' writers groups, Tretyakov was ideally suited to this task.

† Some years later, Brecht and Tretyakov became closely acquainted and Tretyakov was largely responsible for introducing Brecht to the Soviet public. In 1934 under the title *Epic Dramas* he published a translation of *St Joan of the Stockyards*, *The Mother*, and *The Measures Taken*.

events depicted was obscured. In *The Magnanimous Cuckold* and *Tarelkin's Death* the intention was different, but again the results were similar. As Aksyonov wrote at the beginning of 1923:

> So-called 'stage constructivism' started with a most impressive programme for the total abolition of aesthetic methods, but once it appeared on the stage it began to show signs of being only too ready to adapt itself to its surroundings and now it has degenerated almost to a decorative device, albeit in a new style.[39]

Aksyonov's diagnosis of the metamorphosis of Constructivism was quickly to prove all too accurate: by the mid-'twenties many theatres

50. *The Curé and the Cook in* Earth Rampant (*caricatures by Ilya Shlepyanov, 1923*).

throughout the Soviet Union were exploiting it as the latest fashionable decorative style, often with little regard for the play's content, and often to satirise the Western way of life whilst betraying distinct nostalgia for its decadent attractions.

In *Earth Rampant*, Meyerhold and his designer, Popova, sought to eliminate all risk of aesthetic blandishment by resorting to purely utilitarian objects: cars, lorries, motor cycles, machine-guns, field telephones, a threshing machine, a field-kitchen – only that which was required by the dramatic events. The one exception was a stark, life-size wooden model of a gantry-crane which towered up into the flies, built only because a real crane proved too heavy for the stage floor to bear. The sole sources of light were huge front-of-house searchlights. The costumes of the soldiers were naturalistic and the actors wore no make-up.

As in *Mystery-Bouffe*, the negative characters were depicted as grotesque archetypes, performing what Meyerhold still referred to as 'lazzi'.[40] Thus when the 'Emperor' received news of the mutiny he squatted down on a chamber-pot emblazoned with the Imperial eagle and relieved himself to the accompaniment of a band playing 'God save the Tsar', after which an orderly removed the pot, holding his nose. As Meyerhold wrote soon afterwards, 'The actor-tribune acts not the situation itself, but what is concealed behind it and what it has to reveal for a specifically propagandist purpose.'*

On this occasion the tedium of unalloyed virtue was completely overcome by the stirring evocation of civil-war heroism which struck to the hearts of many of the spectators. For them, the receding throb of the lorry which had driven down the gangway of the auditorium and up onto the stage with the coffin of a martyred Red soldier seemed like the finest and most fitting requiem for their own fallen comrades. Dedicated 'to the Red Army and the first Red Soldier of the R.S.F.S.R., Leon Trotsky',[41] *Earth Rampant* was first performed at a special preview on 23 February 1923 to mark the Army's fifth anniversary. Ever since Meyerhold had returned from the Civil War, his theatre had shared a close relationship with the Red Army and had done much to foster the development of military drama groups. It was no empty gesture to dedicate *Earth Rampant* to the Army; at performances of the play regular collections were taken and in 1926 the money accumulated went to purchase a military aeroplane which entered service bearing the name 'Meyerhold'. On the occasion of his jubilee at the Bolshoi Theatre in 1923 Meyerhold was made an honorary soldier of the Moscow Garrison.[42]

Meyerhold conceived *Earth Rampant* in the spirit of a mass spectacle, using the theatre aisles for the passage of vehicles and troops. Subsequently it was performed on a number of occasions in the open-air, being freely adapted for various settings. The most memorable performance was that given in honour of the Fifth Congress of the Comintern in Moscow in June 1924 when a cast of 1500, including infantry and horse-cavalry took part and there was an audience of 25,000. For the occasion Tretyakov adapted the script to give it a victorious rather than tragic ending.[43]

As Fevralsky recalls, Meyerhold looked upon *Earth Rampant* as a production which it was necessary to stage. Apart from Mayakovsky, no Soviet dramatist had yet written a revolutionary play of any quality, and after the experimental ventures of *The Magnanimous Cuckold* and *Tarelkin's Death* the Meyerhold Theatre (as it was now officially known) urgently needed to confirm its reputation with the mass audience as an exponent of

* See p. 192 below.

50A. Meyerhold in his uniform of an honorary soldier of the Red Army (1926).

revolutionary drama.[44] His judgment was confirmed in the summer when *Earth Rampant* was enthusiastically received in a variety of venues during the Theatre's tour of the Ukraine and Southern Russia.

Earth Rampant was conceived as a spectacle with wide popular appeal, and its impact was closely monitored by the Meyerhold Theatre. The integral relationship between the theatre and the Experimental Theatre Workshops placed at Meyerhold's disposal teachers and students who were in a position to pursue organised research into all aspects of theatre production. A number of 'laboratories' were set up, notably a 'dramaturgical laboratory' with the aim of collecting and evaluating objective data relating to plays in performance at the Meyerhold Theatre. Systematic attempts were made to monitor fluctuations in the performances of a given play; for example, audience response was recorded under a wide range of headings, namely: silence, noise, loud noise, collective reading (sic), singing, coughing, banging, shuffling, exclamations, weeping, laughter, sighing, movement, applause, whistling, hissing, the number of people leaving during the performance, the number getting to their feet, throwing objects onto the stage, people getting up onto the stage. As Fevralsky says, however unscientific these methods might appear today, they still represent the first serious attempt to subject performance to scientific analysis.[45]

Another important side to the activities of Meyerhold's company and students was the instruction and supervision of theatre groups in factories, military barracks, and student circles. During his work with Narkompros Meyerhold had become disillusioned with the theatrical activities of the Proletkult movement;* he felt it offered an easy refuge for out of work actors, who furnished the majority of Proletkult's drama instructors, and the general level of amateur theatre reflected their incompetence and outmoded ideas on acting.[46] Consequently, once his theatre and workshop became sufficiently established, he set about forging his own links between the professional and amateur stages without reference to the established Proletkult network.[47] Thus, far more than any other Soviet director of 1920s, Meyerhold took practical steps to open up the theatre to the new actor and the new audience.

During the period of NEP the incursions of private ownership into the legitimate theatre were relatively few; it was in the areas of cinema and light entertainment that the effects were most marked: there was a flood of foreign films, many of them light comedies or crime serials (notably *Judex*, *Fantômas*, *Nick Carter*, and *Pauline*), and a fresh crop of operetta, cabaret, and variety theatres sprang up with such names as 'Trocadero', 'Merry Masks', 'Don't Cry' – even 'Empire'. Beginning in 1923, Meyerhold made the habits and fashions of the 'Nepman' the target of a series of satirical productions, linked either directly or by analogy with the portrayal of Western capitalist decadence.

The first of these was *Lake Lyul*, a 'romantic melodrama' by the young Soviet dramatist Alexei Faiko, which Meyerhold presented at the Theatre of the Revolution on 7 November 1923. Shortly before the play opened Faiko said in an interview:

> In my opinion the modern revolutionary repertoire should not consist
> of schematised slogan-placard productions whose agitatory significance

* Proletkult was set up in 1917 as an association of proletarian cultural organisations sponsored and subsidised by Narkompros as an independent body. In 1922 its theatre groups came under the control of the trade unions, and attracted many directors from the professional stage. However, Meyerhold himself never worked with Proletkult. In 1932 the organisation was disbanded.

is obscured by raucous shouts and which lack any real relevance to the experience of the modern spectator; rather we should aim for entertaining plays, spectacular in conception and effective in performance, with complex subject-matter, involved plots, and stirring emotions.[48]

In other words, Faiko proposed taking on the Nepman at his own dangerous game. Summarising *Lake Lyul*, he writes:

Location: somewhere in the Far West, or perhaps the Far East. Many characters. Crowd scenes. White, yellow and black races. Hotels, villas, shops. Advertisement hoardings and lifts. A revolutionary struggle on an island. An underground movement. Conspiracies. The basis of the plot – the rise and fall of the renegade, Anton Prim.[49]

51. *Scene from* Lake Lyul *at the Theatre of the Revolution* (1923).

The dialogue of the play was terse and the structure episodic, designed to convey the breakneck tempo of life in the 'big city', the dominant motif of the whole production. Faiko describes the setting and costumes:

The back wall of the theatre was bared. Girders stuck out and wires and cables dangled uncompromisingly. The centre of the stage was occupied by a three-storeyed construction with receding corridors, cages, ladders, platforms and lifts which moved both horizontally and vertically. There were illuminated titles and advertisements, silver screens lit from behind. Affording something of a contrast to this background were the brilliant colours of the somewhat more than lifelike costumes: the elegant toilettes of the ladies, the gleaming white of starched shirt-fronts, aiguillettes, epaulettes, liveries trimmed with gold.[50]

The setting designed by Viktor Shestakov bore a distinct resemblance to Popova's construction for *The Magnanimous Cuckold*, though it was cheerfully representational and hardly 'constructivist' in the precise sense. Meyerhold exploited the construction to its limits, using area lighting to switch the action constantly from one level to another, sometimes playing two scenes simultaneously in different places. Its technical sophistication afforded him the flexibility which he had sought through the episodic adaptation of such works as *Columbine's Scarf* and *Masquerade*, and led him on to further experiments in montage at a time when that technique had scarcely been exploited in the cinema.* *Lake Lyul* epitomised the much criticised tendency of 'urbanism', the term used to describe a preoccupation with the dubious attractions of the big city; it closely resembled the work of Tairov at the Kamerny Theatre with such designers as Vesnin and the Stenberg brothers.

A far cry from Meyerhold's earlier productions at his own theatre, it was a huge success with what Erast Garin has called the 'cleaner' public of the Theatre of the Revolution. *Lake Lyul* proved to be Meyerhold's second † and final production at that theatre; in effect, he ceased to be its artistic-director after the 1923–1924 season, handing over the post to his former Petersburg pupil Alexei Gripich.

In January 1924 Meyerhold staged his brilliant reinterpretation of Ostrovsky's *The Forest*.‡ Then with his next production, *D.E.*, presented on 15 June 1924, he showed that his disregard for authors' rights was restricted by no means to the classics. This 'agit-sketch' was an amalgam by Mikhail Podgaetsky of two novels, *The D.E. Trust – The History of the Fall of Europe* by Ilya Ehrenburg and *The Tunnel* by Bernhard Kellermann, with additional material from Upton Sinclair and Pierre Hamp. Podgaetsky's scenario bore little resemblance to Ehrenburg's novel from which the bulk of the material was taken, and after numerous further alterations in the course of rehearsals the connection was attenuated still further. Only two years before Ehrenburg had proclaimed: '*Away with the author!* Theatre shouldn't be written in the study, but built on the stage.'[51] Now he sprang to the defence of his novel, protesting 'I'm not some classic but

---

* Meyerhold's assistant director was Abram Room, soon to make his name as a director in the Soviet cinema.

† The first was Ostrovsky's *A Lucrative Post* (15 May 1923). It is referred to on p. 193 below.

‡ Discussed on pp. 193–200 below.

a real, live person,' and claimed to be working on a stage version of it himself.[52] In an open letter Meyerhold, playing on Ehrenburg's doubtful cosmopolitan status, retorted scornfully:

> . . . even if you had undertaken an adaptation of your novel,* *The History of The Fall of Europe*, you would have produced the kind of play that could be put on in any city of the Entente, whereas in my theatre, which serves and will continue to serve the cause of the Revolution, we need tendentious plays, plays with one aim only: to serve the cause of the Revolution.[53]

D.E. was even more fragmented in structure than Meyerhold's previous episodic productions. It took the form of a political revue in seventeen episodes, of which only two or three featured the same characters twice. There were no less than ninety-five roles divided between forty-five performers, amongst whom the champion quick-change artist was Erast Garin, who appeared as seven different inventors in a scene lasting fifteen minutes. In order that the audience might fully savour Garin's skill, in 1926 Meyerhold introduced a large peep-hole in the screen concealing the actor's on-stage wardrobe.[55]

Here is Fevralsky's synopsis of the bizarre plot:

> The international adventurer Jens Boot organises the 'D.E. Trust' (Trust for the Destruction of Europe), in which he is joined by three of America's most powerful capitalists. By various means the D.E. Trust succeeds in destroying the whole of Western Europe. A large pro-portion of the Western European proletariat manage to escape to the U.S.S.R., which joins with the Comintern to form a secret organisa-tion under the cover-name of the 'U.S.S.R. Radium Trust' in order to build an undersea tunnel linking Leningrad to New York. The building of the tunnel provides employment for the European workers. The D.E. Trust is unable to follow up its triumph over Europe by over-coming the industrious zeal of the Soviet workers and is obliged to support the recognition of the Soviet Union *de facto* and *de jure*. But it is too late: the American proletariat rises in revolt and is supported by the International Red Army, arriving unexpectedly in New York through the tunnel which the capitalists have never discovered. The social revolution prevails.[56]

The production was remarkable for its settings, which were composed entirely of 'moving walls'. Devised by Meyerhold himself, these 'walls'

---

* In his memoirs Ehrenburg says that he had earlier refused Meyerhold's invitation to adapt the novel for the stage.[54]

52. *The Setting for* D.E., *showing the moving walls and screen for projected titles.*

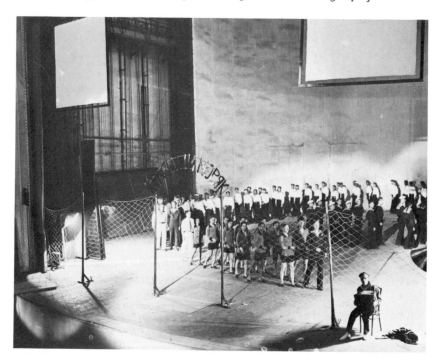

52A. *The Red Fleet in* D.E.

were a series of eight to ten dark red wooden screens, about twelve feet long and nine feet high, which were moved on wheels by members of the cast concealed behind each one. With the addition of the simplest properties, they were deployed to represent now a lecture hall, now a Moscow street, now the French National Assembly, now a sports stadium, and so on. The action never faltered and in some scenes the walls played an active part, their motion emphasised by weaving spotlights. For example, Jens Boot escaping from the Soviet Union fled upstage to be confronted by two rapidly converging walls; managing to squeeze through the narrowing gap just before one crossed in front of the other, he seemed to have disappeared when they separated and moved on across the stage. In fact, he had simply concealed himself behind one wall and left the stage with it.

Once again Meyerhold employed projected captions, this time on three screens. As well as the title and the location of each episode, there were comments on characters, information relevant to the action, and quotations from the written works and speeches of Lenin, Trotsky, and Zinoviev. The aim was to point the political significance of the events on stage and to relate them to as wide a context as possible.

The depravity of the Western world was portrayed in the customary grotesque style, whilst the vigour of the young Soviet state was expressed by marching and singing sailors borrowed from the Red Fleet and real Komsomols performing biomechanics, acrobatic dances, and playing football. Critics were quick to condemn this crude schematisation; not only were the scenes in 'foxtrotting Europe' far more energetic and diverting (helped greatly by the performance of the first jazz band to appear in Soviet Russia),* but there was an obvious danger in representing a deadly political enemy as a collection of emasculated cretins, cowards, and libertines. By all but his most devoted followers Meyerhold was accused once again of 'urbanism' and of 'infantile leftism' – Lenin's term for a naïve conception of the social situation which was bound to foster disastrous complacency. At a public debate shortly after the production's opening, Mayakovsky was particularly scathing in his criticisms. Meyerhold retorted: 'I am glad that Mayakovsky has finally broken his silence. Once he had written *Mystery-Bouffe* he retreated under his bell-jar, and clearly he finds it very comfortable to sit there and watch me fighting alone on the left front.'[57]

Meyerhold was right: no Soviet dramatist had emerged who could begin to rival Mayakovsky in artistic skill and political acumen, and now the repertoire situation was causing acute embarrassment. The time had

---

* The jazz band was assembled by the poet, Valentin Parnakh ('Parnok').

come for more sophisticated material than either Faiko or the collective authors of *D.E.* had offered.[58]

After several months of preparatory work, rehearsals, and revisions, Meyerhold revealed his next production to the public on 29 January 1925: a further play by Faiko called *Bubus the Teacher*. It was hardly the response the critics were demanding: yet another flimsy political farce depicting the exhausted last fling of the rulers of an imaginary capitalist country on the verge of revolution, it prompted the very schematisation of Western decadent types which Meyerhold had already exploited to its limits. The one exception was the character of Bubus himself, an intellectual idealist who vacillated ineffectually between two camps and found himself rejected by the revolution when it finally came. He was an individual embodying the conflict of class loyalties within himself, instead of displaying in two dimensions the attitudes of one particular side. In conception at least he represented a significant advance on the placard style of earlier Soviet theatre, a shift from crude agitation to more reasoned propaganda. Lunacharsky was prompted to coin a new definition for Meyerhold's style: '*sociomechanics*', meaning the study of character in its full social milieu in order to create stage portraits of hyperbolic dimensions which would reveal socio-political causes and effects in all their complexity.[59] But Bubus apart, Faiko's play was so insubstantial that it presented no intellectual challenge whatsoever to Meyerhold. Once more brushing aside the protests of a mere author, he adapted the text to suit his own ends and developed a whole new range of production tricks to invest it with heavy significance, slowing the lively farce tempo to the turgid rhythm of melodrama.[60]

There was no production by Meyerhold which did not reaffirm his conception of rhythm as the basis of all dramatic expression, but in *Bubus* he restored it to the pre-eminence it had enjoyed in such pre-1917 works as *Tristan and Isolde*, *Dom Juan*, and *Orpheus*. With only the occasional break, every movement was synchronised with a musical accompaniment, the text being spoken as a kind of recitative against a melody in counterpoint. As in *D.E.*, lascivious foxtrots and shimmies were danced to jazz accompaniment; but most of the music was taken from Liszt and Chopin and performed by the pianist Lev Arnshtam at a concert Bechstein perched high above the stage in a gilded alcove ringed with coloured lights. Meyerhold intended the effect to be similar to the piano accompaniment in the silent cinema; by revealing the source of the music to the spectator, he hoped to counteract its stupefying effects and reinforce its ironical function.

In contrast to the aggressive angularity of recent productions, the

53. *Bubus the Teacher, Act Two.*

setting, conceived by Meyerhold and executed by Ilya Shlepyanov, consisted of a semicircle of suspended bamboo rods completely enclosing a stage area covered with a circular green carpet. The back wall was adorned with flashing neon signs and the whole picture framed by an ornate false proscenium arch. Properties were few, the most striking being a gilded fountain in the first act. The mellifluous tinkling of the bamboo curtain at the entrance of each character, the soft splashing of the fountain, the rhythmical flashing of the neon all played their part in Meyerhold's complex orchestration.

The languid aristocrats moved in broad leisurely curves within the rounded confines of their fragile stockade, their footfalls silent on the green carpet. Faultlessly turned out, their fans, cloaks, top hats, walking-sticks, and white gloves were the pretext for much elegant by-play. For the first time Meyerhold introduced a device which he called 'pre-acting', whereby the actor employed mime before he spoke his lines in order to convey his true state of mind. Justifying this technique he said:

> Nowadays, when the theatre is once more being employed as a plat-form for agitation, an acting system in which special stress is laid on pre-acting is indispensable to the actor-tribune. The actor-tribune needs to convey to the spectator his attitude to the lines he is speaking and the situations he is enacting; he wants to force the spectator to respond in a particular way to the action which is unfolding before him. . . . The actor-tribune acts not the situation itself, but what is concealed behind it and what it has to reveal for a specifically propa-gandist purpose. When the actor-tribune lifts the mask of the character to reveal his true nature to the spectator he does not merely speak the lines furnished by the dramatist, he uncovers the roots from which the lines have sprung.[61]

Unfortunately, this constant interpolation of mime emphasised rather than made good the vacuity of Faiko's text, and was seen by most critics as a regression to the self-indulged aestheticism of Meyerhold's World of Art period. 'Sadko' of *Evening Moscow* remarked maliciously that 'at times it was like sitting in some provincial offshoot of the Kamerny Theatre'.[62] In 1962 Faiko himself recalled: '. . . it was as though the whole play was duplicated, performed twice, and so assumed a heavy, ponderous, totally decelerated tempo. I saw my light situation comedy transformed into a slow-moving, pretentious, falsely significant production.'[63] Erast Garin writes: 'The public's reception of *Bubus the Teacher* was reserved; they quickly grew tired, just as one grows tired in an unfamiliar museum. It was a spectacle overloaded with skill, a production for the appreciation of actors and directors.'[64] But despite all its shortcomings, *Bubus the Teacher* remained for Meyerhold and his company a valuable exercise in rhythmical discipline which told strongly in subsequent productions. Above all, it marked his 'rediscovery' of music, the vital component in his finest work yet to come.

IV

When Meyerhold staged Ostrovsky's *A Lucrative Post* at the Theatre of the Revolution in May 1923, it was generally taken to be a routine production which as the company's Artistic Director he felt obliged to undertake. Why else should he, leader of the theatrical Left, choose to stage a social comedy written in the 1850s and part of the staple repertoire of the venerable Maly Theatre? In consequence, the production was almost totally ignored by the Moscow critics, but it ran nevertheless – and continued to run for thirteen years. In 1937 Boris Alpers described it as 'one of the most profound and significant productions in the repertoire of the Soviet theatre'.[65]

Meyerhold's approach to the play was relatively straightforward; relying on the virtuosity of a number of his own ex-students in the cast, notably Maria Babanova who had played Stella in *The Magnanimous Cuckold*, he left Ostrovsky's text untouched and devised a scenario of restless movement in order to emphasise the uneasy relationships between the play's characters. In this he was assisted greatly by his designer Viktor Shestakov, who created a clean, functional multi-level construction out of angular beams, plywood, metal, and linoleum. Against these surfaces the exact period costumes and authentic properties sprang into prominence, emphasising their anachronistic quaintness yet pointing the analogy with the nostalgia and materialism of the NEP period.[66] Whether this was the specific reason for the success of *A Lucrative Post* is doubtful, but to Meyerhold at least the production demonstrated the potential vitality of the nineteenth-century repertoire in the Soviet context. Nine months later he applied this lesson to the most spectacular effect.

On 19 January 1924, three weeks before his fiftieth birthday, Meyerhold confounded all expectations with his production of Ostrovsky's most popular comedy, *The Forest*. Shortly before it opened, he told a meeting of Red Army drama organisers: 'We don't need to borrow anything from the theatre of the aristocracy and bourgeoisie, but we must avail ourselves of the experience of the popular theatres of the past. . . . What we need is a Red folk theatre* (but not a Red cabaret), topical folk songs, and

* As in the past, he used his favourite term 'balagan'.

54. *Poster for the premiere of* The Forest, *1924.*

clowns of the kind found in Shakespeare or in travelling shows.'[67] In a debate soon after *The Forest* had opened he said: 'A play is simply the excuse for the revelation of its theme on the level at which that revelation may appear vital today.'[68] The previous year, in an article in *Izvestia* marking the dramatist's centennial, Lunacharsky had called on the Soviet theatre 'to go back to Ostrovsky' in order to learn from his achievements in the depiction of social reality.[69] *The Forest* was Meyerhold's own particular response to this call; but at the same time, it was a resumption of his polemic against the Academic Theatres, in particular against the Maly Theatre's recent traditional version of the same play.

Meyerhold reinterpreted Ostrovsky's genre portrait of the bigoted country gentry of 1870 in the terms of the class war, rejecting character development in favour of the interplay of 'social masks'. The action was adapted to sharpen the conflict between Raissa Pavlovna Gurmyzhskaya, the autocratic mistress of the rich estate 'Tree Stumps', and Aksyusha, her young impoverished relative who serves as a maid of all work. According to Ostrovsky, Gurmyzhskaya, a widow in her early fifties, 'dresses modestly, almost in mourning'. Played by the young Yelena Tyapkina, her fat, ungainly figure was clothed either in a masculine riding habit or in dresses of hideous vulgarity; she brandished a whip, spoke in a gruff, drink-sodden voice, sang sentimental romances off-key, and pawed lasciviously at the foppish young wastrel Bulanov. On the other hand, Meyerhold rejected the conventional view of Aksyusha as 'tearful, sentimental, lyrical in mood'.[70] In Zinaida Raikh's portrayal she displayed all the buoyant energy and industry of a modern 'komsomolka'.

Every principal character was costumed to reveal his or her essential nature: Bulanov adorned the estate in striped singlet and shorts; Milonov, an obsequious neighbour, was transformed into a parish priest complete with full regalia and attendant acolytes. Of less obvious significance were the wigs worn by a number of the characters: Gurmyzhskaya's was bright red, Bulanov's was green, whilst Milonov had both a wig and a beard made of the gold thread used to decorate Christmas trees. A number were discarded soon after the premiere. Ostrovsky's itinerant actors, Arkashka Schastlivtsev, the comedian, and Gennady Neschastlivtsev, the tragedian, were decked out in an odd assortment of garments from the theatrical rag-bag: Schastlivtsev was played as a down-and-out music-hall comic dressed in baggy check trousers, a short toreador's jacket, and jaunty, battered sombrero; his partner resembled a provincial ham in a voluminous dark cloak and broad-sleeved Russian shirt.

In their relationship with each other, their remoteness from the petty everyday world, and their romantic championing of the true love of Aksyusha and her sweetheart Petya, the two actors were a conscious evocation of Don Quixote and Sancho Panza, or as Meyerhold later claimed, of the knight of Spanish 'cloak and sword' drama and the *gracioso* or buffoon of Spanish comedy.[71] It was these characters who above all attracted Meyerhold to *The Forest* in the first place, for as Rudnitsky says, they embodied one of Meyerhold's favourite themes: the triumph of the *comédien* over real life. This is present in Ostrovsky, but in Meyerhold's interpretation they were elevated to the stature of Satan and the Fool, and they controlled not only the fate of the inhabitants of 'Tree Stumps', but the whole mood and tempo of the production itself.[72]

Since the point of the 'mask' is to identify the character immediately and completely, its gradual revelation through behaviour could be discarded. Accordingly, Meyerhold largely ignored the play's original time sequence and rearranged Ostrovsky's text according to the prin-

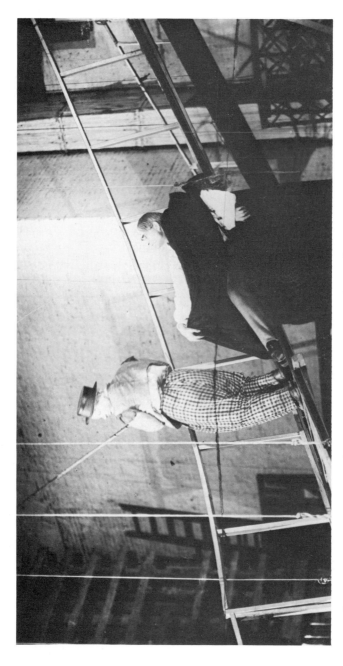

55. The Forest, Episode Seven ('Arkashka and the Governor of Kursk') with Ilinsky as Schastlivtsev and Mikhail Mukhin as Neschastlivtsev.

ciples of cinematic montage. Altering little of the actual dialogue, he divided the original five acts into thirty-three episodes,* shuffling them into new order, and inserting pantomime interludes for the sake of effective contrasts of mood and tempo.

Each episode was preceded by a brief blackout, during which its title was projected onto a screen above the stage. After the prologue in which Milonov led the rest of the local inhabitants in hurried procession across the stage with ikons and religious banners (the traditional comic 'parade'), the play opened with the meeting of the two actors (the original Act Two, Scene Two). This long scene, in which they swap tales of their adventures on tour, was split into seven brief episodes and interspersed with the eight scenes at 'Tree Stumps' from Act One. From episode to episode Arkashka and Gennady gradually descended a curved catwalk suspended above stage-level, arriving finally at a turnstile (forestage left) representing the entrance to 'Tree Stumps'.† The intervening episodes were played on the main stage, area lighting being used (as in *Lake Lyul*) to pick out first one location then the other. The leisurely tempo of the players' progress, further emphasised by the miming of fishing, catching insects, and the like, contrasted abruptly with the domestic bustle on the stage below in a manner which Meyerhold himself later compared both to Eisenstein's use of 'collision montage' in the cinema and to the episodic structure employed by Shakespeare and Pushkin.[73]

The neutral permanent setting with its dynamic function was a refinement of Meyerhold's earlier, more overtly constructivist manner. His use of properties in *The Forest* was based on a similar principle. An assortment of real objects with no obvious relationship was assembled onstage to be utilised as required. The swinging of Aksyusha and her lover Petya on 'giant-strides' ‡ was synchronised with the dialogue to convey their rising elation as they planned their escape; Aksyusha conveyed her disdain of Gurmyzhskaya by rhythmically beating laundry whilst retorting to her strictures; Bulanov betrayed his fatuity by discoursing with Gennady while balancing on two chairs. Every device served both an ironic and a rhythmical function, sometimes helping to gloss over dialogue which was not consistent with Meyerhold's new interpretation of the play, and sometimes investing it with a significance which Ostrovsky had certainly never dreamed of. In his desire to restore the full atmosphere

---

* Soon reduced to twenty-six, and eventually to sixteen.

† The settings and costumes were conceived by Meyerhold and executed by Vasily Fyodorov. Beginning with *The Forest*, the designs for practically all Meyerhold's productions were executed in accordance with his own precise instructions.

‡ Ropes with loops, suspended from a pole.

56. Episode Thirty-three, 'Don Quixote, or Tree-stumps once more'.

of traditional comedy Meyerhold did not shrink from what Rudnitsky
calls 'Aristophanic crudity'. Thus in the episode 'Moonlight Sonata'
Arkashka see-sawed with Gurmyzhskaya's pretentious housekeeper Ulita
while she sang the romance 'Do not tempt me needlessly'; 'Every time
Arkashka came down to the ground at his end of the see-saw and caused

57. *Episode Twenty-three, 'Moonlight Sonata', with Varvara Remizova as Ulita.*

the housekeeper to fly up into the air, squealing and gasping, she was
lifted off her end by the bump and her skirts rode right up, affording the
audience a not altogether decent picture.' The scene ended even less
ambiguously: Arkashka sat on his end of the see-saw and lit a cigarette,
whilst Ulita was left stranded in mid-air gripping the thick beam tightly
between her legs.[74]

Inevitably, with Meyerhold's treatment many of the more subtle
character refinements in Ostrovsky's text were obscured, not least in the
tragi-comical clown figure of Arkashka – which did not prevent Igor
Ilinsky from enjoying his greatest success of all in the part. But the
production pleased few critics: those on the 'left' could see little point in

reviving *The Forest* in the Soviet context, regarding the production as a resurgence of Meyerhold's Petersburg aestheticism and accusing him of 'revisionism'; those on the 'right', predictably enough, were outraged at the barbarous liberties they felt he had taken with Ostrovsky's text. However, neither side succeeded in gauging the public's reaction or in influencing its opinion: *The Forest* remained permanently in Meyerhold's repertoire for the next fourteen years, being performed over 1700 times.*

In fact, as Rudnitsky points out, the attitude towards Ostrovsky which Meyerhold had adopted was consistent with the changing mood of the left avant-garde: 'The days of wanton assaults on the classics were past, and the revolutionary poets were declaring their love for them. . . . In their attitude one sensed a cheerful and rather vulgar familiarity.'[75] This

58. Ivan Pyriev as Bulanov with Mukhin as Neschastlivtsev.

is as good a description as any of Meyerhold's approach to the several nineteenth-century masterpieces which he was to stage over the next eleven years. But in his case the familiarity was invariably the product of the closest acquaintance, which was more than could be said of the host of ill-conceived 'reinterpretations' of the classics now perpetrated by his imitators. The habit quickly assumed epidemic proportions and acquired

* 1700 plus is the figure given by Rudnitsky and Garin. Presumably this includes the number of performances given on tour, since the number at The Meyerhold Theatre was 1328 (*Meyerhold II*, p. 528). In any case, it places *The Forest* ahead of any other Soviet production of the period in popularity.

the name of 'meyerholditis'. Ironically, in the course of time it was Meyerhold himself who was accused of propagating it.[76]

V

Less than three months after the ill-received *Bubus* Meyerhold staged a production which won acclaim from all sides and marked a crucial advance in his production style. By the spring of 1925, the New

59. The Warrant. *Varka (Zinaida Raikh) and Valerian (Sergei Martinson).*

Economic Policy had restored the Soviet economy to solvency and the time had come to revoke the alliance with private enterprise. To mark the closing of this era, Meyerhold put on *The Warrant* (20 April 1925), the first full-length play by the young Nikolai Erdman. A satirical fantasy in the style of Gogol and Sukhovo-Kobylin, it depicted a typical group of 'internal émigrés' of the NEP period who still dreamt of the restoration of the monarchy, and preserved all the trappings and customs of the old

60. The Warrant. The wedding of Valerian Smetanich to 'The Grand Duchess Anastasia' (centre). Note Meyerhold seated at bottom right-hand corner.

order within the undignified confines of a communal flat in Moscow. In a series of hilariously involved peripeteia, Nadezhda Gulyachkina and her son Pavel seek to restore the family fortunes by arranging the marriage of Pavel's unprepossessing sister Varka to Valerian Smetanich, the son of prosperous bourgeois neighbours. As a dowry they offer Pavel's Party membership and the protection against the shocks of Communism that it will guarantee. Pavel's sole proof of his status is a warrant bearing his signature as chairman of the house committee, which, as it transpires, is forged by himself. The plan is foiled when Valerian chooses instead as his bride the Grand Duchess Anastasia, the miraculously surviving heir to the Romanov dynasty – only to discover that she is the Gulyach-kins' cook Nastya Pupkina from Tula. A lodger reveals all to the militia, but is sent packing: they have better things to do than to arrest these pathetic remnants of the past.*

As Rudnitsky says, the emblematic portrayal of character, the 'social masks', which Meyerhold had employed in all his productions of the Soviet period was entirely unsuited to *The Warrant*. Erdman's characters did not divide into the sharply contrasting social categories of *The Forest*, *D.E.*, or *Bubus*; instead they were all drawn from within the same narrow class, a series of subtly inflected variations on the one theme. The secret of Erdman's style lay in his ability to translate scrupulously noted details of petty bourgeois speech and behaviour into the most extravagant and arresting hyperbole without any sacrifice of authenticity. In effect, this was the style which Meyerhold had defined as 'the grotesque' fourteen years earlier in his essay *Balagan*, and which had so coloured his sub-sequent work. *The Warrant* gave him full opportunity to draw on all those years of accumulated experience and to apply it to a work of acute social observation.

Inevitably mime played a vital role in the production, in particular, sudden freezes which seemed to convey the characters' horrified sub-conscious awareness of their inescapable dilemma. Thus, says Rudnitsky:

> In Act One when Garin as Gulyachkin, in a kind of Khlestakovian ecstasy, surprised himself by blurting out the menacing and solemn words 'I am a Party man!', the fatal phrase made those around him and Gulyachkin himself freeze in horror. Ivan Ivanovich, the lodger, at whom the threat was addressed, shrank back and cowered to the floor. Gulyachkin's mama and sister stood with their mouths gaping wide. Gulyachkin himself, unhinged by his own heroism, remained motion-

---

* For a translation of *The Warrant* see Nikolai Erdman, *The Mandate and The Suicide* (trans. Genereux, Volkov and Hoover, Ann Arbor, 1975).

less in an unnatural pose which suggested both pride and terror. And then immediately this entire 'sculptural group', this monumental photograph of the explosion which had rocked the petit bourgeois world, glided slowly and smoothly into the depths of the stage on the revolve.[77]

Meyerhold and his designer Shlepyanov devised a deep circular stage-area with two large concentric revolves and a series of tall varnished wooden screens which enclosed the action. Telling effects were achieved with these simple mechanical means: a petrified group would silently

61. Madam Gulyachkina at prayer before her horn-gramophone.

retreat, a gap would materialise in the seemingly impassable wall, and they would be 'hurled from the stream of life onto the rubbish dump of history'.[78] The revolves were also used to bear on the properties, employed sparingly but effectively 'both as an instrument of acting and as a symbolic generalisation of a way of life'.[79] A domestic altar complete with votive candles and horn-gramophone, a wrought-iron treadle sewing-machine, a piano decorated with paper flowers, a banquet table with epergne and candelabra: these were the objects the doomed 'nepmen' relied on to preserve their delusion of permanency.

But Meyerhold's production was more than a merciless jest at the expense of a helpless foe; there was little laughter at Pavel Gulyachkin's closing line 'What's the point of living, mama, if they don't even bother to arrest us?' It was a glimpse of the tragic aspect of the grotesque, which recalled Blok's bewildered Pierrot playing mournfully on his pipe at the end of *The Fairground Booth*. It was a significant change in mood from the derisive lampoons which had gone before. As Boris Alpers wrote:

> Meyerhold's satirical theatre, merry and irreverent in mood and capable of malicious ridicule at the expense of those individuals who were receding into the past, suddenly paused for reflection, broke off its laughter. Its performances began to move one. In its voice there began to predominate the note of tragedy.[80]

62. Erast Garin as Pavel Gulyachkin.

A deep significance lay behind Erast Garin's interpretation of Pavel Gulyachkin, his first major role with the company. Igor Ilinsky had just left following a dispute with Meyerhold, and his place was now filled by Garin. Rudnitsky writes:

> The buoyant, mischievous, charming Ilinsky, full of youthful energy, was replaced by the nervous, fragile, disturbingly grotesque Garin, with his sudden freezes into immobility. Energy was replaced by trance, the dynamic by the static, high-spirited playful humour by sombre and bitter satire. The highly talented Garin threw into sharp relief the growing divergence between Meyerhold's theatre and a changing reality.[81]

The Warrant marked Meyerhold's effective rejection of placard drama and his return to a theatre of disturbing complexity; as Pavel Markov wrote, 'The production makes you think. It questions premises and proceeds by deduction.'[82] Significantly, Stanislavsky, who had not even taken the trouble to see *The Forest*, was deeply impressed and commented on the last act: 'In this act Meyerhold has accomplished what I myself am dreaming of.'[83]

VI

The following season, for the first and only time Meyerhold entrusted a production to one of his pupils, Vasily Fyodorov. It was Sergei Tretyakov's 'drama of fact' *Roar, China!*, a play based on an actual incident on the Yangtse River in 1924 in which the captain of a British gunboat demanded the summary execution of two Chinese coolies following the death in a brawl of an American business representative.

Shortly after the premiere on 23 January 1926, Fyodorov publicly disowned the production and resigned from the company. Subsequently, it transpired that large sections of the work were the result of Meyerhold's revision, notably the highly realistic portrayal of the Chinese coolies. By contrast, the scenes involving the Navy and the European business community were a throwback to the style of *Lake Lyul* and *D.E.*, emphasised the more by a setting divided across the middle by a strip of water with the looming gunboat upstage and the 'Chinese quarter' downstage.

Due largely to the interest provoked by the issues raised in the play at a time when the Chinese revolutionary movement was gaining momentum, *Roar, China!* was highly successful and formed part of the Meyerhold Theatre's repertoire when it went on its first foreign tour in 1930. Subsequently, the play was performed in numerous theatres throughout the Soviet Union and other countries.

Apart from *Roar, China!*, almost twenty months passed after *The Warrant* before Moscow saw another production by Meyerhold. His time was divided between work on Pushkin's *Boris Godunov* at the Moscow Art Theatre's Third Studio (Vakhtangov's theatre until his death in 1922) and on *The Government Inspector* at his own theatre. Sadly, *Boris Godunov* was never completed; Meyerhold returned to it with his own company in 1936, but again succeeded only in rehearsing certain scenes. The notes and eye-witness accounts of rehearsals which remain suggest that he might well have succeeded in achieving the long-overdue recognition of a dramatic masterpiece.[84]

8. 1926
The Government Inspector

———◆———

In his review of *The Forest* Meyerhold's old Petersburg opponent Alexander Kugel wrote '. . . amongst us there are still many who were brought up on the exemplary works of Russian literature, and we regard such treatment of our great poets as unexampled barbarism'.[1] The charge was not new: many critics had protested in similar terms against the outrages perpetrated on *The Storm*, on *Masquerade*, and on *Tarelkin's Death*. But Meyerhold remained true to Mounet-Sully's dictum, 'Chaque texte n'est qu'un prétexte,' claiming that '. . . the art of the director is the art not of an executant, but of an author – so long as one has earned the right'.[2] No production demonstrated this more emphatically than *The Government Inspector* on 9 December 1926. After the first performance of the play in April 1836, Gogol was so terrified by the outraged protests of conservative critics that he denied all satirical intent, saying 'Put two or three rogues on the stage and everyone flies into a rage and cries "we are not rogues!" '[3] Rejecting this excuse as disingenuous, Meyerhold attached far greater significance to what Gogol said eleven years later in his *Author's Confession*:

> In *The Government Inspector* I decided to gather into one heap everything rotten in Russia as I then saw it, all the injustices which are perpetrated in those places and in those circumstances where justice is most required of a man; I decided to hold up everything to ridicule at once.[4]

As Meyerhold's co-adaptor, Mikhail Korenev said:

> The theatre was faced with the task of making *The Government Inspector* an accusatory production. Needless to say, our target was not merely peculation in some miserable little town in the middle of nowhere which has never got onto any map, but as far as possible the entire Nicholayan era, together with the way of life of its nobility and its officials.[5]

In fact, Meyerhold went so far as to project his whole production on the scale of the Russian capital, arguing that when Gogol was working on *The Government Inspector*, 'he was burning with the desire to depict something from the life of Petersburg'.

In the original Petersburg production the cast paid little attention to Gogol's notes on character portrayal, reducing the play to a trivial farce involving stock characters, and with Khlestakov played, in Gogol's words, 'like some vaudeville rogue . . . the conventional swindler, that drab character who has appeared in exactly the same costume for the past two hundred years'.[7] It must have been harmless, because even stolid Tsar Nicholas was vastly amused and instructed the entire Royal Family and Privy Council to see it.

In Moscow a month later the play fared no better, even though the great Shchepkin played the Mayor. Gogol was deeply depressed and fled the country, to return only occasionally over the next twelve years. He continued to work on the text, seeking to eradicate the farcical elements which he considered had contributed to the burlesque of the first production. The final version published in 1842 contains numerous amendments, notably the insertion of the epigraph, 'Don't blame the mirror if your own mug is crooked', and the Mayor's aside to the audience in the final scene, 'What are you laughing at? You're laughing at yourselves!' Although this version is now accepted as canonical, it was not performed until 1870, by which time, says Korenev:

> Tradition unwittingly or perhaps, on the contrary, with most cunning malice aforethought, set *The Government Inspector* on the rails of vaudeville and simple rib-tickling comedy and obscured its social significance; in their customary interpretation, the characters scarcely ever rose above the level of the conventional masks of light comedy.[8]

But new efforts were made to define Gogol's dramatic style, leading to the emergence of two further schools of opinion at the beginning of the twentieth century. First, there was the 'neo-naturalistic' interpretation which identified his theatre as the forerunner of the genre works of Ostrovsky, Tolstoy, Turgenev, and others, and was exemplified by the Moscow Art Theatre production of 1908. Second, there were the attempts of the symbolists (notably Rozanov's *Legend of the Great Inquisitor*, Bely's *Gogol*, and Merezhkovsky's *Gogol and the Devil*) to reinterpret *The Government Inspector* in the light of the writings of Gogol's late 'mystical' period, in particular the *Dénouement* to the play (1846), in which he represents it as an allegory of the Last Judgment with Khlestakov the personification of man's 'venal, treacherous conscience'.[9]

In 1908, Meyerhold expressed his admiration for Merezhkovsky's article, recommending it as a corrective to the entrenched views of the senior members of the Alexandrinsky company. The manner of his work with Komissarzhevskaya suggests strongly that his planned production of *The Government Inspector* at her theatre in 1907 would almost certainly have followed the symbolist reading.

However, in 1926 Meyerhold rejected all such narrow interpretations, seeing the play as a unique synthesis of realism, hyperbole, and fantasy, and arguing that whereas Gogol's treatment was comic, the overall effect was disturbingly lachrymose. During a rehearsal he told his company:

> When Gogol read Pushkin the opening chapters of *Dead Souls*, Pushkin (who, incidentally, loved a good laugh) grew steadily more and more gloomy until finally he was totally downcast. And when the reading was finished he said in a voice filled with melancholy: 'God, what a sad place our Russia is!' Gogol had achieved the desired effect: although the treatment was comic, Pushkin understood at once that the intention was something other than comic.[10]

These remarks set the tone for the whole production; early on, Meyerhold said 'We must avoid everything which is pure comedy or buffoonery. We must be careful not to borrow any commedia tricks, and try to express everything in terms of tragi-comedy. We must steer a course for tragedy.'[11]

II

In his earlier interpretations of the classics Meyerhold, for all his startling innovations, had remained faithful to the printed text. Even in his 'montage' of *The Forest*, he altered little of the actual dialogue and added nothing to it. But the breadth of his conception of *The Government Inspector* forced him to adopt an altogether freer approach. As the actor and director Mikhail Chekhov wrote:

> He realised that to stage *The Goverment Inspector* and only *The Government Inspector* would be to torment himself with an unbearable vow of silence. *The Government Inspector* started to grow and swell until it split wide open; through the cracks there gushed a raging torrent: *Dead Souls*, *The Nevsky Prospect*, Podkolyosin, Poprishchev, the dreams of the Mayoress, horrors, guffaws, raptures, the screams of ladies, the fears of petty bureaucrats. . . .[12]

In his now customary manner, Meyerhold divided the play into fifteen

titled episodes, a sequence of fifteen separate vignettes which mainly
followed the chronological sequence of Gogol's plot.[13] Whilst drawing
on all six extant versions of the play, he took as the foundation for his
grand design the first draft of the play which dates from 1835. He
restored the scene in which Anna Andreevna boasts to her daughter of the
cavalry captain driven to despair by her flashing eyes; the speech in which
the Sergeant's wife offers to lift her skirts to show Khlestakov the bruises
she has received from the Mayor's flogging; the comic dialogue where
Khlestakov tries in vain to penetrate Doctor Hübner's German in order

63. *Episode Five: 'Filled with Tenderest Love'. With Raikh as Anna Andreevna*
(left).

to extract a bribe from him. He introduced isolated lines from *The
Gamblers*, *Marriage*, and *Vladimir of the Third Degree*, together with
unmistakable touches from the *Petersburg Stories*. Moreover, on the departure of Khlestakov and Osip at the close of Act Four the theatre was made
to echo with the ghostly jingling of harness bells, reminding the audience
of the flight of Chichikov's celestial troika at the end of the first part of
Dead Souls.

At first glance, the majority of these amendments seem to contradict
Gogol's own revisions of the play, restoring its farcical elements; but
they were thoroughly consistent with the satirical style developed by

Meyerhold in recent productions, in which pantomime and precise visual 'business', often with props, were employed to bring out the true significance of the action and the character's awareness of it. Thus, the scale of Anna Andreevna's amorous fantasies about the Cavalry Captain was demonstrated by the sudden materialisation from behind furniture and out of cupboards of a band of adoring young officers serenading her to imaginary guitars, with the climax coming when the last of them emerged like a jack-in-the-box from the top of a cupboard and histrionically shot himself. When Khlestakov informed the Mayor that he lived 'to pluck flowers of pleasure', he immediately relieved himself of a gobbet of phlegm. Then during his drunken recital of his Petersburg exploits he idly drew Anna Andreevna's entranced little finger to his lips on a teaspoon.

The merest commonplace action was transformed into a studied pantomime: the ruminative, unison puffing of long pipes by the town dignitaries in the opening scene, the elaborate toilette of the Mayor before setting off for the inn, even the proffering of bribes to Khlestakov – all assumed the precision of a familiar ceremony, which exactly suggested the ossified daily round of petty officialdom.

This emphasis on reiterated gestures formed the basis for the inter-pretation of character. In his notes to his actors Meyerhold supplied each character with a wealth of biographical detail which would have pleased Stanislavsky. The difference was that it was more idiosyncratic, more 'Gogolian' than Stanislavsky would have countenanced; he advised his actors 'to find a certain eccentricity within the limits of your own personalities'.[14] The intention was not so much to furnish a broad base for the psychological interpretation of the role as to fix distinctive movements, poses, details of costume, and so on. Thus, Pavel Markov, then principal dramaturg of the Moscow Art Theatre, commented:

> Meyerhold looks at men and actors with the eye of a painter, a draughtsman, or a cinema cameraman. He almost willingly sacrifices the effect of gradually uncovering the inner kernel of a personality. In a fleeting glance, a single movement, the drop of a hand, he reveals more than a normal observer would notice; he shows (or seeks to show) the fate of a man unfolding, and at the same time achieves a dazzling theatrical effect. . . . The actor plays one and the same situation throughout an entire episode on the basis of the most precise rhyth-mical scheme which the director has presented to him.[15]

In working with his actors on this laconicism of style, Meyerhold urged them to study the films of Charlie Chaplin, Buster Keaton, and James Cruze, whose *Fighting Coward* was currently showing in Moscow.[16]

III

Proceeding from the assumption of a much grander location than Gogol's original small town, Meyerhold's portrayal of character was far removed from the traditional 'hemming and hawing idiots dressed up to look more idiotic still'.[17] For his visit to Khlestakov in his rat's nest under the stairs of the inn, the Mayor was arrayed in an ornate shako and voluminous cloak, looking like some august field-marshal from the glorious campaign

64. Episode Four: 'After Penza'. With Nikolai Mologin as Dobchinsky (left), Pyotr Starkovsky as the Mayor (top left) and Erast Garin as Khlestakov (right).

against Napoleon. The transformation of Anna Andreevna from the accepted stereotype was even more striking: Gogol's 'provincial coquette, not quite beyond middle age, educated half on novels and verses in visitors' books and half in fussing over the pantry and the maids' room . . .' became a 'provincial Cleopatra', a 'Russian Venus' with a lustrous black chignon, and shoulders of gleaming alabaster rising from the rich silks which swathed her voluptuous figure. It was a conception which certainly showed off Zinaida Raikh to the best advantage, but as Andrei Bely pointed out, she was in any case a creature straight from Gogol's own febrile imagination, one of the ladies from 'the town of N', who so excited Chichikov's erotic fancy at the Governer's ball in *Dead Souls*.[18]

The theme of sexuality was announced in the scene in Anna Adreevna's boudoir which immediately preceded the materialisation of her band of admirers. Seizing on Gogol's note that 'She has four complete changes of costume during the play', Meyerhold made the Mayoress try on a whole series of dazzling silk gowns, stepping into the huge mahogany wardrobe to change them and rustling provocatively as she pivoted in front of the mirror. Her movements were eyed furtively by Dobchinsky, who was so bemused by the whole erotic sequence that he made a blind exit into the cupboard, from whence there emerged the first of the love-stricken officers.

But true to the spirit of Gogol, this was hyperbole with a purpose. Whether all the finery represented a true picture of remote provincial life or Petersburg high society was beside the point; what it did represent was the bombastic Mayor and his feather-brained wife as they pictured themselves in their social-climbing dreams. When finally, the subterfuge was exploded, the Mayor lost his wits, to be removed raving in a strait-jacket by his own cloddish policemen, whilst Anna Andreevna was borne away senseless on the shoulders of her faithful entourage of subalterns, like some fallen Racinian heroine. To such heights had their deluded fantasies soared, that this grotesquely tragic end seemed fitting, even inevitable, and the audience had no need of the Mayor's chilling whisper 'What are you laughing at? You're laughing at yourselves!' to freeze the smiles on their faces.* Farce turned into nightmare as the church bells, ordered to celebrate Maria Antonovna's betrothal to Khlestakov, boomed louder and louder, police whistles shrilled, and a disembodied Jewish band sent the guests on a frenzied *galop* through the auditorium. Simultaneously, a white screen rose in front of the stage, bearing the fatal announcement of the true inspector's arrival and then slowly disappeared aloft to disclose life-size terror-stricken effigies of the towns-people – condemned to eternal petrifaction.†

What of Khlestakov, the engineer of this whole nightmare? Meyerhold drew attention to his affinity with the card-sharper, Ikharyov, in *The*

---

* In October 1846 Gogol wrote to Shchepkin: 'Pay particular attention to the closing scene; it is absolutely necessary for it to be vivid, even startling. The Mayor must be completely distraught and not at all funny.' (Quoted by Meyerhold – *Meyerhold II*, p. 146).

† In his *Dénouement* to the play Gogol describes the Dumb Scene as '. . . the petri-faction into which everybody is frozen by the announcement of the arrival of the true inspector who will exterminate all of them, wipe from the face of the earth, destroy them utterly . . .'

65. Garin as Khlestakov.

Gamblers,[19] but he gave him as many more aspects as he had once identified in Arlecchino and Don Juan.* Leonid Grossman describes his first entrance:

> He appears onstage, a character from some tale by Hoffmann: slender, clad in black, with a stiff, mannered gait, strange spectacles, a sinister old-fashioned tall hat, a rug and a cane, apparently tormented by some private vision. He is a flâneur from the Nevsky Prospect, a native of Gogol's own Petersburg. . . .[20]

And he had a double, an 'Officer in Transit' (sprung from Khlestakov's passing reference in the play to an infantry captain who had fleeced him at cards in Penza) with a pale lugubrious visage and a cynical daring reminis-

* See pp. 113–114 above.

cent of Lermontov's Pechorin from *A Hero of our Time*. He was Khlestakov's taciturn accomplice in every enterprise. At the inn he set to work marking a pack of cards; immediately Khlestakov's air of distraction vanished and he, too, became a sharp-witted swindler. On sensing the Mayor's servility towards him at their opening encounter, Khlestakov borrowed his companion's tunic, fur-collared cape, and tall shako, and 'Before our very eyes this timorous little fop, this most servile of civil servants was transformed into the phantasmagorical figure of the imposter.'[21] Later the pair of them danced a quadrille with Anna Andreevna and her daughter Maria: whilst Khlestakov played the love-smitten gallant to mother and daughter in turn, his double looked on with a disdainful sneer, revealing the whole tawdriness of these amorous manoeuvres.

The 'Officer in Transit' was seen on the one hand as 'a mystical representation of everything which took place behind the scenes of Khlestakov's soul',[22] and on the other as 'an animated piece of furniture',[23] ready to provide the accessories for every transformation, an attentive ear for a soliloquy – even the occasional phrase in the rare event of words failing his garrulous companion.

Khlestakov had a different mask for every situation: Nevsky flâneur, ingenious card-sharper, timorous clerk, imperious general, adroit adventurer. He was all of these plus a Russian Munchhausen who elevated the lie to an art form. Yet on the words, 'Well how are things, Pushkin, old friend?' he lapsed into the melancholic reverie of a solitary poet and for a fleeting moment the audience was given a glimpse of Gogol himself. Much was made of Meyerhold's 'mystical' interpretation of Khlestakov, but a thoroughly rational justification for it is supplied by Gogol:

> In a word he should be a type containing traits found scattered in a variety of Russian characters but which happen here to be combined in one, as is often the case in nature. There is nobody who for a minute, not to say several minutes, has not changed or does not go on changing into a Khlestakov, although naturally he is reluctant to admit it. We even make fun of this habit – but only, of course, when we see it in someone else. Even the smart guards officer, even the eminent head of the family, even our friend, the humble man of letters, will sometimes turn into a Khlestakov. In short, there's hardly a single man who won't become him at least once in his lifetime – the only point is that he'll change back again and carry on as though it had never happened.[24]

Erast Garin, who played Khlestakov, writes: 'In the interpretation of the director there was hyperbole but no mysticism . . . the mystical interpretation of Meyerhold's Khlestakov by a section of the critics was a

66. Episode Seven: 'Over a Bottle of Fat-Belly'. Khlestakov recounts his Petersburg exploits with the Blue Hussar (centre) seated next to Maria Antonovna and the Officer in Transit reclining extreme left.

product of their own biographies; they were over-conscientious in the application of their literary education'.[25]

As a counterweight to the unrelieved corruption of the townspeople and the fiendish machinations of Khlestakov, Meyerhold interpreted his valet, Osip, as a vigorous positive character rather in the spirit of Aksyusha and Petya in *The Forest*. Rejecting the traditional picture of the scrofulous drunken rascal, he made him a red-cheeked country lad who sang traditional folk songs and emanated robust common sense. The text of his reminiscences of Petersburg (at the opening of Act Two) was not changed, but he was furnished with the audience of a charwoman borrowed by Meyerhold from *The Gamblers*, who pealed with laughter throughout.* Like the 'Officer in Transit' and Anna Andreevna's young officers – to say nothing of Doctor Hübner and his ministrations to the Mayor in Act One† – the charwoman both served a practical theatrical purpose (helping to avoid the soliloquy which Meyerhold considered outmoded) and accentuated the irony of the dialogue (Osip's contempt for Petersburg society). But further to that, her laughter served as a coloratura accompaniment to Osip's tenor recitative; one instance of the production's musical conception which is discussed below.

Meyerhold's most enigmatic addition was the figure of the 'Blue Hussar', a small captain in a light-blue uniform who appeared in three scenes and spoke no lines, representing perhaps yet another neglected suitor of the Mayoress and her daughter. 'What is this little officer, an empty space in the production?' – asked Mikhail Chekhov – 'Yes, of course, though not in the production but in man himself. *The Idea* of the emptiness and pointlessness of life, is conceived and manifested by Meyerhold to a degree of nightmarish reality.'[26]

IV

Meyerhold's version of *The Government Inspector* was considerably longer than the original, and his extensive use of pantomime and *tableaux vivants* made it longer still. In performance with two intervals it ran a fraction over four hours, ending after midnight. Meyerhold wanted to use elaborate settings to evoke the atmosphere of the 1830s, but needed to avoid lengthy scene changes which would have been inimical to the psychological effect of montage, and which would have made the running

---

* 'We invented the Charwoman and then found a Charwoman in Gogol himself' (*Meyerhold II*, p. 132). In Scene Eight of *The Gamblers* Uteshitelny says: 'And on the stairs some charwoman, an absolute fright . . .'

† For a record of a rehearsal of this scene see *Braun*, pp. 221–230 (in this version the name 'Hübner' is rendered in the literal form 'Giebner').

time quite intolerable. Accordingly, he devised a method of kinetic staging, similar in principle to the double revolve in *The Warrant*.

The stage was enclosed by a semi-circular, imitation polished mahogany screen containing a series of eleven double-doors (plus two more at either wing), surmounted by a dull green border and with three large suspended green lights. The centre section of the screen opened to admit a tiny truck-stage (about fourteen feet by twelve feet with a one-in-eight rake) which rolled silently forward on runners to face the audience with actors and setting ready assembled. At the end of the scene the screen reopened and the truck retreated, to be replaced by another similarly prepared. All but four scenes were played on these trucks, with the inn scene ('After Penza') alone lowered from the flies. The remainder occupied the full stage area, with the final 'grand rond' overflowing into the auditorium. Bobchinsky's headlong tumble down the stairs of the inn continued right out of sight into the orchestra pit – a 'mise *hors* scène', as Eisenstein called it.

The full stage was used to striking effect in the episode entitled 'Procession' (the return from the hospital to the Mayor's house) when a tipsy Khlestakov in voluminous cloak steered an erratic course the length of a balustrade with a sycophantic *corps de ballet* of town dignitaries matching his every stagger. In 'Bribes' (Act Four, Scenes Three to Nine, staged simultaneously) the wooden screen was transformed into a cunning 'bribe machine': as Khlestakov lay stupefied on the empty stage in a flickering half-light, eleven hands, seemingly conjured up by his drunken imagination, materialised simultaneously from eleven doors and apprehensively tendered eleven· wads of banknotes which Khlestakov pocketed with the mechanical gestures of a clockwork doll.

Each scene on the truck-stage glided forward from the gloom like the reincarnation of a long-buried past, an exquisitely composed engraving projected out of its gleaming mahogany frame; a long pause was held for the image to register, then the tableau came to life. In a newspaper interview Meyerhold commented: 'Thanks to the method of staging which we have employed in the production, we have been able, in the language of the cinema, to shoot the principal scenes in close-up.'[27] This is well illustrated by Sergei Radlov's description of the scene where Khlestakov drunkenly expatiates on his Petersburg exploits:

Crystal sparkles, blue and translucent; heavy silk, gleaming and flowing; the dazzling black hair and dazzling white breast of a grand stately lady; a dandy, romantically gaunt and drunk as only a Hoffmann could imagine, lifts a cigar to his languid lips with the movement of a

67. Episode Nine: 'Bribes'.

somnambulist. A silver bowl filled with pieces of fat, succulent water-melon. Enchanted objects, wobbling slightly, float from hand to hand, passed by servants in a trance. Huge splendid divans, like elephants carved from mahogany, stand poised in majestic slumber. What is this – *Caligari* run in slow motion by some lunatic projectionist?[28]

To some casual observers the profusion of lifelike detail seemed to suggest a rapprochement with Moscow Art Theatre naturalism, but in

68. Episode Fourteen: 'A Fine Celebration!' The reading of Khlestakov's letter by the Postmaster, with the Mayor and Mayoress seated right and the Blue Hussar (Vladimir Maslatsov) extreme right.

truth the picture was anything but naturalistic. The pot-belly of a ward-robe, the voluptuous curve of a Récamier couch, the deep rose-patterned back of a divan: they were all subtly exaggerated to enhance the poses of the characters and to impinge more firmly on the retina of the spectator.

Above all, the truck-stage afforded no space for ill-considered, 'inspirational' movement. With as many as thirty characters pressed together in a human pyramid, the merest deviation in timing or movement could destroy the whole ensemble. By this most practical device Meyer-hold compelled his company to exercise physically the self-discipline which had always been the ultimate objective of biomechanics and all the experiments which preceded the formulation of that system.

V

The powerful atmosphere and the sense of period of the production owed much to the complex musical score which accompanied it throughout.* It included arrangements of works by nineteenth-century Russian composers, in particular romances by Glinka and Dargomyzhsky, and music specially composed by Mikhail Gnesin. Gnesin describes how the music heard during the ball celebrating Maria Antonovna's betrothal to Khlestakov was based on the little Jewish bands which Meyerhold recalled from the balls and weddings of his youth in Penza. It was similar to the music that Chekhov specified as an accompaniment to Ranevskaya's agony in Act Three of *The Cherry Orchard*.[29]

Twenty years earlier, in his analysis of that same act Meyerhold had defined its musical structure, treating the actual music as one element in an overall rhythmical harmony designed to reveal the 'sub-text' of the drama.† Now he analysed and interpreted *The Government Inspector* in precisely the same manner, exploiting to perfection the lessons he had learnt originally from Appia and Wagner. Emmanuel Kaplan describes Meyerhold's orchestration of Gogol's score in the opening scene:

Introduction. Dark. Somewhere, slow quiet music begins to play. In the centre of the stage massive doors swing silently open of their own accord and a platform moves slowly forward towards the spectator, out of the gloom, out of the distance, out of the past – one senses this immediately, because it is contained in the music. The music swells and comes nearer, then suddenly on an abrupt chord – *sforzando* – the platform is flooded with light in unison with the music.

On the platform stand a table and a few chairs; candles burn; officials sit. The audience seems to crane forward towards the dark and gloomy age of Nicholas in order to see better what it was like in those days.

Suddenly, the music grows quiet – *subito piano* – gloomy like the period, like the colours of the setting: red furniture, red doors and red walls, green uniforms and green hanging lampshades: the colour scheme of government offices. The music is abruptly retarded and drawn out expectantly; everybody waits – on the stage and in the audience. Smoke rises from pipes and chibouks. The long stems 'cross out' the faces of the officials lit by the flickering candle flames; they are

---

* In common with other major Soviet theatres, Meyerhold had at his disposal an orchestra to provide a musical accompaniment for productions.

† See *Meyerhold on Theatre*, p. 28.

like fossilised monsters: crossed out and obliterated, once and for all. There they sit, wreathed in a haze with only the shadows of their pipes flickering on their faces; and the music plays on, slower and quieter as though flickering too, bearing them away from us, further and further into that irretrievable 'then'. A pause – *fermata* – and then a voice: 'Gentlemen, I have invited you here to give you some most unpleasant news. . . .' like Rossini in the Act One *stretto* with Doctor Bartholo and Don Basilio, only there the tempo is *presto*, whilst here it is very slow. Then suddenly, as though on a word of command, at a stroke of the conductor's baton, everyone stirs in agitation, pipes jump from lips, fists clench, heads swivel. The last syllable of 'revizor' (inspector) seems to tweak everybody. Now the word is hissed in a whisper: the whole word by some, just the consonants by others, and somewhere even a softly rolled 'r'. The word 'revizor' is divided musically into every conceivable intonation. The ensemble of suddenly startled officials blows up and dies away like a squall. Everyone freezes and falls silent; the guilty conscience rears up in alarm then hides its poisonous head again, like a serpent lying motionless, harbouring its deadly venom.

The dynamics of this perfectly fashioned musical introduction fluctuate constantly. The sudden *forte-fortissimo* of the Mayor's cry 'send for Lyapkin-Tyakpin!' The terrified officials spring up in all directions, hiding their guilty consciences as far away as possible – under the table, behind each other's backs, even behind the armchair where the Mayor was just sitting. It is like a dance-pantomime of fright. The District Physician begins to squeal on the letter 'i', first a long drawn-out whistle then jerkily on 'e' *staccato*, then the two 'notes' alternately rising and falling, whilst the next lines are 'embroidered' onto this background. In orchestral terms, it is like a piccolo with double bass *pizzicato*, just like the comic scenes in Rimsky-Korsakov's *May Night*. A sudden screech *glissando* from the Doctor and a new 'dance of terror' begins. The plastic pattern of the characters' movements corresponds to the rhythmical pattern of their voices. Their brief pauses seem to foretoken the dumb scene of the finale.[30]

Perhaps more than anything else it was this concept of 'musicality' that characterised Meyerhold's style and set him apart from every other stage-director of his time.*

* For a scene-by-scene reconstruction of the production by Nick Worrall see *Theatre Quarterly*, Vol. II, No. 7, pp. 75–95.

VI

There can be no doubt that Meyerhold's *Government Inspector* inspired a greater volume of critical literature than any other production in the history of the Russian theatre.[31] In the most unpredictable way, former allies and opponents of Meyerhold found themselves ranged up on the same side, both in support and in condemnation of his interpretation. Thus, the praise of Andrei Bely was predictable enough, but he could hardly have expected to be joined by both Kugel and Mayakovsky. Meyerhold found the attacks of the 'left' especially hard to bear, particularly when they were directed at the performance of Zinaida Raikh. His retorts in open debate descended to a level of personal invective which drove the Association of Theatre and Cinema Critics to publish a protest against his 'unexampled anti-social attacks'.[32] The outcome of the affair was a lasting animosity which Meyerhold could well have done without in the years to come.

However, despite the violent criticism of its alleged 'mysticism', the attempts to discredit its author's political integrity, the hysterical protests at the liberties taken with Gogol's hallowed text, and the fears that it was too complex to be accessible to the average spectator, the work was performed regularly up to the very day of the theatre's liquidation in 1938. Not only did it establish once and for all the creative autonomy of the stage director, it gave new impetus to the reappraisal of Gogol and the other Russian classics. A notable product of this was Shostakovich's first opera, *The Nose*, composed in 1928–1929 when he was working at Meyerhold's theatre. The libretto, based on Gogol's story of the same name plus fragments from *Diary of a Madman*, *Dead Souls*, *Nevsky Prospect*, and *Old-world Landowners*, has a similar episodic structure to Meyerhold's *Government Inspector*.

When the Moscow Art Theatre was preparing Bulgakov's version of *Dead Souls* in 1930, Stanislavsky took the production out of Vasily Sakhnovsky's hands because he objected to its Meyerholdian 'symbolism'.[33] It is Stanislavsky's version staged finally in 1932, virtually as a polemic against Meyerhold's *Government Inspector*, which has remained in the Moscow Art Theatre repertoire to this day.

9.   1927–1931
The New Repertoire

When the Moscow Art Theatre opened its 1925–1926 season with Konstantin Trenyov's *The Pugachov Rising*, it confirmed the adoption of the new Soviet repertoire by every major Russian theatre except the Kamerny. This tendency was consolidated over the next two years by the widespread success of such plays as Trenyov's *Lyubov Yarovaya*, Gladkov's *Cement*, Bulgakov's *The Days of the Turbins*, and Vsevolod Ivanov's *Armoured Train 14–69*. Yet after *The Warrant* in April 1925 nearly four years passed before the production of another Soviet play by Meyerhold. Whilst Soviet society had outgrown the need for schematised propaganda pieces, few dramatists were writing with the social insight and poetic inspiration which Meyerhold demanded, and those who were all failed to deliver a completed script. A new play by Mayakovsky, to be called *A Comedy with Murder*, was promised first for 1926 then for 1928, but was never written;[1] plans to stage Andrei Bely's dramatic adaptation of his novel *Moscow* in 1927 were abandoned three years later when the final draft had still not been completed;[2] an attempt to lure Bulgakov away from the Moscow Art Theatre was politely resisted;[3] despite Meyerhold's urgent pleas, Erdman took three years to complete his next play after *The Warrant*, and then it was banned by the censor.

One dramatist who did complete a play that fired Meyerhold's imagination was Sergei Tretyakov. His *I Want a Child* submits traditional attitudes towards love and sexuality to rational scrutiny, and concludes by advocating selective breeding, based on criteria of political (as opposed to racial) purity. The communist heroine, Milda Griegnau is 'an agronomist who relieves her sexual tension by giving birth to a baby, whilst paying due regard to the demands of practical eugenics'.[4] Having accepted the play in 1926, Meyerhold tried for almost four years to overcome the censor's resistance to the text. In view of the controversial subject, he proposed staging it in the form of an illustrated discussion which the spectators would be free to interrupt. In keeping with this conception, the brilliant constructivist designer El Lissitsky devised a setting which embraced the whole interior of the theatre, completely obliterating the division between stage and audience. So complex was the project that Meyerhold decided to postpone it until the rebuilding of his outmoded and inadequate theatre. This he never lived to see, and a production was lost which, to judge from the surviving model and plans, would have

69. *El Lissitsky's setting for* I Want a Child, *1928–1929. (Model reconstruction from the Arts Council Exhibition 'Art in Revolution', Hayward Gallery, 1971. Photograph John Webb.)*

exemplified the spatial and functional concepts of Constructivism to a degree which the theatrical work of Popova, Stepanova, and Shestakov never did.[5]

Such was the repertoire crisis at the Meyerhold Theatre in the late twenties that Meyerhold himself staged no new work to mark the tenth anniversary of the October Revolution. A plan to adapt John Reed's *Ten Days That Shook the World* did not materialise, and the best the theatre could offer was *A Window on the Country*, a 'political review' in the style of *D.E.* produced by twelve of Meyerhold's pupils. Aimed at propagandising the drive to modernise agriculture, it comprised a series of jejune sketches of peasants engaged in their traditional tasks and pastimes, interspersed with filmed illustrations of the latest technological achievements.

In January 1928 Meyerhold revived *The Magnanimous Cuckold*, introducing amendments designed, as he said, to reduce the predominance of form over content. Babanova had now left the company, and the part of Stella was played by Raikh. Dimitri Talnikov, a penetrating critic if no great supporter of Meyerhold, wrote in *Contemporary Theatre*:

> Raikh moves ponderously over the construction and speaks her lines lifelessly; she lacks Stella's fire, her spiritual infectiousness, her youth. She is a woman of experience simulating naïveté and innocence, but no matter how much she rolls her eyes, nobody is likely to believe her.[6]

The tone of Talnikov's review is a sample of what Meyerhold could now expect from many critics, but the substance of his criticism holds good: despite Meyerhold's claims that Raikh had helped him to reveal the tragic essence of Crommelynck's play,[7] the part of Stella was not within her range and the production itself hardly ripe for revival at this time.

II

At length Meyerhold returned to the classics for his only new production of the 1927–1928 season. This time he chose *Woe from Wit*, Griboedov's satirical portrayal of Moscow society in the 1820s. The production was a reinterpretation, no less free than *The Government Inspector* had been, and was inspired, said Meyerhold, by a letter from Pushkin to the Decembrist Alexander Bestuzhev, in which he wrote:

> Who is the intelligent character in *Woe from Wit*? Answer: Griboedov. And do you know what Chatsky is? A passionate, honourable, decent young fellow who has spent some time in the company of a very intelligent man (namely, Griboedov) and has absorbed his thoughts, his witticisms and his satirical remarks. Everything he says is very intelligent, but to whom does he say it? Famusov? Skalozub? The old Moscow grannies at the ball? Molchalin? That is unpardonable. The first test of a man's intelligence is his ability to recognise whom he is dealing with, and to avoid casting pearls before swine like Repetilov.[8]

Proceeding from this, Meyerhold's aim was to set Chatsky apart from the rest of society and relate him to the young radicals of the ill-fated Decembrist movement with whom Griboedov himself had been in sympathy. As they had done with *The Government Inspector*, Meyerhold and Mikhail Korenev took the three extant texts of Griboedov's play, and by cutting, rearranging, and adding other material they produced a new version in seventeen episodes. One scene contained inflammatory verses by Pushkin and Ryleev which Chatsky and his fellow Decembrists were seen declaiming in the adjacent library. Meyerhold chose the more unequivocal title of the first draft *Woe To Wit*, implying 'woe to him who is incautious enough to exercise his intelligence'.

All but the first of the episodes were given the title and setting of a part of Famusov's extensive mansion,* thereby unfolding before the spectator a panoramic view of the manners and pursuits of Griboedov's society. However, in a number of episodes Meyerhold's interpolations had no organic relationship with the text, but served merely to heighten the local colour. Thus, a dancing lesson, a game of billiards, and target practice in the shooting gallery had neither the dynamic quality of the physical action in *The Forest* nor the complex metaphorical imagery of the tableaux in *The Government Inspector*. The one notable exception was the scene ('*The Dining Room*') where thirty-two dinner guests, seated bolt upright at a long table directly facing the audience, slowly relayed the false rumour of Chatsky's madness to the accompaniment of a tranquil nocturne by John Field; with the appearance of the solitary figure of Chatsky, they all raised their napkins as though in self-defence, hissing menacingly like snakes at bay.

In the interpretation of Chatsky by Garin, the utmost was done to emphasise his sense of isolation from Sophie, Molchalin, Famusov, and the rest. When he did speak to them, it was often whilst improvising at the piano. The music, selected and arranged by the composer Boris Asafiev, was designed to reflect the various aspects of Chatsky's character: Beethoven – his militant reforming zeal, Mozart – his Byronic welt-schmerz, Bach – his exalted humanity, John Field – his tender dreams of Sophie.[9] The device found little sympathy amongst the critics, one of whom compared Garin to 'a piano-player at the pictures, illustrating his emotions'.[10] They were similarly perplexed by Meyerhold's depiction of Moscow society: on this occasion, he completely rejected the grotesque and presented Griboedov's gentry as robust, decisive and confident in their philistinism, leaving no hope that Chatsky's somewhat pallid ideal-ism would prevail – which in the light of the 1825 débâcle of the Decem-brist revolt was accurate enough.

The basic setting was a supposedly practicable construction by Victor Shestakov, which was a typical example of the degeneration of construc-tivism to a design idiom devoid of all architectonic logic, since in perform-

* For details of Meyerhold's version and a reconstruction of the production by Alma H. Law see *The Drama Review*, Vol. 18, No. 3 (T–63), pp. 89–107.

70. Woe to Wit, 1928 : Episode Fourteen (The Dining Room).

ance the upper level and staircases were scarcely used. Its arbitrariness typified the production in general which, as Meyerhold himself admitted, was not an artistic success, suffering from 'false academicism' and a disproportionate emphasis on certain episodes. He later called it the 'Petersburg version' in order to emphasise its affinity with his pre-revolutionary work, and in September 1935 produced a second version, the 'Moscow version', which was dedicated both to the pianist, Lev Oborin (the original dedicatee), and to the Chinese actor, Mei Lan-fang, who had recently visited Russia and whose mimetic skill and rhythmical discipline Meyerhold held up as models to his actors.[11] The dedication provides a clue to the production's comparative failure: the cast of the richest verse play in the Russian language was exhorted to emulate the plastic skills of the greatest living exponent of Chinese dance-drama.

III

In July 1928, Meyerhold and Zinaida Raikh left the Soviet Union on holiday and spent the next five months in France. At that time, audiences at his theatre had dropped to less than three-quarters capacity, with box-office receipts falling at times to forty per cent. This was due largely to the staleness of the repertoire which contained such long familiar works as *The Forest* and *The Magnanimous Cuckold*. With the failure of *A Window on the Country*, the theatre's financial position was all the more precarious. Scorning all available Soviet plays except the controversial *I Want a Child*, Meyerhold preferred to wait for the new works long promised by Erdman and Mayakovsky, and a Civil War tragedy commissioned from the poet Ilya Selvinsky. Meanwhile, he sought to bridge the gap by arranging a season for his theatre in Paris. But 'Glaviskusstvo', the newly-formed state authority which controlled all the arts, twice ordered him to discontinue negotiations and even threatened to close his theatre if he failed to return and improve its position. After a violent controversy which rallied widespread support for Meyerhold and split even the ranks of Glaviskusstvo, a special government commission was formed to investigate the theatre's affairs. It condemned Meyerhold's negligence, but recommended a subsidy to cover outstanding debts and running costs for a further two months up to the end of November,* delaying its final decision on the theatre's future until his return.[12] The recommendations amounted to an ultimatum, which may have been motivated by the fear that Meyerhold was considering following the example of Mikhail

* Since 1926 the theatre had borne the title 'State Meyerhold Theatre', and had qualified for regular state subsidy.

Chekhov, the celebrated actor and artistic director of the Second Moscow
Art Theatre and a close friend of Meyerhold, who had decided to emigrate
in August 1928.

   Rather than risk losing his theatre, Meyerhold abandoned his plans for
a Paris season and returned to Moscow on 2 December 1928, having been
ordered by his French doctors to convalesce in Vichy and Nice after a
serious illness which had affected his heart and liver. Far from admitting
his own financial negligence, Meyerhold straightaway complained of the

71. The Bed Bug (*1929*). *Publicity leaflet by Mavakovsky.*

state of the old Sohn Theatre (where only a hundred and fifty out of three
hundred and ninety seats in the circle were usable) and demanded more
storage and rehearsal space. On this, he said, depended the repertoire for
the season, which he hoped would include *I Want a Child*, Erdman's
Suicide, and Selvinsky's *The Second Army Commander*.[13]

   However, the first production proved to be the recently completed
Bed Bug, which Mayakovsky read to the company for the first time on
28 December. Announcing his plan to stage it as quickly as possible,
Meyerhold declared 'The repertoire crisis has been completely overcome
(at least for the present). The theatre's confidence in the foremost
experimental dramatist of the Revolution remains steadfast.'[14] After only
six weeks' rehearsal, the play was presented on 13 February 1929.

   In terms of theatrical innovation, *The Bed Bug* was one of Meyerhold's
less significant productions, but of all the Soviet plays staged by him it is

the one which has been most frequently revived. Contrasting him with Stanislavsky, 'the novelist-director', Pavel Markov has described Meyerhold as 'the poet-director' par excellence.[15] Not only does this convey the essence of his allusive, rhythmical style, it also refers to the remarkable proportion of poets amongst the dramatists staged by him. But apart from Blok, Meyerhold held none of them in such high esteem as Mayakovsky. His immediate reaction to *The Bed Bug* was to hail it as 'a work as great and significant as Griboedov's *Woe from Wit* was in its day',[16] and he immediately invited Mayakovsky to supervise the linguistic side of the production.

72. The Bed Bug. *Scene One. Left to right: Bayan (Alexei Temerin), Madam Renaissance (Natalya Serebryanikova), Prisypkin (Igor Ilinsky).*

The first half of the play, which culminates in the riotous nuptials of lapsed party member Prisypkin and his manicurist bride Elzevira Renaissance, is a deadly accurate grotesque portrayal of the Soviet petit bourgeoisie. At Mayakovsky's suggestion, the young 'Kukryniksy' cartoon group was invited to design the settings, costumes, and make-up. Nearly all the costumes and properties were bought over the counter in Moscow shops in order to demonstrate the pretentious ugliness of current fashions and the all too discomforting topicality of the satire – rammed home at the final curtain by the de-frosted Prisypkin's joyful recognition of a whole audience of fellow bourgeois.

Mayakovsky sets Part Two of the play fifty years in the future in a gleaming utopian paradise. Starting work on the play, Meyerhold said:

> The main purpose is to castigate the vices of the present day. In projecting us forward to 1979, Mayakovsky is forcing us to examine not a world transformed, but the very same sickness that is afflicting society today . . . Mayakovsky's aim is to show us that illnesses have deeply rooted causes, and take a great deal of time and a vast amount of energy to overcome.[17]

73. The Bed Bug. *Part Two. The defrosting of Prisypkin.*

The costumes and settings for Part Two were designed by the constructivist Alexander Rodchenko, and depicted an antiseptic, utilitarian vision of the future which seemed to contain a distinct hint of self-parody, entirely consistent with the ironic view of Meyerhold and Mayakovsky. But the critics were confused: some saw it as an inspired vision of advanced technology, some found it a lifeless abstraction, whilst some even suspected that it was a parody of the achievements of socialism.[18]

The music was composed by the young, little-known Dmitry Shostakovich, then employed as a pianist at Meyerhold's theatre. As he recalls, the score was based on the marches of fire-brigade bands much admired by Mayakovsky.[19] Its strident cacophony was less to the taste of most critics. There was an ominous ring to the words of Robert Pelshe in *Contemporary*

Theatre, the official organ of 'Glaviskusstvo': '. . . we recommend Comrade Shostakovich to reflect more seriously on questions of musical culture in the light of the development of our socialist society according to the precepts of Marxism'.[20]

Despite widespread criticism, particularly of the contributions of Rodchenko and Shostakovich, *The Bed Bug* was a huge popular success, due

74. Meyerhold and Shostakovich, 1928.

largely to the inspired portrayal of Prisypkin by Igor Ilinsky. For another season at least, the Meyerhold Theatre was secure.

IV

Ever since the success of Bill-Belotserkovsky's heroic drama *The Storm* in 1925, the Civil War play had become a staple item of the Soviet repertoire: with its clear distinction between Reds and Whites, its epic heroism and suffering, and the personal memories which it evoked for many of its audience, it was a dramatic genre in its own right. Meyerhold had been the first to demonstrate its emotive power with his staging of Tretyakov's *Earth Rampant* in 1923, since when he had devoted his energies exclusively to comedy and satire. But in July 1929 he staged *The Second Army Commander*,* a Civil War tragedy in verse by the young poet Ilya

* In *Meyerhold on Theatre* and elsewhere the title is translated wrongly as 'Commander of the Second Army'. The point of the play is that one commander (Chub) is replaced by a second (Okonny).

Selvinsky. Selvinsky's aims were considerably more complex than those of most previous dramatists who had tapped the same source. Shortly after the premiere he wrote:

> In my play one can trace the problem of the leader and the masses, the problem of ideological imposture, the problem of technology opposed to poetic inspiration. There is the collision between the petit bourgeois revolutionary impulse and the proletarian, the contrast between misguided genius and competent ordinariness, the development of socialism into revolutionary praxis, and much more besides. . . . But if you are looking for the general shape of the tragedy, its philosophical architecture, then I would say it is to be found in its dialectic.[21]

The play is set around the battle for the town of Beloyarsk in the early stages of the Civil War when the Red Army was still little more than a

75. The Second Army Commander. *'The Firing Squad.'*

loose grouping of guerrilla units. The thesis and antithesis of Selvinsky's dialectic are represented by Chub, a partisan leader of peasant origins thrown up by the masses, and Okonny, an army clerk and one-time book-keeper who sees in the Revolution the means of self-realisation and glory. The one is laconic, straightforward, and limited in his horizons, the other is expansive, boldly imaginative, and highly versed in revolutionary rhetoric. Okonny usurps Chub's command by winning over the army with the appeal of his strategy, then causes the death of hundreds in gaining a victory of doubtful military value. He is arrested, and Chub, now more flexible and far-sighted, is restored to a new command, but only to be confronted by a 'new' Okonny, called Podokonny, the inference being that the dialectical process will continue. Selvinsky's portrayal of the two commanders is equally ironic, suggesting that the behaviour of both has its positive and its negative aspects. Taking the view that this simply obscured the intended 'dialectic', Meyerhold insisted on sharpening the antithesis by enhancing Chub's heroic stature and depicting Okonny as an egocentric adventurer riding to glory on the back of the Revolution. The character of Podokonny was eliminated and Okonny faced a firing squad at the end of the play. The changes were the outcome of long and bitter wrangles between the implacable director and the inexperienced dramatist. Selvinsky complained in the press that Meyerhold had reduced his text to 'agitational primitiveness', and broke off all relations with him. In 1967 Selvinsky recalled: 'He wasn't capable of arguing. He bombarded his opponent with paradoxes, disarmed him with humour, and always stuck rigidly to his principles.' Yet at the same time he confessed himself entranced by many of the effects which Meyerhold achieved, and conceded the considerable influence of the production on his later work.[22]

Meyerhold's production was a conscious revolt against the prevailing genre representations of the Civil War; it was an attempt to create, in Pavel Markov's words, 'a monumental musical tragedy'. The setting was of suitably heroic proportions and severity: the acting area was enclosed by a towering leaden-coloured screen which functioned as a sounding board for the frequent choral effects. Against it, a flight of steps descended from stage-left to right in a gradual spiral. Props were kept to a bare minimum, and the maximum emphasis was placed on costumes and weapons. The setting was executed by Sergei Vakhtangov (the director's son) and the costume consultant was the prominent artist Petrov-Vodkin. In their furs and skins, criss-crossed with weighty ammunition belts, their assorted accoutrements and headgear sharing little in common save the Red Guard insignia, the partisans, ancestors of the modern Red Army, looked like the resurrected warriors of some ancient epic of the Steppe. Boris Alpers wrote:

They are men who disappeared on the battlefields of 1918–19, the legendary heroes of a legendary time. If you removed their Caucasian hats and their sheepskin jerkins, you would find half-severed skulls, cloven heads, gaping breasts, torsoes disfigured with a five-pointed star.

76. '*The Sentries.*'

That is why they stand so still, holding their tall lances; that is why they move with such a slow and measured tread, the imprint of some strange reverie on every face.[23]

Meyerhold's scenic compositions possessed a hieratic grandeur strongly reminiscent of his production of *The Dawn* nine years earlier. Aided by a powerful musical score by Vissarion Shebalin, he kept a strict regard for the metre of Selvinsky's text and created what was virtually a dramatic oratorio. Much as critics objected to the play's historical inaccuracy, the schematised characterisation, the prolixity of Selvinsky's verse, and the feeble portrayal of Okonny, they were unanimous in their admiration for Meyerhold's staging of the ensemble scenes. In particular, they singled out the recounting of the Battle of Beloyarsk by a narrator with a refrain in mazurka time chanted by the entire company of fifty using megaphones, like the masks in Greek tragedy, to amplify their voices to awesome power.

The production was given its premiere on 24 July 1929 when the company was on tour in Kharkov. Contrary to Meyerhold's gloomy expectations, it proved successful and when it was staged in Moscow in the autumn it was recognised as the first serious attempt to create a Soviet tragedy.[24]

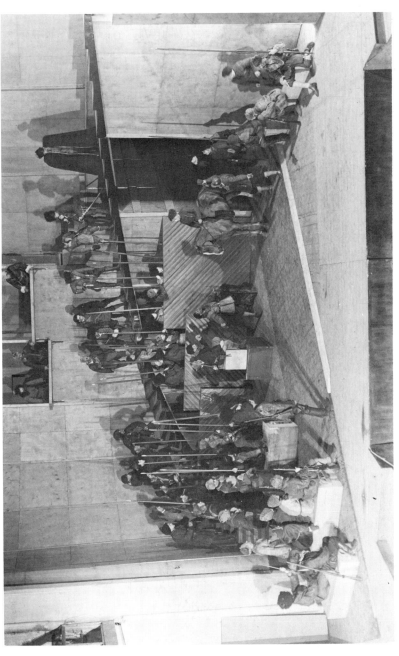

77. 'The Meeting.'

V

The huge popular success of *The Bed Bug* completely overcame all Mayakovsky's reservations about play-writing; within seven months of its opening he had completed another play, *The Bath House*, described as 'a drama in six acts with circus and fireworks'. According to Mikhail Zoshchenko, Mayakovsky's first reading of the text to the company and Artistic Soviet* of the Meyerhold Theatre on 23 September 1926 '. . . was a triumph. The actors and writers laughed uproariously and applauded the poet. They grasped the point of every single phrase. I have seldom seen such a positive reaction.'[25] But the state censorship body, 'Glavrepertkom', failed to share their enthusiasm; it considered the satire far too provocative, and demanded numerous cuts before it passed the text for performance.[26] This reaction was a direct reflection of the opinion propagated by the Russian Association of Proletarian Writers ('RAPP') that satire did nothing but harm the cause of socialism, and that art should depict only 'real life'. It is precisely this attitude that Mayakovsky is lampooning in Act Three of *The Bath House*, where the arch-bureaucrat, Pobedonosikov, and his retinue have just seen the play, and failed to recognise themselves in it. Pobedonosikov instructs the director on the theatre's proper function:

> In the name of every worker and peasant, I beg you not to disturb my peace of mind. What do you think you are, an alarm clock? Perish the thought! Your job is to beguile my eye and ear, not to assault them. . . . We need to rest after the discharge of our obligations to the state and society. Back to the classics! Study the great geniuses of the accursed past.

In the last act, when they are all ejected from the Phosphorescent Woman's time machine which bears away the inventor and his proletarian friends to a Communist future in the year 2030, Pobedonosikov cries to the hack painter, Belvedonsky:

> Hey artist, seize the opportunity! Paint a real, live man as he is mortally insulted![27]

By 1930, the influence of RAPP and its associated bodies in the other arts threatened to dominate Soviet criticism. As Rudnitsky writes, 'Using

---

* From 1928 onwards 'artistic soviets' were set up in all theatres. Their function was to supervise the selection and presentation of plays. In most cases, the chairman was nominated by the Party. The Soviet at the Meyerhold Theatre comprised over sixty members.

78 and 79. The Phosphorescent Woman (Zinaida Raikh) and Pobedonosikov (Maxim Shtraukh).

channels accessible only to themselves, they cleverly secured official support for nearly all their concrete recommendations, critical appraisals, and assessments of individuals.' [28] Their programme, essentially a rehash of Proletkult principles, advocated the true-to-life, positive portrayal of Soviet reality in a style easily accessible to the broad masses. Eventually, RAPP overreached itself in promoting its members' interests and in 1932 it was disbanded by the Central Committee of the Party. However, by that time its influence had been crucial in the evolution of the new, rigid code of Socialist Realism which was to stifle artistic expression for the next twenty-five years and still dominates much of Soviet criticism.

Meyerhold and Mayakovsky had already come under heavy fire from RAPP when they staged *The Bed Bug*. Now the bombardment was resumed even before *The Bath House* was seen by the Moscow public. Before Meyerhold's production, the play had its first performance on 30 January 1930 at the State People's House in Leningrad; it was greeted in the press with wholly negative criticism which made little effort to examine the problems posed by Mayakovsky's text. Then in the February number of *On Literary Guard* the RAPP critic Vladimir Yermilov published a preview totally condemning the play, even though he admitted to having read only a published fragment of the text.[29] For all its flagrant tendentiousness, Yermilov's article was republished in greatly abridged form in *Pravda* on 9 March, thereby ensuring that the production opened on 16 March 1930 in an atmosphere of mistrust and hostility.

Almost without exception, the reviews were destructive; the play itself was seen as a malicious misrepresentation of Soviet officialdom, and its presentation a regression to the heavy-handed knockabout style of the early twenties. In so far as it is possible to tell from photographs and the

80. The Bath House, *Act Three.*

objective accounts published, the production does seem in some respects to have resembled the 1921 version of *Mystery-Bouffe*, not to mention the agit-prop shows of the 'Blue Blouse' collectives which had come into being since then. Once again the 'Clean' were portrayed as a series of preposterous grotesques, whilst the 'Unclean' were an ill-differentiated series of komsomols in uniform blue overalls whose wholesome vigour recalled Meyerhold's students in *The Magnanimous Cuckold*. Zinaida Raikh as the Phosphorescent Woman appeared in a gleaming flying helmet and an alluring close-fitting space suit, the not altogether convincing harbinger of a perfect socialist future.

Sergei Vakhtangov designed a setting which featured a towering scaffolding with a series of steps and platforms. In a number of scenes a huge screen in the form of a venetian blind with each slat bearing a

81. The Bath House, *Act Six. The Departure of the Time Machine.*

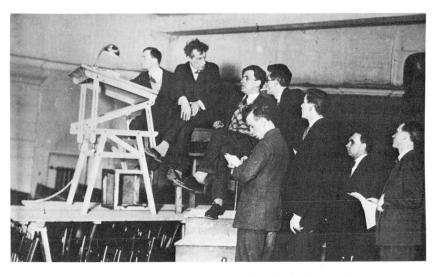

82. Meyerhold and Mayakovsky rehearsing The Bath House (*in conversation centre*).

political slogan was lowered from the flies. The walls of the auditorium too bore rhyming slogans by Mayakovsky, broadcasting the policies of the theatrical left and ridiculing the bureaucrats, the censor, RAPP, the critics, and the Moscow Art Theatre. Forced onto the defensive, Meyerhold and Mayakovsky had made the production as much a statement of their own principles as a denunciation of state bureaucracy.

Whilst conceding its imperfections, Meyerhold regarded *The Bath House* as the best of his four productions of Mayakovsky. Nevertheless, it was coolly received by the public, possibly because it seemed like a throwback to the agitatory clichés of the early twenties, possibly (as Rudnitsky and Fevralsky have both suggested) because its style was ahead of its time. In any case, poor attendances compelled the theatre to drop the production. It was a loss that hit Meyerhold hard, but incalculably greater was the loss of Mayakovsky himself, who on 14 April 1930 shot himself at the age of thirty-six. What drove Mayakovsky to this will always remain a matter for speculation, but some years later, recalling the campaign against *The Bath House*, Meyerhold said: 'It was nothing short of a stab in the back of Mayakovsky, the revolutionary – both by RAPP and by Yermilov, who clearly played the role of a modern D'Anthès to Mayakovsky's Pushkin.'[30]

So close were Meyerhold and Mayakovsky – both as men and as artists – that to read Mayakovsky today is to sense the true atmosphere of Meyerhold's theatre. There were many reasons for Meyerhold's troubles in the thirties, but as significant as any was the loss at their very outset of his truest friend and ally, the only living dramatist he ever treated as his equal.

VI

Early in 1930, Meyerhold was finally granted permission to take his theatre abroad on tour. A section of the company left Moscow shortly after the premiere of *The Bath House* and spent six weeks in Germany, performing in nine cities including Berlin, Breslau, and Cologne. The repertoire consisted of *Roar, China!*, *The Government Inspector*, *The Forest*, and *The Magnanimous Cuckold*.[31] The critical reception was mixed, but public interest was enormous: a performance of *Roar, China!* at the Rheinlandhalle in Cologne was watched by an audience of six thousand.[32]

In May the company arrived in Paris, where it gave ten performances, starting on 16 June. With the exception of *Roar, China!*, which was banned due to its revolutionary content, the plays presented were the same. The premiere of *The Government Inspector* was the occasion for a vociferous demonstration by a section of the Russian émigré community, which protested at Meyerhold's 'mutilation' of Gogol. But nevertheless, that opening night at the modest little Théâtre de Montparnasse was a triumph. Ilya Ehrenburg recalls:

> There was Louis Jouvet, Picasso, Dullin, Cocteau, Derain, Baty . . . And when the performance ended, these people, gorged with art – one would have thought – and in the habit of carefully measuring out their approval, rose to their feet and united in an ovation.[33]

At the end of June the company returned to Moscow, while Meyerhold and Raikh remained in France on holiday until September. According to the artist, Yury Annenkov, who knew him from his Petrograd days, Meyerhold was thinking seriously of going to work in America at that time, but was persuaded by Raikh to return to Moscow first. In a letter dated 6 September 1930 and reproduced in Annenkov's memoirs, Meyerhold writes '. . . soon to Moscow. Then to New York (November 1930).' A note in the recently published volume of Meyerhold's correspondence suggests that this might refer to an American tour which Meyerhold was hoping to arrange for his theatre.[34]

Certainly a further tour at this time would have come as a welcome relief from the ever-pressing problem of finding suitable new plays. In November 1930, Meyerhold could find nothing better to mark the thirteenth anniversary of the Revolution than a revised and updated version of the political review *D.E.* (called *D.S.E.*). Shortly afterwards he turned to Vsevolod Vishnevsky, another of the new generation of Soviet writers, whose play *The First Cavalry Army* had been staged with great success at the Central Red Army Theatre the previous year. Vishnevsky's credentials could scarcely have been bettered: the son of an engineer, he joined the army when still a schoolboy at the outbreak of war, and then in 1917 fought for the Bolsheviks; enlisting in the Red Navy, he was involved in some of the toughest campaigns of the Civil War as well as contributing dispatches to the Communist press. Subsequently, he recorded his experiences in a series of essays and short stories.

There is no doubt that when Meyerhold decided to stage Vishnevsky's *The Final Conflict*,* it was in the hope that he had found a dramatist to replace Mayakovsky. What appealed to him was the extreme freedom of the play's form, which defied categorisation: it began with an elaborate

---

* Also translated as 'The Last Decisive'. The title is a quotation from the chorus of *The Internationale*.

production number which parodied the Bolshoi Theatre's highly successful staging of Glier's ballet, *The Red Poppy*, a ludicrously idealised picture
of life in the Red Navy. This was interrupted by sailors appearing from
the audience and promising a real play about navy life. There followed a
series of loosely connected episodes contrasting the adventures of
debauched 'anarchist' sailors on the spree in Odessa with the cultured
atmosphere of a seamen's club and the discipline and readiness of the
Baltic Fleet.

The production as a whole was a dazzling display of theatrical tricks,
but in the final scene Meyerhold surpassed himself: a detachment of
twenty-seven frontier guards and sailors held a beleaguered position on
the first day of an imagined future war. Machine guns fired blanks directly
at the spectators, artillery thundered from the back of the theatre,
searchlight beams darted, and on cue an actress planted in the audience
was convulsed with sobbing. As the last survivor gasped away his life, a
radio receiver blared out a trivial song by Maurice Chevalier. Summoning
his remaining strength, the sailor painfully chalked on a screen:

$$162,000,000$$
$$-27$$
$$\overline{}$$
$$161,999,973$$

thereby demonstrating the value of the sacrifice and the will of the rest
of the Soviet people to fight on. His task accomplished, the sailor died
with a smile on his lips – then immediately stood up, advanced to the
forestage and said 'Men and women – everyone who is ready to join in the
defence of the U.S.S.R. – stand up!' The audience stood without
exception – but as one critic sourly observed, they would have stood at
the end of Glinka's *A Life for the Tsar*.[35]

The impact of the final scene was conceded by most critics, but at the
same time the play's ideological incoherence was heavily criticised. The
most cogent opinion came from Pavel Markov:

Just as in *The First Cavalry Army*, Vishnevsky employs the difficult and
dangerous method of contrast, but contrast does not necessarily
equal dialectical contradiction. On the contrary, it can easily turn into
mechanical juxtaposition and the monotonous interplay of two or
three colours. . . . So far, Vishnevsky has composed only the sketches
for a future symphony; put together to make a unified dramatic text,
they jar on the ear because of their lack of inner harmony.[36]

83. The Final Conflict, *Last Episode.*

But for all its incoherence and crude effects, *The Final Conflict*, with its combination of burlesque, low comedy, genre realism, melodrama, and tragedy, was a style of popular theatre which was near to Meyerhold's heart. The production opened on 7 February 1931. Ten days later Meyerhold wrote to Vishnevsky:

> . . . Amongst Soviet dramatists you have every right to occupy the first place. Knowing your capacity for work, knowing your genuine ability to learn and improve yourself, I am convinced that your new play will be even more remarkable than the one we are performing with such pleasure at the present time.[37]

Sadly, their friendship quickly turned sour when Vishnevsky's next work *Fighting in the West* failed to live up to Meyerhold's expectations and they disagreed violently over its revision.[38] Eventually it was staged at the Theatre of the Revolution, and in 1933 Vishnevsky gave his most celebrated play *An Optimistic Tragedy* to Tairov of all people, who staged it with enormous success. In 1937 Meyerhold and Vishnevsky finally settled their differences and agreed to collaborate on a play about the Spanish Civil War.[39] But their rapprochement was too late, coming as it did barely three months before the closure of Meyerhold's theatre.

Yury Olesha's *A List of Benefits*, first performed on 4 June 1931, was remarkable for being one of Meyerhold's very few 'chamber works', a production in which he made scarcely any attempt to stretch the resources of the traditional stage. The play tells the story of a fictitious Soviet tragedienne Yelena Goncharova who, feeling her creativity stifled by 'rectilinear, schematised works devoid of imagination', considers emigrating to Paris, the city of her dreams. But once there, she finds herself propositioned by a lecherous impresario, invited to perform a pornographic sketch in a music hall and enveigled into émigré society. Disenchanted and filled with remorse, Yelena finally joins a demonstration

84. Goncharova (Zinaida Raikh) auditioning Hamlet *for Margeret, manager of the Globe Music Hall.*

of unemployed workers, only to be accidentally killed protecting a French communist leader from an assassination attempt by a White émigré.[40]

The play's discursive style and its emphasis on the psychological complexity of the main characters made it very different from anything attempted previously by Meyerhold. However, the theme was only too familiar: Yelena Goncharova, who appropriately played Hamlet, was an intellectual, an artist, whose sense of individuality and capacity for reflection placed her at odds with society. The genealogy was unmistakable: Konstantin Treplev, Pierrot, Ivar Kareno, Arbenin, Bubus, Khlestakov, Chatsky, even Okonny. It was not surprising that Meyerhold was drawn to the character of Goncharova (who was finely played by Zinaida Raikh); her dilemma was familiar enough in Soviet society of the

twenties and reflected the doubts of many artists close to Meyerhold.
In particular, there was Mikhail Chekhov, the greatest of Soviet Hamlets,
whose thoughts and experiences, relayed by Meyerhold to Olesha, were
crucial to the play's composition.[41] Unlike *The Second Army Commander*,
Olesha's material was in no way amenable to ideological polarisation, for

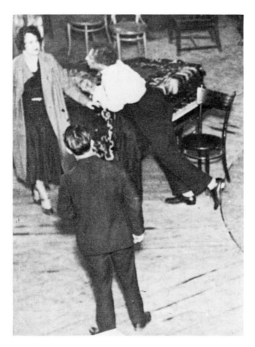

85. Meyerhold rehearsing Raikh in the role of Goncharova (1931).

its ambivalence lay within the very personality of Goncharova, and
Meyerhold's interpretation remained true to her dilemma. At the close
of the play the dying Yelena asks for her body to be covered with the
Red Flag, but all the banners are raised by the strikers to confront the
mounted police. Olesha's final stage direction reads: 'The unemployed
march. Yelena's body remains lying in the street uncovered. There are
heard the strains of a march.' It would have been simple enough for
Meyerhold to cover her and to play 'The Internationale', but on this
occasion there was to be no optimistic tragedy, no stirring call to arms, no
affirmation of solidarity. This time the audience was allowed to remain
seated.

In October 1931 the old Sohn Theatre was closed finally for renovation. In fact, it never reopened, so *A List of Benefits* became Meyerhold's
last production in the building which had witnessed his greatest triumphs.

10.   1932–1938
Responses to Criticism

When the Sohn Theatre closed in 1931 Meyerhold and his company were left homeless until they moved into premises in Tver Passage (now the Yermolova Theatre in Gorky Street) in summer, 1932. The time was spent on tour, first in Leningrad and later in Tashkent, no new productions being staged.

Originally, Meyerhold was allocated money only for essential repairs to the existing theatre; but he wanted nothing less than a completely new building, designed to his specification, with seating for three thousand spectators. This he announced only after demolishing the old building, calculating that the state would finance his new project rather than tolerate a ruined theatre in the very centre of Moscow.[1] His supposition proved correct, but it led to endless delays and the building was only just approaching completion when the Meyerhold Theatre was liquidated in January 1938. In consequence, Meyerhold was compelled to spend the final years of his life struggling to overcome the inadequacies of a theatre which was inferior even to the ramshackle Sohn. The Tver Passage Theatre was a miserable little box which seriously inhibited the selection of plays; in fact, it was almost as responsible for the gradual stagnation of the company's repertoire as the mediocrity of contemporary dramatic literature in the stifling climate of Socialist Realism.

The new theatre on Old Triumphal (later Mayakovsky) Square was designed by Sergei Vakhtangov and Mikhail Barkhin under the direct supervision of Meyerhold. In its third and final variant it took the form of a steeply raked, horseshoe-shaped amphitheatre seating one thousand six hundred spectators. The thrust stage was pear-shaped (approximately eighty feet deep and twenty-five feet at the widest point) with two revolves (the smaller downstage), both of variable level. There was no fly tower, scene changes being carried out on lifts beneath the stage. The entire auditorium was covered with a glass canopy with provision for stage-lighting from above. Immediately behind the stage was a wide arc of dressing-rooms affording direct access onto the acting area. Directly above them was an orchestra gallery. To either side and to the rear of the main revolve there were gaps wide enough to allow the passage of motor vehicles. A configuration closer to a conventional proscenium stage could be obtained by installing portable seating downstage, up to the forward edge of the main revolve.* After Meyerhold's death the theatre was extensively modified by another architect and opened in October 1940 as

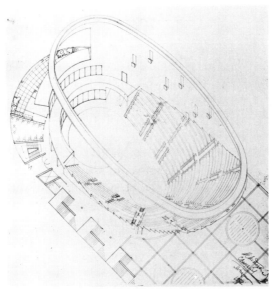

86. The new Meyerhold Theatre, second variant (1932). Axonometric drawing by Barkhin and Vakhtangov.

the Tchaikovsky Concert Hall. Since then, it has been used only occasionally for dramatic productions.

Estranged from Selvinsky and Vishnevsky, and despairing of finding any other Soviet dramatist worthy of production, Meyerhold commissioned the young novelist Yury German to adapt his novel, *Prelude*, for the stage. The result was a dramatic text, much altered in rehearsal, which was set in Germany and amounted almost to a mirror image of *A List of Benefits*: A brilliant scientist Kelberg witnesses with growing horror the moral collapse of the German intelligentsia under the pressures of the capitalist system, and in the end feels compelled to emigrate to Soviet Russia. The

* For an account of the project by the architects see *Theatre Quarterly*, Vol. II, No. 7, pp. 69–73.

production at the Passage Theatre (28 January 1933) exhibited all Meyer-hold's impeccable style and sense of theatre; once again the critics remarked on the surprising degree of psychological penetration in the portrayal of the main characters. However, it was modestly conceived and of historical significance only in so far as it was the last work by a Soviet author to be shown publicly at the Meyerhold Theatre.

Beginning with *The Bed Bug* in 1929, the last seven productions by Meyerhold of Soviet plays had all suffered severe criticism, whatever the public response had been. Of them all, only the two by Mayakovsky ever entered the repertoire of other Soviet theatres; the rest were staged only by Meyerhold. At the party purge of his theatre carried out later that year, Meyerhold showed no signs of committing the anticipated act of contrition; on the contrary, he attributed his alleged shortcomings to external circumstances, excusing himself by saying:

> I cannot represent the great advances of socialist reconstruction with plywood scenery. I need new technical resources in a new building. The problems facing the theatre are problems of technology.[2]

Meanwhile, he once more sought refuge in the classics. In December 1932 he revived his production of *Dom Juan* at the Pushkin (ex-Alexand-rinsky) Theatre in Leningrad with Yury Yuriev, now sixty, again playing the leading role. A year later, he produced a revised version of *Masquerade* (also with Yuriev) in the same theatre. Between the two, in April 1934, he staged *Krechinsky's Wedding* by Sukhovo-Kobylin at his own theatre, and invited Yuriev to play Krechinsky.

By comparison with Meyerhold's earlier versions of the Russian classics, *Krechinsky's Wedding* was exceptionally restrained: the settings were simple, with lighting the predominant means of expression, and pride of place was given to the minutely studied performances of Yuriev and Igor Ilinsky (who played Rasplyuev). Ilinsky writes:

> . . . with this production, Meyerhold undoubtedly advanced a further step towards profound psychologism and inner development of character. A new period seemed to have begun at the Meyerhold Theatre. This departure from the familiar Meyerhold of sensational bluff, the urge to shock and scandalise, might in the future have had a decisive influence on the development of his theatre.[3]

However, in 1937 when Meyerhold was showing visitors round the growing building of his new theatre, he enthusiastically described his plans for *Boris Godunov*, a new version of Mérimée's *Carmen* by Babel and Erdman, a revival of *Mystery-Bouffe*, *Othello*, and *Hamlet* – possibly with settings by Picasso.* With that repertoire, one wonders just what course his work might have taken, once away from the confines of the Passage and out on the deep arena of the grand auditorium in Mayakovsky Square.

II

Alexandre Dumas' melodrama, *The Lady of the Camellias*, which was presented at the Meyerhold Theatre on 19 March 1934, seemed a curious, not to say dubious choice; Meyerhold justified it in an interview with Harold Clurman:

> I am interested in showing the bad attitude of the bourgeoisie to women. Marguerite is treated like a slave or a servant. Men bargain over her, throw money in her face, insult her – all because they say they love her. I was interested to show this because we, too, in the Soviet Union, have had a wrong conception of love and of women. Our attitude has been too biologic [sic]. . . .[4]

He gave a similar explanation in an interview in *Izvestia*, citing the occasion in Geneva when Lenin was moved to tears by the play, and suggesting that he was responding to 'the artistic portrayal of the slavery of women under capitalism'.[5] But Joseph Yuzovsky was probably closer to the truth in his review of the production when he imagined Meyerhold saying:

> I no longer desire ascetic self-denial of my heroes, my settings and my costumes. I wish my spectator joy; I want him to possess the world of beauty which was usurped by the ruling classes.[6]

Rudnitsky does not disagree with this, but suggests that it was Meyerhold's considered response to the demands for harmony and balance, for optimism and a sense of joie de vivre, which the 'times' were now imposing on Soviet artists.[7] There may be some truth in this, but equally *The Lady of the Camellias* may be seen as an admission of weariness after years of struggling to extract something of worth from the contemporary Soviet repertoire. Perhaps above all, Meyerhold desired to see his beloved Zinaida in the classic bravura role of Marguerite Gautier. He readily acknowledged that his conception of Marguerite was based on the performance of Eleonora Duse whom he had seen in his early days in

---

* According to his assistant, Alexander Gladkov, Meyerhold discussed this project with Picasso in Summer 1936 (see *Moskva teatralnaya*, ed. I. Kuznetsova, Z. Pekarskaya, Moscow, 1960, p. 365). Zinaida Raikh mentions a similar discussion in December 1928 (*Teatr*, 1974, No. 2, p. 34).

Petersburg. Even so, the production was by no means imitative or traditional; Leonid Varpakhovsky, who worked with Meyerhold on it, recalls:

> Instead of the feverish flush, the weak chest and the coughing, all suggesting sickness and a sense of doom, there was recklessness, gaiety, eagerness, energy, no hint of illness. Once more one found oneself recalling Meyerhold's words: 'In order to shoot the arrow, one must first draw the bowstring.' Marguerite's first entrance was preceded by a static

87. Zinaida Raikh as Marguerite with Mikhail Tsaryov as Armand (1934).

scene showing her companion Nanine and the Baron de Varville in conversation. They spoke without exchanging glances from positions on opposite sides of the stage. Their conversation was desultory, with Nanine sewing and de Varville playing the piano. It was a mise en scène which gave this purely expository scene the necessary sense of alienation and frigidity. Marguerite's unexpected appearance was in sharp contrast, dynamic in the extreme. She was returning home from the opera in the company of some young people whom she had invited to a fancy-dress evening. Marguerite, shouting words in Italian, rushed right across the stage from corner to corner, holding reins in which she had harnessed two of her youthful admirers. The two boys held top-hats high in their hands, whilst Marguerite brandished an imaginery whip.

In making this entrance so stunningly unexpected, Meyerhold increased the distance which the actress has to travel in the course of the performance – from illness to death. And in order to indicate the illness of the heroine from the very beginning, he made Kulyakbo-Koretskaya, who played Marguerite's companion, follow her closely, holding a warm shawl as though trying to prevent her catching cold.[8]

Many critics complained that Meyerhold, after all his 'reinterpretations' of the Russian classics, did not lay a finger on Dumas' highly questionable text. This was not true: his stage version included additional material from the original novel, as well as fragments from Flaubert and Zola, though this is not to say that the ideological balance of the play was significantly altered. However, the level of society was raised to the haute bourgeoisie, with Armand Duval's father becoming a 'powerful industrialist' instead of an assessor of taxes.[9]

The period was transposed from the 1840s to the late 1870s which, according to Meyerhold, 'offer a more expressive stage of this particular phase of bourgeois society'.[10] They also offered greater artistic possibilities, being the age of Manet, Degas, and Renoir: their works – particularly Renoir's – were carefully studied and copied in the scenery, properties, costumes, and even the actors' movements and poses. The basic settings were simple and flexible, consisting largely of screens and drapes, but the properties were all exquisite period pieces, each serving a specific function and each made to register with the aid of spot-lighting. Dismissing the charges of contemporary critics that all this finery was either a substitute for good acting or simply aesthetic self-indulgence, Rudnitsky suggests that Meyerhold's true aim was to contrast the splendour of the clothing and furnishings with the meanness and cruelty of their owners.[11]

In Act Four, Meyerhold employed his favourite device of the staircase, this time a graceful spiral in wrought iron. Throughout, the limitations of the cramped box-stage were minimised by setting the scenes at a sharp angle to the proscenium line, thereby giving the spectator the impression of watching from the wings.* Most of the actors' movements, following the line of the setting, were diagonal, ensuring the spectator a three-quarters view which was more plastic and free from masking, even in extreme close-up. Thus, the production was conventionally representa-

* Meyerhold employed this device first in *A List of Benefits*.

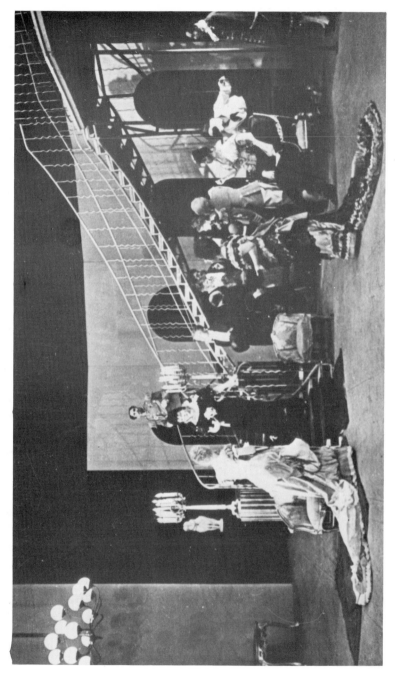

88. The Lady of the Camellias, *Act Four.*

tional yet conceived in the three-dimensional terms more commonly associated with the open stage.[12]

Once more music was a crucial element in Meyerhold's production. The insight and precision with which he employed it are conveyed by these two extracts from a letter to his composer Vissarion Shebalin:

> . . . Act Four begins with music. A can-can (or galop) begins before the lights come up. . . . The character of this short introduction must be reminiscent of a traditional operetta finale in a scheme such as this:
>
> 8 beats: forte: major key; 16 beats: piano: major key; 8 beats: forte: minor key; 8 beats: piano: minor key; 8 beats: forte: major key; 16 beats: piano: major key; 8 beats: fortissimo: major key.
>
> You hear the music from behind the scenes, giving you the impression that several rooms separate us from the orchestra and that the intervening doors are being constantly opened and shut. Before the music has ended, it has served as a background for the first scene of his act. Length: 1 minute, 10 seconds. . . .
>
> Supper-music: 'music for dessert'. Very graceful. Ice-cream cakes of different colours, garlanded with fruits, are served. You feel like saying: Shall they play a scherzo? No! Yes, a scherzo! No, not quite that. More expressive. Sober, with an undercurrent of a lyrical beat. Ah, how expressive music can be! This music should be divided into parts. It is a whole play in itself. Expressively tense (saturated with subtle eroticism). It should not soften the scene. On the contrary, it should be intensified, growing into a powerful finale, when Armand throws Marguerite to the floor, bringing everyone onto the stage as he throws the money in Marguerite's face. No longer is this a scherzo. Everything has gone wrong. Someone has put his foot in the ice-cream cake. Length: 3 minutes, 10 seconds.[13]

Zinaida Raikh was a born Marguerite. So often Meyerhold had been accused of distorting his productions for her benefit, but on this occasion her grace, beauty, and stage presence made *The Lady of the Camellias* the one unquestionable public triumph of the Meyerhold Theatre in the thirties – despite the predictably sour response from the majority of critics. In the same year a dramatic adaptation of Balzac's novel, *A Bachelor's Establishment*, was presented by the Vakhtangov Theatre. But the ironic advice given to visitors was: 'If you want Balzac go to Meyerhold, for Dumas fils go to the Vakhtangov.'[14]

III

With the site of his new theatre still little more than an empty space, and with no clear-cut plans for any new productions, Meyerhold accepted an invitation to direct Tchaikovsky's *The Queen of Spades* at the Leningrad Maly Opera for the 1934–1935 season, where it had its premiere on 25 January 1935. Under its Artistic-Director, Samuel Samosud, the Maly Opera had established a reputation for innovation, being responsible for the first productions of Shostakovich's operas, *The Nose* (1930) and *Lady Macbeth of Mtsensk* (1934). Samosud agreed readily with Meyerhold's proposal for a complete revision of *The Queen of Spades*. Meyerhold reasoned that the libretto by Tchaikovsky's brother, Modest, was a crude distortion of Pushkin's original text, wholly motivated by his desire to gratify the prevailing taste for cheap romantic spectacle. Accordingly, he set out 'to saturate the atmosphere of Tchaikovsky's wonderful music . . . with the ozone of Pushkin's even more wonderful tale',[15] enlisting the aid of a young poet, Valentin Stenich, to compose a new libretto.*

At the suggestion of the Director of Imperial Theatres, Modest Tchaikovsky had moved the period of the opera back from the 1830s to the last years of Catherine the Great's reign, since it afforded greater opportunities for elaborate costumes and spectacle. To avoid the social anomaly of Hermann, a poor officer of the Engineers, consorting with the nobility, he was transformed into an Hussar. But this completely obscured a crucial point in Pushkin's story: the Countess exemplifies the hereditary society from which Hermann feels excluded; to penetrate it he needs the wealth which only luck at cards can bring him. He pursues Liza not because he loves her, but because through her he can discover the secret of the fatal three cards. Liza kills herself because she realises this, not because Hermann has killed the Countess.

Meyerhold restored the action to the 1830s and made Hermann once more Pushkin's poor Engineers officer, emphasising his isolation by depicting him as a brooding solitary of the kind who had dominated so many of his earlier productions. In his article on Meyerhold's revision of the opera Ivan Sollertinsky describes Hermann as 'a remarkable synthesis of the unbridled romantic hero: the "young man of the nineteenth century" consumed with Napoleonic ambition, demonic passions, the melancholy of Childe Harold and the introspection of Hamlet . . .'[16] Meyerhold himself compared him to Lermontov's 'Hero of Our Time',

* For a translation of Meyerhold's account of his revision and the production see *Braun*, pp. 278–289.

Pechorin, and to Pushkin's Yevgeny in *The Bronze Horseman*.[17] Stenich based his libretto on the poetry of Pushkin and his pleiad, in places incorporating actual fragments of their verses, elsewhere retaining Modest's original text. Inevitably, the result was uneven, and few critics conceded any stylistic improvement. But dramatically the new plot was far closer to Pushkin, with Liza assuming a role properly subordinate to the central Hermann–Countess conflict. Scenes devised by Modest Tchaikovsky simply for the adornment of the Imperial stage were removed entirely, and new words were set to the original music. Thus the opening scene in the Summer Garden, in which the exposition of the Hermann–Liza–Yeletsky triangle is interspersed with the irrelevant coming and going of children and their wet-nurses, was replaced by Pushkin's original scene of the young officers gambling at Narumov's house with Hermann as an onlooker. The soldiers' song which is sung by the children in Modest's libretto was given to a girl wearing Hussar's uniform, entertaining Narumov's guests before they got down to the serious business of cards. The ball was staged not with hosts of splendidly costumed extras, but as a series of intimate scenes with Hermann ever present, so that the audience could follow his conflicting emotions. In the final scene at the gaming house Hermann's fatal challenge was taken up neither by Yeletsky (as in Tchaikovsky) nor by Pushkin's famous Muscovite gambler Chekalinsky, but by a figure called 'The Stranger' invented by Meyerhold – a characteristic flourish which stirred memories of the infernal emissaries of his Petersburg days, yet was in no way inconsistent with the mood of Pushkin's tale.

The settings were broadly representational, properties being employed with the same expediency as in *The Government Inspector* and *The Lady of the Camellias*. The designs by Chupyatov were not at all to Meyerhold's liking; they could not compare in elegance or architectural flair with what he was accustomed to in Moscow, though once again (in the Countess' bedroom scene) the curved staircase was in evidence. However, he compensated for the settings' limitations with his brilliant deployment of the huge chorus, rehearsing them with a care to which they were totally unaccustomed, but to which they responded with enthusiasm.[18] Meyerhold describes his new approach to the problem of music and movement compared with his previous operatic work:

> In *Tristan* I insisted on the actor's movements and gestures synchronising with the tempo of the music and the tonic scheme with almost mathematical accuracy. But in *The Queen of Spades* I tried to allow the actor rhythmical freedom within the limits of the musical phrase (like

Chaliapin), so that his interpretation, whilst remaining dependent on the music would have a contrapuntal rather than a metrically precise relationship to it, sometimes even acting as a contrast, a variation, anticipating or lagging behind the score instead of simply keeping in unison.[19]

The one almost unanimous criticism of the production was that the new libretto deprived Tchaikovsky's score of much of its thematic logic,

89. The Queen of Spades. *The Countess's Bedroom. Hermann and Liza after the death of the Countess.*

particularly in the exposition of the Hermann–Liza relationship. But scarcely anyone disputed the dramatic gains or the opera's overall fidelity to Pushkin. Here is Meyerhold's description of the closing scene:

Hermann stakes such a huge sum of money that he cannot get the notes out of his pocket; he has to chalk the amount on the table. The others are afraid to play with him; many back away and he is left almost alone. He issues a general challenge.

A character steps forward who has not appeared before. I call him 'The Stranger'. He steps forward and announces: 'I will play. . . .' He comes up to the table and starts to deal. But whilst the Stranger is approaching the table and all attention is fixed on him and Hermann, the yellow-clad figure of the Countess materialises unnoticed at the table; she sits with her back to the audience, following the cards. Hermann cries: 'My ace!' . . . A long pause. Then the silence in the orchestra is broken not by the Stranger but by the old woman saying 'Your Queen loses.'

Hermann shrieks: 'What Queen?' A further pause. Then again, the Old Woman: 'The one in your hand, the Queen of Spades.' Pointing at the card, the ghost of the Countess staggers back slightly, as though about to fall. Hermann sees her in the same dress that she was wearing in the bedroom and falling just as she did when he pointed the pistol at her.

Blackout. Immediately a new setting: a ward in the Obukhov Hospital with a bed jutting on to the forestage. Hermann is sitting on the bed. We hear the same music as we heard in the barracks before the appearance of the Countess's ghost. Hermann speaks the same words that she spoke then, as though playing her role.

So ends Tchaikovsky's *Queen of Spades*. So ends Pushkin's *Queen of Spades*.[20]

Meyerhold's achievements were considerable enough for the Maly Opera to invite him to direct Mussorgsky's *Boris Godunov* the following season, considerable enough too for Stanislavsky to invite him to work at his Opera Theatre in 1938. Apparently the Meyerhold–Stenich version of *The Queen of Spades* is preserved in the archives – awaiting an opera company with sufficient enterprise to revive it.

IV

Two months after *The Queen of Spades*, on 25 March 1935, to mark the seventy-fifth anniversary of Chekhov's birth the Meyerhold theatre staged three of his one-act farces: *The Anniversary*, *The Bear*, and *The Proposal*, under the collective title *33 Swoons*. According to Meyerhold's calculations, there are no less than thirty-three occasions in the course of the three plays when a character swoons; hence his decision to make this the linking motif of the whole production. Each swoon was accompanied by special music – brass for the men and strings for the ladies – which subsided once the victim had recovered. Meyerhold was anxious to justify this as more than a mere theatrical device. The swoons, he claimed, were:

the manifestation of neurasthenia, which was most prevalent in Chekhov's day. Neurasthenia is a clear indication of the lethargy, the loss of will-power which is typical of Chekhov's characters. . . . In the course of studying the age and society depicted by Chekhov, we assembled a large variety of material which confirms the unusually high incidence of neurasthenia amongst the intelligentsia of the eighties and nineties (in the theatre there was even the special *emploi* of 'neurasthenic'). We know well enough what the social preconditions for such a phenomenon are.[21]

The explanation is laboured and unconvincing: it might perhaps be applied to Chekhov's full-length plays, in particular to a number of the roles that Meyerhold himself played, such as Treplev, Tusenbach, and Trofimov; and indeed his portrayals were often described by the critics as 'neurasthenic'; but lethargy and loss of'will-power are not the obvious

90. The Bear. Smirnov (*Nikolai Bogolyubov*) and Popova (*Zinaida Raikh*).

terms to spring to mind when considering the violent eruptions which typify the characters' behaviour in Chekhov's farces. Convinced that the farces are more 'tragic grotesques' than 'jokes' (as Chekhov described them), Meyerhold equipped his actors with an abundance of hand-props, and invented endless business designed to help them betray the characters' inner emotions, whilst at the same time 'increasing the circulation of their vaudeville blood'. Thus, in *The Proposal*, Natasha and Lomov were made to fight over a napkin and tray while disputing the ownership of the meadows; in *The Anniversary*, the deputation of shareholders presented the Chairman Shipuchin not with an address and silver tankard but with a huge stuffed bear; at the close of *The Bear*, when the grief-stricken widow Popova finally ensnared the landowner Smirnov, she embraced him and with her free hand removed from the piano a bouquet of red roses which had lain there throughout, evidently left by another suitor.[22]

Meyerhold's tricks certainly yielded some hilarious moments, but the overall effect was to slow the pace with the sheer weight of ideas. He himself admitted to Alexander Gladkov: 'We tried to be too clever and consequently lost sight of the humour. We must look the truth in the face: the audience at any amateur production of *The Proposal* would laugh more than they did at ours, even though Ilinsky was acting and Meyerhold was the director. Chekhov's light, transparent humour was crushed beneath the weight of our theories and the result was a disaster.'[23]

Sadly, this uncharacteristic production was to prove the last new work ever to be seen by the public at the Meyerhold Theatre. In 1935, the full implications of the First All-Union Congress of Soviet Writers held the previous year were becoming clear. Membership of the Union of Soviet Writers was to be mandatory for any writer who hoped to publish, and the recognition of the tenets of Socialist Realism a pre-condition of membership.[24] Thus Party control was extended directly and formally to every area of literature, including of course the theatrical repertoire.

At the beginning of 1936 the Party's campaign against 'formalism' in the arts took an ominous turn. Shortly after the creation of a new, considerably more powerful central controlling body, the All-Union Committee for Art Affairs, there appeared in *Pravda* two editorial articles condemning productions of Shostakovich's opera, *Lady Macbeth of Mtsensk*, and his ballet, *The Clear Stream*.[25] Both were promptly removed from the repertoire. Then at the end of February, Mikhail Chekhov's former theatre, the Second Moscow Art Theatre, and the Leningrad Young Workers' Theatre were both liquidated at the command of the Supreme Soviety and the Central Committee of the Communist Party.

With few exceptions, stage-directors took the first available opportunity to confess their past aberrations and affirm their faith in Socialist Realism. On 14 March 1936, Meyerhold spoke in Leningrad on the theme 'Meyerhold against Meyerholditis': far from admitting his mistakes, he accused his imitators of propagating 'meyerholditis', the plagiarising and indiscriminate application of his formal devices with no comprehension of their logical motivation. Whilst acknowledging that some elements in his productions may have been unclear to the audience, he condemned unprincipled critics who made no serious attempt to interpret them. What is more, he boldly defended Shostakovich against the attacks in *Pravda*, and affirmed his right and the right of all artists to experiment.[26]

Simultaneously, a conference of 'workers in the arts' was convened in Moscow to discuss the implications of the attacks on Shostakovich and later articles condemning formalism which had appeared in *Pravda*. Meyerhold was the target of many assaults, notably from the principal speaker, Johann Altman (the editor of *Teatr*), and Radlov and Okhlopkov, two of the directors he had charged in Leningrad with meyerholditis. When he replied on 26 March 1936, he yielded absolutely nothing to his critics; indeed, what he said was tantamount to a total rejection of Socialist Realism and the official interpretation of the term 'formalism'. No one who heard it could have missed the withering sarcasm behind Meyerhold's remarks on simplicity in art, or have failed to be shaken by the fine arrogance with which he asserted his creative independence. At a time of craven hypocrisy, self-humiliation, and universal suspicion, his open intransigence was without parallel amongst artists of his standing.[27] In the next number of *Soviet Theatre*, the organ of the All-Union Committee for Art Affairs, the crudely-phrased, unsigned editorial stated that '. . . Beginning with his breakaway from the Art Theatre, Meyerhold in practice has always opposed his method not only to the naturalistic theatre but to the realistic theatre as well. To this day he has not rid himself of elements of the symbolist and aesthetic theatre, and most important of all, he continues to uphold them.'[28]

In response to charges that his was the only theatre in the entire Soviet Union without a Soviet play in its repertoire, Meyerhold announced plans for staging a modernised version of *The Bed Bug*, to be called 'A Fantastic Comedy', Mayakovsky's original sub-title. This was to be followed by a dramatic adaptation of Nikolai Ostrovsky's novel, *How the Steel was Tempered*. The Mayakovsky project was abandoned after preliminary rehearsals,[29] whilst *One Life* (as Ostrovsky's work was retitled) needed textual revision and was deferred to the following season. After a revival of *The Government Inspector* in April 1936, the second half of the year was devoted to rehearsals of Pushkin's *Boris Godunov*, for which Prokofiev composed the music. Only some scenes were rehearsed, but the production outgrew the Passage stage and finally was laid aside to await the opening of the new theatre. The accounts of the rehearsals reveal Meyerhold's profound insight into Pushkin's drama, and suggest that the production could well have challenged *The Government Inspector* as his theatrical masterpiece.[30]

Before he resumed work on *One Life* Meyerhold made a further half-hearted attempt early in 1937 to stage a play which would meet with Party approval. Lydia Seifullina's *Natasha* is a chronicle play of a style which was becoming all too familiar in the Soviet Union at that time. Natasha is the orphan of parents tortured and murdered by the Whites in the Civil War who shakes off the oppression of a kulak employer to become a labour hero on a collective farm. Meyerhold strove to reproduce the rural setting in all its lifelike detail, complete with apple trees and cabbage patches, but the result was an unworthy and embarrassing fiasco which was dropped immediately following the first dress-rehearsal. Unfortunately, Meyerhold's opponents could now seem justified in their claims that he was incapable of staging a modern Soviet play.[31]

The need to make a success of *One Life* was now more acute than ever. Nikolai Ostrovsky, half-blind and crippled by wounds and illnesses incurred in the Civil War and the service of the Party, had inspired many millions of Soviet readers with his example, and at his death in December 1936 had become a national hero. The hero of *How the Steel was Tempered*, published in 1935, is Pavel Korchagin, a poor Ukrainian boy whose story follows closely that of Ostrovsky himself. No subject could have been more suitable for a play to mark the twentieth anniversary of the October Revolution. There can be little doubt that Meyerhold was profoundly moved by Ostrovsky's example in the course of their meetings in the final months of the writer's life, and unlike *Natasha*, the production of *One Life* was one which fired the imagination of the entire company. The author of the scenario, Yevgeny Gabrilovich, writes:

> It was truly the birth of a new revolutionary production, far removed from the earlier eccentricism, yet still with echoes of it in its depths. It was harsh, turbulent, romantic, violent – no other production of Nikolai Ostrovsky, either on the stage or on the screen, has approached it in my experience.*
>
> I vividly recall the episode when Pavka Korchagin was urging his comrades to resume work on the new railway line. They were all dog-tired, hungry, discouraged and bad tempered; nobody wanted to go out onto the site in the rain and cold. Then, after exhausting his vocabulary with descriptions of the international situation, jokes, and exhortations, Pavka slowly and tentatively began to dance. He danced all alone in the dim light of the damp barrack room, whilst his comrades on their bunks looked first with amusement then with growing amazement. He danced on and on, faster and faster, livelier and livelier, spinning and knee-bending, with no music, not even his own voice to accompany him. And then someone began to beat time with his hand on his bunk; then another, and then a third joined in the accompaniment. Another jumped down on to the floor and began to dance

---

* There was a second version staged at the Moscow Young Workers' Theatre in 1937, followed since by numerous productions (including a ballet version). The novel has been filmed twice: by Donskoy in 1942, and by Alov and Naumov in 1957 (under the title *Pavel Korchagin*).

alongside Pavka. Others joined them, and the noise of the accompaniment grew louder and louder, with some of the lads now banging with
their fists. And now it wasn't only Pavka dancing, but ten, fifteen,
twenty others as well. Then slowly at first, but gradually more quickly
and more violently, the beams of the spotlights began to move about
the stage, as though they too were dancing. And now everything
seemed to join in – the men, the lights, the drums, even the walls of
the barrack room. Still there was no music – just the rhythmical
sound of hands, fists, and drums. Then suddenly amidst this whirlwind
and thunder, you heard from somewhere, very softly, as though in the
very depths, in the heart of the hut, an old revolutionary song. It
swelled and strengthened, and now the dancing and the banging fell
silent. The men, hot and sweating from dancing, in their torn clothes
and their remnants of boots, joined in this marvellous song, made up by
their brothers and fathers in prison and exile. Then still singing, in the
now motionless beams of the spotlights, they went out into the rain
and the cold to work.[32]

Shortly before the anniversary celebrations in November the production
was viewed by representatives from the Glavrepertkom; no serious
criticisms were made and general approval was expressed by those
present. However, it was suggested that the work needed further polish-
ing, and in any case there was no need to rush it on in time for the actual
anniversary. So two weeks later, the production was shown again – this
time to be severely criticised, not only by the President of the Committee for Artistic Affairs, Platon Kerzhentsev, but also by those who
previously had voiced enthusiasm.[33] It was clear that a decision had
already been taken about the Meyerhold Theatre's future which the
likely success of an indisputably revolutionary, not to say Socialist Realist,
production could not be allowed to prejudice. In short, it seems that it
was necessary to conceal *One Life* from public view and public opinion. On
17 December 1937 *Pravda* published an article signed by Kerzhentsev,
entitled 'An Alien Theatre'. The style was familiar enough:

On the occasion of the twentieth anniversary of the Great Socialist
Revolution only one out of the seven-hundred Soviet professional
theatres was without a special production to commemorate the
October Revolution and without a Soviet repertoire. That theatre was
Meyerhold's Theatre. . . .
    Almost his entire theatrical career before the October Revolution
amounted to a struggle against the realistic theatre on behalf of the
stylised, mystical, formalist theatre of the aesthetes, that is, the theatre

which shunned real life. . . . [In its production of Verhaeren's *Dawn*]
his theatre made a hero out of a Menshevik traitor to the working
class. . . . *The Government Inspector* was treated not in the style of the
realistic theatre, but in the spirit of the White émigré Merezhkovsky's
book, *Gogol and the Devil*.

It has become absolutely clear that Meyerhold cannot and, apparently, will not comprehend Soviet reality or depict the problems
which concern every Soviet citizen. . . .

For several years [he] stubbornly tried to stage the play, *I Want a
Child*, by the enemy of the people, Tretyakov, which was a hostile slur
on the Soviet family. . . .

Systematic deviation from Soviet reality, political distortion of that
reality, and hostile slanders against our way of life have brought the
theatre to total ideological and artistic ruin, to shameful bankruptcy.
. . . Do Soviet art and the Soviet public really need such a theatre?

By now, the answer to that question was clearly considered beyond
debate. On 8 January 1938, after a matinée performance of *The Government
Inspector*, the Meyerhold Theatre was liquidated, and the rewriting of
Meyerhold's biography began. The theatre's repertoire for the final week
tells it own story: *The Government Inspector*, *The Lady of the Camellias*, *Woe
to Wit*, *Krechinsky's Wedding*, *The Forest*.

Conclusion: 1938–1940

In the weeks following the liquidation of Meyerhold's theatre, few of his friends and associates visited him and Zinaida Raikh in their flat off Gorky Street:* some felt it tactful to stay away, others were anxious to avoid the risk of guilt through association.[1] Amongst those who spurned the danger were three in particular. Pasternak, by no means a close friend of the Meyerholds was one of the first to call. Eisenstein, although himself extremely vulnerable since the banning of his film *Bezhin Meadow* the previous year, secreted the vast Meyerhold archive in the walls of his dacha, thereby ensuring its survival to this day.[2] Finally Stanislavsky, long regarded as Meyerhold's antipode, astonished all Moscow when in March 1938 he invited him to work as his assistant at his Opera Theatre.

This apparent reconciliation of opposites was much less surprising than it seemed from the outside. For a start, though the two men rarely met for thirty or more years after the failure of the Theatre-Studio, and though Stanislavsky was very seldom seen at the Meyerhold Theatre, they shared a strong mutual respect, and Meyerhold never lost an opportunity to express his love and gratitude towards his first and only teacher. By contrast, the breach with Nemirovich-Danchenko seems never to have been truly mended, and Nemirovich made no secret of his dislike for Meyerhold's productions. From the mid-thirties Meyerhold and Stanislavsky had begun to see more of each other, and there was even a plan to take *33 Swoons* for performance in Stanislavsky's flat when he was confined to bed through illness.

However, there is little evidence of any significant artistic rapprochement between the two. In recent years some Soviet critics have sought to demonstrate Meyerhold's increasing preoccupation with 'psychological realism' in his late productions, but as Rudnitsky rightly observes, the fiasco of *Natasha* suggests that Meyerhold felt little commitment in that

* In Bryusov Lane. The building now bears a memorial plaque.

direction.[3] It is significant that even when describing Meyerhold's 'chamber' works staged within the confines of the Passage stage, critics invariably recalled the sudden arresting image or theatrical stroke, seldom the complete psychological creation. On the other hand, although Stanislavsky may latterly have shown a serious concern with the physical aspects of acting, notably in his book *Building a Character*, it was aimed primarily towards the greater stimulation of the actor's creative imagination, and in practice led to no radical change in production style. The ultimate objective remained the creation of an illusion of life; the relationship between performer and spectator was always rooted in empathy. As for Meyerhold, whilst it is true that, like Brecht, he was by no means averse to the emotional identification of the spectator with the character, he employed it consciously as a means of deepening the understanding of the production's overall significance, as one element amongst many. With Meyerhold the character was never more than a fragment of the play's total meaning; with Stanislavsky the merest servant or foot-soldier carried his autobiography complete with him on stage.

It was for this reason that with Meyerhold the basic dramatic unit was the episode, whereas with Stanislavsky it remained the act; the one dismantles reality, the other reproduces its flow. Then again, nowhere in Stanislavsky's writings does one find any analysis of audience psychology, the assumption being that if the actor's performance is 'truthful', then the spectator will recognise the truth and identify with it.* With Meyerhold, from as early as *The Fairground Booth* in 1906, the entire production was structured to stimulate and exploit audience reaction, confounding its expectations as often as it confirmed them. There is no reason to suppose that Meyerhold's theatrical philosophy would have changed had his dream come true, and he had gained the freedom of the 'empty space' on Mayakovsky Square.

On 7 August 1938, Stanislavsky died. Yury Bakhrushin, his deputy at the Opera Theatre, recalls him saying shortly before his death: 'Take care of Meyerhold; he is my sole heir in the theatre – here or anywhere else.'[4] Two months later, Meyerhold succeeded Stanislavsky as the theatre's artistic director.

Prevented by failing health from leaving his home, Stanislavsky had entrusted Meyerhold with the rehearsals of what was to be his last production, *Rigoletto*. It was presented under Meyerhold's supervision on 10 March 1939. The projected repertoire for the following season

* In *An Actor Prepares* Stanislavsky writes: 'the spectator . . . is like a witness to a conversation. He has a silent part in [the actors'] exchange of feelings, and is excited by their experiences' (trans. E. Hapgood, London, 1959, p. 197).

included productions by Meyerhold of Mozart's *Don Giovanni* and Prokofiev's *Semyon Kotko*.

*   *   *

On 13 June 1939 the All-Union Conference of Stage-Directors opened in Moscow with an address by Andrei Vyshinsky, Vice-President of the Soviet of People's Commissars, Attorney-General and chief prosecutor in the infamous 'show trials' of the thirties. Two days later, the debate on

91. Meyerhold addressing the All-Union Conference of Stage-Directors, 15 June 1939.

the main speeches began and the fourth speaker was Meyerhold. In their reports on the conference on 17 June neither *Pravda* nor *Izvestia* made mention of his speech, except to say that it was severely criticised by Johann Altmann. According to the official published record of the conference which appeared the following year,[5] Meyerhold did not even attend, still less speak.

To this day the full contents of his speech remain a mystery. In his biography *The Dark Genius*, Yury Yelagin includes a version which he claims is based on notes made by himself at the conference.[6] It indicates that Meyerhold, far from admitting his errors, rejected the tenets of Socialist Realism in more unequivocal terms than ever before. However, so factually inaccurate and tendentious is Yelagin in the rest of his book, that one hesitates to trust his memory in this instance. In *Soviet Poets and Poetry* (Los Angeles, 1943), Alexander Kaun, without revealing his source, quotes extracts of the speech totally at variance with Yelagin's version and indicating that, whatever else Meyerhold said, he also committed the act of contrition long demanded of him. Trustworthy Soviet sources suggest that Kaun is closer to the truth.* In February 1974 the Soviet periodical *Teatr* included in its Meyerhold centenary section a partial transcript of his final speech, but cut in such a way as to exclude any admissions of failure or reassertion of principles that might ever have been there.[7] It was a cravenly evasive piece of editing, totally unworthy of the director's memory.

Yet whatever Meyerhold said, it can detract in no way from the courageous defence of his principles which he pursued right up to the day of his theatre's untimely dissolution. On 20 December 1937, reporting the official discussion at the Meyerhold Theatre of the *Pravda* article 'An Alien Theatre', the *Izvestia* correspondent wrote:

> Vsevolod Meyerhold completely refused to admit that he had encouraged sycopathy and suppressed criticism, and that his false political and artistic policies had led his theatre to total disaster.[8]

Immediately after the conference of stage-directors Meyerhold returned to Leningrad to complete his direction of a display by the Lesgaft Institute of Physical Culture to be included in national parades in Leningrad and Moscow. On 20 June he was arrested and was never again seen at liberty. He was shot in a Moscow prison on 2 February 1940. Shortly after his arrest, Zinaida Raikh's body was discovered in their Moscow flat, mutilated with numerous knife wounds. Of the property in the flat only papers were missing. The assailants, described officially as 'thugs', were never caught.[9] Today, the bodies of Meyerhold and Raikh lie not in the Novodevichy Cemetery, the pantheon of Russian artists, but in the lesser known Vagankovskoe, near the grave of Yesenin.

What was Meyerhold's particular contribution to the modern stage? The twentieth century, in the theatre as in the other arts, can be distinguished by its recognition and pursuit of the irrational and the contradictory, for its rejection of the reassurance provided by custom and outward show. The audience is forced to take issue with its preconceptions, to question the values that endorse the existing order. No director has ever shaken his public's composure more thoroughly and more consistently than Meyerhold. Given the climate of lies, blandishments, false optimism and hypocrisy that prevailed in the Soviet Union after the 1920's, Meyerhold's fate can now be seen as inevitable, and the enormity of the crime against him becomes a grim testimony to his great power as an artist.

* In conversation with myself in Moscow, July 1967 (EB).

Notes

The following abbreviations are used for works cited frequently in the footnotes:

V. E. Meierkhold – Statyi, pisma, rechi, besedy (Moscow, 1969, vols. I & II) – *Meyerhold I & II*.
V. E. Meierkhold – Perepiska 1896–1939 (Moscow, 1976) – *Perepiska*.
Braun, E. (trans. & ed.), *Meyerhold on Theatre* (London–New York, 1969) – *Braun*.
Valentei, M. A. and others (ed.), *Vstrechi s Meierkholdom* (Moscow, 1967) – *Vstrechi*.
Rudnitsky, K. L., *Rezhisser Meierkhold* (Moscow, 1969) – *Rudnitsky*.
Volkov, N. D., *Meierkhold* (Moscow–Leningrad, 1929, vols. I & II) – *Volkov I & II*.

Chapter One

1. The details of Meyerhold's early years are taken from Nikolai Volkov's biography, which is the only existing source.
2. *Volkov I*, p. 54.
3. Ibid., p. 57.
4. Ibid., p. 70.
5. Ibid., pp. 88–89.
6. Stanislavsky, K. S., *Sobranie sochinenii* (Moscow, 1954–1961), Vol. V, pp. 174–175.
7. *Perepiska*, p. 21.
8. *Meyerhold I*, p. 119 (*Braun*, p. 29).
9. Ibid., p. 120 (Ibid., p. 30).
10. *The Seagull*, Act One.
11. *Meyerhold I*, p. 75.
12. *Rudnitsky*, p. 17.
13. *Perepiska*, p. 29.
14. Stanislavsky, K. S., *Moya zhizn v iskusstve*, (Moscow, 1962), pp. 306–307 (this passage does not appear in the English edition).
15. *Meyerhold I*, p. 73.
16. See the exchange of letters between Meyerhold and Stanislavsky in January 1902 (*Perepiska*, pp. 35–37).

17. Nemirovich-Danchenko, V. I., *Teatralnoe nasledie*, Vol. II (Moscow, 1954), p. 225.
18. *Volkov I*, pp. 138–139.
19. Quoted in *Rudnitsky*, p. 15.
20. Kugel, A. R., *Profili teatra* (Moscow, 1929), p. 66.
21. For a complete list of all Meyerhold's productions see *Meyerhold II*, pp. 598–610 (a translation of this list from 1905 onwards is contained in Hoover, M. L., *Meyerhold – The Art of Conscious Theater* (University of Massachusetts Press, 1974).
22. See Pevtsov, I. N., 'Beseda ob aktere' in Tsimbal, S. L., *Tvorcheskaya sudba Pevtsova* (Leningrad–Moscow, 1957), pp. 213–214.
23. *Perepiska A. P. Chekhova i O. L. Knipper*, Vol. II (Moscow, 1936), p. 371.
24. *Perepiska*, p. 39.
25. Quoted by Alexander Gladkov, 'Meierkhold govorit' in *Tarusskie stranitsy* (Kaluga, 1961), p. 302.
26. Cf. *Rudnitsky*, pp. 33–34; Welsford, E., *The Fool – His Social and Literary History* (London, 1935), pp. 305 ff.
27. 'Tovarishchestvo novoy dramy' in *Vesy*, Moscow, 1904, No. 4, p. 37.
28. See West, J., *Russian Symbolism* (London, 1970), pp. 137–146.
29. Remizov, op. cit., pp. 38–39.
30. *Perepiska*, p. 45. For an expanded version of this analysis see *Braun*, pp. 28–29.
31. 'Vishnevy sad' in *Vesy*, Moscow, 1904, No. 2, pp. 47–48.
32. See Polotskaya, E., 'Chekhov i Meierkhold' in *Literaturnoe nasledstvo* (*Vol. LXVIII*) – *Chekhov* (Moscow, 1960), pp. 432–433.
33. Bolotin, Y., 'Provintsialnaya letopis' in *Teatr i iskusstvo*, 1904, No. 8, p. 178.
34. *Perepiska*, p. 45.
35. Ibid., p. 48.
36. Unsigned review in *Tiflissky listok*, 28 September 1904, p. 2.
37. *Teatr i iskusstvo*, Petersburg, 1904, No. 42, pp. 749–750.

Chapter Two

1. For Meyerhold's reaction to this production see *Braun*, pp. 24, 31.
2. Nemirovich-Danchenko, V. I., op. cit., p. 283.
3. Stanislavsky, K. S., op. cit., pp. 337–341.
4. Quoted in Stroeva, M. N., *Rezhisserskie iskania Stanislavskogo 1898–1917* (Moscow, 1973), p. 148.
5. Stanislavsky, K. S., op. cit., p. 341. (In *My Life in Art*, London, 1962, pp. 429–430.)
6. See *Rudnitsky*, pp. 48–49.
7. See *Meyerhold II*, pp. 30–34 (*Braun*, pp. 175–180); Freidkina, L., *Dni i gody VI. I. Nemirovicha-Danchenko* (Moscow, 1962), pp. 207–210, 352 ff., 462.
8. Quoted in *Rudnitsky*, p. 49.

9. 'Nenuzhnaya pravda', *Mir iskusstva*, Petersburg, 1902 (Vol. VII), No. 4, pp. 67–74.

10. See *Meyerhold I*, pp. 123–128 (*Braun*, pp. 34–39).

11. Ibid., p. 107 (Ibid., p. 41).

12. Ibid., p. 110 (Ibid., p. 45).

13. *See* Gray, C., *The Great Experiment – Russian Art 1863–1922* (London, 1962), Chapters 1–2.

14. *Meyerhold I*, pp. 108–109 (*Braun*, p. 43).

15. Ibid., p. 109, (Footnote, loc. cit.).

16. Ibid., pp. 109–110 (Ibid., p. 44).

17. Pozharskaya, M. N., *Russkoe teatralno-dekoratsionnoe iskusstvo* (Moscow, 1970), p. 159.

18. Meyerhold spoke little or no French before he visited Paris in 1913 (see *Perepiska*, p. 153). However, Maeterlinck's 'Le Tragique quotidien' was published in Russian translation in *Mir iskusstva*, 1899, No. 2. *Le Trésor des humbles* appeared in its entirety in 1901 (translated by L. Vilkina as *Blazhenstvo dushi*), and was followed in 1903 by the first of six volumes of his complete writings, (Moscow, 1903–1909). Amongst the early critical writings devoted to him were: Hannibale Pastore, 'Maurice Maeterlinck', *Vestnik inostrannoy literatury*, 1904, September; Adolphe van Bever, *Maurice Maeterlinck – Kritiko-biografichesky ocherk* (Petersburg, 1904).

19. See Robichez J., *Le Symbolisme au théâtre – Lugné-Poe et les debuts de L'Oeuvre* (Paris 1957).

20. The passages are quoted from *Le Trésor des humbles* (Paris, 1896, 4th edition), pp. 181 ff.

21. *Meyerhold I*, p. 133 (*Braun*, p. 54).

22. Loc. cit.

23. Ibid., pp. 135–136 (*Braun*, p. 56).

24. 'Po dorogam iskanii' in *Vstrechi*, p.33.

25. For an account of Sada Yakko and Kawakami's tour see Pronko, L. C., *Theater East and West* (University of California, 1967), pp. 120–123.

26. Quoted in *Volkov II*, p. 51.

27. *Meyerhold II*, p. 84.

28. *Meyerhold I*, p. 244.

29. Ibid., p. 245.

30. Stanislavsky, K. S., *Sobranie sochinenii*, cit., vol. VII, p. 325.

31. *Rudnitsky*, p. 49.

32. Quoted in *Rudnitsky*, p. 62.

33. Stanislavsky, K. S., *Moya zhizn v iskusstve*, cit., p. 346.

34. *See* Pevtsov, I. N., op. cit., p. 227.

35. Quoted in Stroeva, M. N., op. cit., pp. 178–179.

36. Under the pen-name 'Avrelii' in *Vesy*, Moscow, 1906, No. 1, p. 74.

37. Dated 31 January 1906 in *Perepiska*, pp. 60–61.

Chapter Three

1. Gladkov, A., 'Meierkhold govorit', *Novy mir*, 1961, No, 8, p. 226.
2. *Volkov I*, pp. 217–220.
3. Ibid., p. 236.
4. Fuchs, G., *Die Schaubühne der Zukunft* (Berlin, undated but published 1904–1905).
5. See *Volkov I*, pp. 240–241.
6. Fuchs, op. cit., pp. 38–39.
7. Ibid., pp. 15–16.
8. Ibid., pp. 46–56.
9. Ibid., p. 66.
10. Ibid., pp. 72–73.
11. Ibid., pp. 77–79.
12. Ibid., p. 105.
13. For accounts of the Munich Künstlertheater see Fuchs, G., *Die Revolution des Theaters* (Munich–Leipzig, 1909), pp. 236–291; Fuerst, W. R. and Hume, S. J., *Twentieth-Century Stage Decoration* (New York, 1929 and 1967), Vol. I, pp. 45–48.
14. *Meyerhold I*, p. 244.
15. Loc. cit.
16. Quoted by Meyerhold, loc. cit.
17. *Meyerhold I*, p. 104.
18. Quoted in Freidkina, L., 'U istokov formalizma v russkom teatre', *Teatr*, Moscow, 1937, No. 6, p. 72.
19. Letter (undated) quoted in Talnikov, D., *Komissarzhevskaya* (Moscow–Leningrad, 1939), p. 268.
20. Znosko-Borovsky, Ye., *Russky teatr nachala XX veka* (Prague, 1925), p. 271.
21. See *Perepiska*, pp. 73 ff.
22. Ibid., p. 367.
23. Yartsev's description, published in 1907, was quoted in full by Meyerhold in his *O Teatre*, Petersburg, 1913 (see *Meyerhold I*, pp. 239–242, *Braun*, pp. 65–68).
24. Kugel, A., 'Teatralnie zametki', *Teatr i iskusstvo*, Petersburg, 1906, No. 48, pp. 748–750.
25. Fuchs, G., *Die Schaubühne der Zukunft*, cit., p. 76.
26. See Kugel, A., op. cit., pp. 731–732; Rostislavov, A., 'Prizraki na stsene', *Teatr i iskusstvo*, 1906, No. 49, p. 768.
27. Matskin, A., *Portrety i nablyudenia* (Moscow, 1973), p. 201.
28. Berdyayev, N., *Sub specie aeternitatis* (1900–1906) Petersburg, 1907, pp. 31, 32 (quoted in *Rudnitsky*, p. 78).
29. For accounts of these productions see Sayler, O., *Max Reinhardt and his Theatre* (New York, 1924); Duncan, I., *My Life* (London, 1928 and 1968).
30. See *Meyerhold I*, pp. 132–133 (*Braun*, pp. 53–54).

31. Ibid., p. 247.
32. Tairov, A., *Zapiski rezhissera* (Moscow, 1921), p. 27.
33. *Meyerhold I*, p. 248.
34. Znosko-Borovsky, Ye., op. cit., pp. 281–282.
35. 'Khudozhniki v Teatre V. F. Komissarzhevskoy', *Alkonost*, Book I (Petersburg, 1911) p. 129.
36. See *Meyerhold I*, p. 248.
37. 'Moskovskie teatry – spektakli Peterburgskogo Dramaticheskogo teatra' *Zolotoe runo*, Moscow, 1907, No. 7–9, p. 150.
38. The following contain English translations of *Balaganchik*: Kisch, Sir Cecil, *Alexander Blok; Prophet of Revolution* (London, 1960); Reeve, F., *An Anthology of Russian Plays*, Vol. II (New York, 1963).
39. See Blok, A., *Sobranie sochinenii v 8 tomakh* (Moscow–Leningrad, 1960–1963), Vol. I, pp. 210, 227, 277, 287, 322.
40. *Meyerhold I*, pp. 228, 250 (*Braun*, pp. 70–71, 141).
41. Quoted in *Volkov I*, p. 280.
42. *Vstrechi s Meyerholdom*, cit., p. 40.
43. Ibid., p. 41.
44. *Rudnitsky*, pp. 92–93.
45. 'Moi portrety. Meierkhold', *Teatr i muzyka*, Moscow, 1923, No. 1–2, pp. 427–428.
46. Letter to Alexander Gippius (20 January 1907) in Blok, op. cit., Vol. VIII, p. 176.
47. *Meyerhold I*, pp. 208–209.
48. *Obozrenie teatrov*, Petersburg, 1907, No. 39, p. 6.
49. Blok, op. cit., Vol. IV, p. 425.
50. See Bely, A., *Arabeski* (Moscow, 1911), pp. 311–312.
51. Blok, op. cit., Vol VII, p. 13.
52. See Beketova, M., *Aleksandr Blok* (Petersburg, 1922), p. 105.
53. *Rudnitsky*, p. 91.
54. *The Banquet Years* (London, 1959), p. 30.
55. *Meyerhold I*, pp. 226–227 (*Braun*, pp. 137–139).
56. Loc. cit.
57. Matskin, A., op. cit., p. 209.
58. See especially *Meyerhold II*, pp. 231 ff.
59. *Meyerhold I*, p. 251 (*Braun*, pp. 71–72).
60. Simonson, L., *The Stage is Set* (Revised and amended edition, New York, 1963), pp. 358–359.
61. See Volbach, W., *Adolphe Appia. Prophet of the Modern Theatre* (Wesleyan University Press, 1968), pp. 82–93.
62. Quoted in *Volkov I*, p. 284.
63. Quoted in Stroeva, M., op. cit., pp. 219–220.
64. See *Perepiska*, pp. 82–84.
65. *Meyerhold I*, pp. 105–142 (*Braun*, pp. 23–64).

66. See *Volkov*, pp. 305, 308, 311.
67. For Meyerhold's impressions of Reinhardt's work see *Meyerhold I*, pp. 162–166; *Perepiska*, pp. 85–86.
68. Volkova, N., (ed.), *Vstrechi s proshlym-sbornik TsGALI* (Moscow, 1972), pp. 321–322.
69. Blok, op. cit., Vol. V, pp. 194–195.
70. Quoted in *Volkov I*, p. 332.
71. *Obozrenie teatrov*, Petersburg, 1907, No. 200, p. 14.
72. Valentina Verigina in *Vstrechi*, p. 44.
73. In *O Teatre* (Meyerhold I, pp. 237–257).
74. Leyda, J., *Kino* (London, 1960), p. 82.
75. *Volkov I*, pp. 334–335.
76. Blok, op. cit., Vol. V, p. 200.
77. Quoted in *Alkonost*, (Petersburg, 1911), Kniga I, p. 70.
78. Quoted in *Volkov I*, p. 335.
79. Ibid., pp. 341–343.
80. Ibid., p. 344.
81. Ibid., pp. 345–346.
82. *Moskovsky ezhenedelnik*, 1907, No. 48, pp. 33–34.
83. Quoted in *Volkov I*, p. 346.
84. *Perepiska*, p. 108.
85. See *Vstrechi*, pp. 45–46.
86. See Deich, A., *Golos pamyati* (Moscow, 1966), p. 58; *Meyerhold I*, p. 97.
87. *Perepiska*, p. 111.

Chapter Four

1. *Teatr. Kniga o Novom teatre*, Petersburg, 1908. (*Meyerhold I*, pp. 105–142; *Braun*, pp. 23–64).
2. *Meyerhold I*, p. 141 (*Braun*, p. 62).
3. Ibid., p. 142 (Ibid., p. 63–64).
4. *Peterburgskaya gazeta*, 24 April 1908, p. 2.
5. See *Rudnitsky*, pp. 114–115; Telyakovsky, V., *Vospominania* (Leningrad–Moscow, 1965), p. 167.
6. For a vivid evocation of the Alexandrinsky Theatre at this time see Petrov, Nikolai, *50 i 500* (Moscow, 1960), pp. 74–93.
7. Included in *Meyerhold I*, pp. 170–174.
8. Loc. cit.
9. See *Meyerhold I*, p. 338.
10. See *Volkov II*, p. 26.
11. Osipov, I. in *Obozrenie teatrov*, Petersburg, 1908, No. 535, pp. 5–6.
12. *Vstrechi*, p. 48.
13. See *Rudnitsky*, pp. 117–120.
14. See *Perepiska*, p. 121.
15. *Volkov II*, pp. 40–41.

16. Ibid., pp. 83–84.
17. Ibid., pp. 35–39.
18. Letter to Lyubov Gurevich, *Perepiska*, p. 122.
19. See *Volkov II*, pp. 43–50; *Perepiska*, p. 123.
20. *Meyerhold I*, pp. 167–169.
21. *The London Mercury*, October 1935, Vol. 32, No. 192, p. 537.
22. 'V. E. Meyerhold i russky operny impressionizm', *Istoria sovetskogo teatra –* tom pervy (Leningrad, 1933), p. 310.
23. *Meyerhold I*, pp. 143–161 (*Braun*, pp. 80–98).
24. Quoted from the English translation – Corrigan, R. W. and Dirks, M. D. (trans.) *Music and the Art of the Theatre* (University of Miami, 1962), pp. 14 ff.
25. Ibid., pp. 17–18.
26. *Meyerhold I*, p. 160 (*Braun*, p. 97).
27. Appia, op. cit., p. 46.
28. *Meyerhold I*, pp. 198–199.
29. See *Rudnitsky*, p. 126; *Perepiska*, p. 131.
30. 'Elgur' in *Obozrenie teatrov*, Petersburg, 31 October 1909, p. 7.
31. 'V. S.' in *Teatr i iskusstvo*, Petersburg, 1909, No. 45, pp. 793–794.
32. *Vstrechi*, p. 74.
33. Znosko-Borovsky, Ye., op. cit., p. 337.
34. For accounts of the Ancient Theatre see Stark, E., *Starinny teatr* (Petersburg, 1922); Znosko-Borovsky, Ye., op. cit., pp. 333–343.
35. *Meyerhold I*, pp. 189–191.
36. For a further account of *The Adoration of the Cross* see Pyast, V., *Vstrechi* (Moscow, 1929), pp. 169–180.
37. Znosko-Borovsky, Ye., op. cit., pp. 311–312.
38. *Volkov II*, pp. 237–238.
39. See especially Matskin, A., op. cit., pp. 284 ff., Davydova, M. V., *Ocherki istorii russkogo teatralno-dekoratsionnogo iskusstva XVIII – nachala XX vekov* (Moscow, 1974), pp. 164–168.
40. 'Die Abenteuer der Sylvester Nacht', *Fantasiestücke in Callot's Manier* (*Sämtliche Werke*, Munich–Leipzig, 1908, Vol. I, pp. 339–375).
41. *Meyerhold I*, p. 228 (*Braun*, pp. 140–141).
42. Znoski-Borovsky, Ye., op. cit., p. 303.
43. In 'K postanovke *Don Zhuana* Moliera' (1910) – *Meyerhold I*, pp. 192–197 (*Braun*, pp. 98–103).
44. Loc. cit.
45. See Simonson, L., op. cit., pp. 204–216; Mantzius, K., *A History of Theatrical Art*, trans. von Cossel, L. (London, 1905), Vol. IV, pp. 100–104.
46. *Vstrechi*, p. 79.
47. See Kugel, A., 'Teatralnie zametki', *Teatr i iskusstvo*, 1910, No. 47, pp. 901–903; Benois, A., 'Balet v Aleksandrinke', *Rech*, 19 November 1910, p. 3.
48. *Meyerhold I*, pp. 195–196 (*Braun*, pp. 102–103).
49. Loc. cit.

50. Znosko-Borovsky, Ye., op. cit., p. 308.
51. See Malyutin, Ya., *Aktery moego pokolenia* (Leningrad–Moscow, 1959), pp. 112–113; *Aleksandr Yakovlevich Golovin – Vstrechi i vpechatlenia* . . . (Leningrad–Moscow, 1960), pp. 328–329.
52. Khodotov, N., *Blizkoe-dalekoe* (Leningrad–Moscow, 1962), p. 251.
53. *Meyerhold I*, p. 221 (*Braun*, pp. 133–134).
54. Ibid., pp. 218–219 (Ibid., p. 131).
55. Ibid., p. 221 (Ibid., p. 133).
56. See Matskin, A., op. cit., pp. 244–245, *Rudnitsky*, p. 139.
57. Op. cit., p. 3.
58. Volkonsky, S. M., *Chelovek na stsene* (Petersburg, 1912), p. 78.

Chapter Five

1. See *Volkov II*, pp. 161–166; *Vstrechi*, p. 75.
2. See *Meyerhold I*, pp. 144–145 (*Braun*, pp. 82–83).
3. *Meyerhold I*, p. 256 (*Braun*, p. 106).
4. Loc. cit.
5. See Golovin, A., op. cit., p. 163.
6. Fokin, M., op. cit., pp. 500–501.
7. See Volkonsky, S. M., *Khudozhestvennye otkliki*, (Petersburg, 1912), pp. 185–190.
8. Fokin, M., op. cit., pp. 501–503.
9. *Volkov II*, p. 269.
10. Quoted in *Rudnitsky*, p. 162.
11. Gladkov, A., 'Meierkhold govorit', *Neva*, Leningrad, 1966, No. 2, p. 204.
12. *Yezhegodnik Imperatorskikh teatrov*, Petersburg, 1913, Vypusk IV, p. 136.
13. Diary entry 20 April 1913 (Blok, op. cit., Vol. VII, p. 239).
14. Quoted in *Volkov II*, p. 273.
15. For an account of these productions see Tomashevsky, K., 'Victory over the Sun', *The Drama Review*, New York, Vol. 15, No. 4 (T-52), pp. 92–106.
16. *Meyerhold I*, pp. 252–253 (*Braun*, pp. 144–145).
17. *Meyerhold I*, pp. 207 ff. (*Braun*, pp. 119 ff.)
18. Ibid., p. 212. (Ibid., p. 124).
19. *Volkov II*, p. 291.
20. *Perepiska*, pp. 154–156.
21. Reprinted in Lunacharsky, A. V., *O Teatre i dramaturgii*, Vol. II (Moscow, 1958), p. 165.
22. For a detailed account of *La Pisanelle* and Meyerhold's visit to Paris see Abensour, G., 'Meyerhold à Paris', *Cahiers du Monde Russe et Soviétique*, Paris, 1964, Vol. V, No. 1, pp. 5–31.
23. *Lyubov k tryom apelsinam*, *Zhurnal Doktora Dapertutto*, Petersburg, 1914, No. 1, pp. 61–62.
24. Ibid., 1914, No. 4–5, p. 90. For extracts from later Studio curricula see *Braun*, pp. 146–149, 153–156.

25. *Perepiska*, p. 154, 388.
26. Blok, A., op. cit., Vol. IV, p. 576.
27. *Sovremennik*, Petersburg, 1914, June, pp. 120–121.
28. See Verigina, V., 'Vospominania o Bloke', *Uchenie zapiski Tartuskogo gosudar-stvennogo universiteta*, Vypusk 104 (Tartu, 1961), pp. 361–363.
29. *Sovremennik*, loc. cit.
30. Gripich, A., 'Uchitel stseny' in *Vstrechi*, p. 137. (Gripich was a member of the Studio company.)
31. *Meyerhold II*, p. 18.
32. For a detailed description of the programme see *Braun*, pp. 149–151.
33. For Meyerhold's comments on this project see *Lyubov k tryom apelsinam*, 1915, No. 4–7, pp. 208–211 (*Braun*, pp. 151–153).
34. See *Volkov II*, pp. 428–430.
35. *Meyerhold I*, pp. 221–222.
36. Leyda, J., op. cit., p. 58.
37. *Teatralnaya gazeta*, Moscow, 31 May 1915, p. 7.
38. See Levitsky, A., *Rasskazy o Kinematografe* (Moscow, 1964), pp. 78–106.
39. Leyda, J., op. cit., p. 59.
40. Ibid., p. 81.
41. Ginzburg, S., *Kinematografia dorevolyutsionnoy Rossii* (Moscow, 1963), p. 303.
42. Yutkevich, S., 'V. E. Meierkhold i teoria kinorezhissury', *Iskusstvo kino*, Moscow, 1975, No. 8, p. 75. For an account of *The Picture of Dorian Gray* by Meyerhold see *Iz istorii kino*, No. 6 (Moscow, 1965) –*Braun*, pp. 305–311.
43. Interview in *Teatralnaya gazeta*, Moscow, 7 August 1916, p. 15.
44. *Novy zritel*, Moscow, 1925, No. 18, p. 15.
45. *Perepiska*, p. 421; Yutkevich, S., op. cit., p. 76.
46. See also Fevralsky, A., 'Meierkhold i kino', *Iskusstvo kino*, Moscow, 1962, No. 6, pp. 105–113.
47. For accounts of *The Storm* see *Meyerhold I*, pp. 285–293; *Volkov II*, pp. 403–415; *Vstrechi*, pp. 106–108; Kogan, D., *Golovin* (Moscow, 1960), pp. 38–41; *Rudnitsky*, pp. 185–192.
48. *Meyerhold I*, p. 298.
49. Ibid., p. 299.
50. Yuriev, Yu., *Zapiski*, (Leningrad–Moscow, 1963), Vol. II, pp. 201–202.
51. Malyutin, Ya., op. cit., pp. 99–100.
52. See *Volkov II*, p. 183.
53. *Meyerhold I*, p. 300.
54. *Meyerhold II*, p. 440.
55. For colour reproductions of many of the settings, costumes, and properties see Lansere, E. (ed.), *Maskarad Lermontova v teatralnykh eskizakh A. Ya. Golovina* (Moscow–Leningrad, 1941–1946).
56. Under the pseudonym 'Homo novus', *Teatr i iskusstvo*, 1917, No. 10–11, p. 192.
57. *Rudnitsky*, p. 203.

58. Yuriev, Yu., op. cit., Vol. II, p. 239.
59. For further accounts of *Masquerade* in works other than those cited see Matskin, A., op. cit., pp. 273 ff.; Petrov, N. V., op. cit., pp. 128–139; *Vstrechi*, pp. 111–113, 149–153, 159–163.

Chapter Six

1. See *Volkov I*, pp. 189, 227–229.
2. See *Meyerhold I*, pp. 95–96, 318.
3. Lunacharsky, A., 'Yeshcho ob iskusstve i revolyutsii', *Obrazovanie*, Petersburg, 1906, No. 12, p. 82.
4. Interview with 'N. M.', *Teatr*, Moscow, 24 October 1913, p. 5.
5. Report by 'VI. S.', *Apollon*, Petersburg, 1914, No. 6–7, p. 109.
6. *Lyubov k tryom apelsinam*, 1915, No. 1–3, p. 140.
7. *Meyerhold I*, p. 318.
8. See *Ocherki istorii sovetskoy dramaturgii*, Vol. I (Leningrad–Moscow, 1963), p. 8.
9. *Nashi vedomosti*, 12 January 1918 (Quoted in *Rudnitsky*, p. 223).
10. See *Meyerhold II*, p. 590.
11. Matskin, A., op. cit., pp. 300, 320.
12. See *Vstrechi*, pp. 137–145; *Vremennik Teatralnogo otdela NKP*, Petrograd, 1918, No. 1 (November), pp. 24–29.
13. See Fevralsky, A., *Pervaya sovetskaya piesa* (Moscow, 1971), pp. 60–62.
14. See Zolotnitsky, D., *Zori teatralnogo oktyabrya* (Leningrad, 1976), pp. 64–65.
15. *Petrogradskaya pravda*, 5 November 1918, p. 2.
16. Zolotnitsky, D., op. cit., p. 76.
17. Eye-witness account quoted by Fevralsky, A., op. cit., p. 73.
18. Fevralsky, A., 'Misteria-buff', *Spektakli i gody* (ed. A. Anastasiev, E. Peregudova, Moscow, 1969), p. 13.
19. Loc. cit.
20. *Zhizn iskusstva*, Petrograd, 11 November 1918, p. 2.
21. Quoted by Zolotnitsky, op. cit., p. 75.
22. See Fevralsky, A., *Pervaya sovetskaya piesa*, cit., pp. 201 ff.
23. For accounts of this period in Meyerhold's life see *Vestnik teatra*, Moscow, 1920, No. 68, pp. 4–5; *Teatralnaya zhizn*, Moscow, 1964, No. 14, pp. 28–29.
24. Ilinsky, I., *Sam o sebe* (Moscow, 1962), p. 106.
25. See Zolotnitsky, op. cit., p. 82.
26. See Matskin, op. cit., p. 319.
27. At a public debate reported in *Vestnik teatra*, 1920, No. 78–79, p. 16.
28. See *Perepiska*, pp. 191–192.
29. On 31 October 1920, quoted in *Vestnik teatra*, 1920, No. 72–73, pp. 19–20 (*Braun*, pp. 169–170).
30. Zolotnitsky, op. cit., pp. 107–108. For other versions see *Rudnitsky*, p. 244;

Khersonsky, Kh., 'Vzyatie Perekopa i *Zori*; *Teatr*, Moscow, 1957, No. 5, pp. 90–91.

31. *Vestnik teatra*, 1920, No. 72–73, p. 10, No. 75, p. 14. (*Braun*, pp. 173–174).
32. Quoted by Zolotnitsky, op. cit., pp. 102–103.
33. *Pravda*, Moscow, 10 November 1920, p. 2.
34. Reported in *Vestnik teatra*, 1920, No. 75, p. 12.
35. *Vestnik teatra*, 1920, No. 76–77, p. 4.
36. For discussions of the role of Narkompros and the Theatre Department see Fitzpatrick, S., *The Commissariat of Enlightenment* (Cambridge University Press, 1970).
37. *Meyerhold II*, p. 360.
38. For an English translation of *Mystery-Bouffe* see *The Complete Plays of Vladimir Mayakovsky* (trans. Daniels, G., New York, 1968 and 1971).
39. *Pervaya sovetskaya piesa*, cit., p. 158.
40. Ibid., p. 170.
41. *Vestnik teatra*, 1921, No. 93–94, p. 23.
42. For a detailed account of the liquidation of the R.S.F.S.R. Theatre No. 1 see Fevralsky, A., 'Teatralny oktyabr i *Zori*', *Sovetsky teatr*, Moscow, 1931, No. 1. pp. 4–9.

Chapter Seven

1. See Markov, V., *Russian Futurism* (London, 1969), pp. 270–274.
2. Volkov, N., *Teatralnye vechera* (Moscow, 1966), p. 285.
3. *Vestnik teatra*, 1922, No. 80–81, p. 22; No. 83–84, p. 22.
4. For a summary of Taylorism and Reflexology and a detailed exposition of Meyerhold's biomechanical 'études' see Gordon, M., 'Meyerhold's Bio-mechanics', *The Drama Review*, New York, Vol. 18, No. 3 (T-63), pp. 73–88. Further photographs of the études are contained in *The Drama Review*, Vol. 17, No. 1 (T-57).
5. From Fyodorov, V., 'Aktyor budushchego', *Ermitazh*, Moscow, 1922, No. 6, pp. 10–11 (for a complete version see *Braun*, pp. 197–200).
6. *Vstrechi*, pp. 322–323.
7. Meierkhold, V., Bebutov, V., Aksyonov, I., *Amplua aktyora* (Moscow, 1922), p. 4. For a complete translation of *Amplua aktera* see Hoover, M., op. cit., pp. 297–310. Hoover also includes full biomechanics programmes and the curricula of Meyerhold's Workshop for the years 1922–1923 and 1927–1928.
8. *Teatr*, Moscow, 1922, No. 5., pp. 149–151.
9. *Teatr i muzyka*, Moscow, 1922, No. 7, pp. 23–24.
10. For the relevant passages from Coquelin see Cole, T., Chinoy, H. (ed.), *Actors on Acting* (New York, 1949), pp. 195–206.
11. Garin, E., *S Meierkholdom* (Moscow, 1974), pp. 28 ff.
12. *Vstrechi*, p. 125.

13. Ibid., p. 76. For a description of 'The Leap onto the Chest' see Gordon, M., op. cit., p. 85.
14. *Theatre Arts Monthly*, New York, 1935, November, p. 874.
15. See Gvozdev, A., 'Istorichesky rol teatra Meierkholda', *Sovetsky teatr*, Moscow, 1931, No. 1, p. 2.
16. Interview in *Teatr*, Moscow, 24 October 1913, p. 6.
17. Quoted by Sergei Yutkevich in *Vstrechi*, p. 212.
18. *Teatralnaya Moskva*, 1922, No. 37, p. 10.
19. *Meyerhold II*, p. 47 (*Braun*, p. 204).
20. *Rudnitsky*, p. 261.
21. See Ilinsky, I., op. cit., p. 148.
22. 'Zritelnoe oformlenie v GOSTIMe' (unpublished), quoted in *Rudnitsky*, pp. 261–262.
23. Gvozdev, A., *Teatr imeni Vs. Meierkholda – 1920–26* (Leningrad, 1927), p. 28.
24. *Isvestia*, 14 May 1922, p. 4.
25. Garin, E., op. cit., p. 50.
26. Meyerhold Archive, quoted in *Rudnitsky*, p. 269.
27. Alpers, B., *Teatr sotsialnoy maski* (Moscow–Leningrad, 1931), p. 34.
28. Ilinsky, I., op. cit., p. 154.
29. *Ermitazh*, Moscow, 1922, No. 8 (4–10 July), pp. 3–4, 11–12.
30. *Teatralnaya Moskva*, 1922, No. 46 (27 June–2 July), p. 8.
31. Sukhovo-Kobylin, A., *Trilogia* (Moscow, 1966), p. 348.
32. Previously unpublished article in Trabsky, A. (ed.), *Russky Sovetsky Teatr 1921–1926* (Leningrad, 1975), p. 202.
33. See Garin, E., op. cit., pp. 58–61.
34. See Khersonsky, Kh., *Stranitsy yunosti kino* (Moscow, 1965), pp. 110–124.
35. See Zharov, M., *Zhizn, teatr, kino* (Moscow, 1967), p. 154.
36. For accounts of Eisenstein's work in the theatre see Eisenstein, A., *Izbrannye proizvedenia v shesti tomakh*, Vol. V (Moscow, 1968), pp. 68 ff; Barna, Y., *Eisenstein* (London, 1973), pp. 46–72.
37. *Braun*, p. 311.
38. See *Perepiska*, pp. 218–219.
39. *Zrelishcha*, Moscow, 1923, No. 21, p. 8.
40. *Perepiska*, pp. 225–226.
41. *Zrelishcha*, 1923, No. 21, p. 8.
42. Fevralsky, A., *Zapiski rovesnika veka* (Moscow, 1976), p. 239, 246.
43. Ibid., p. 238–239.
44. Ibid., p. 236.
45. Ibid., pp. 268–271. For an analysis of the records of audience reaction see the articles by V. F. Fyodorov and subsequent discussions in *Zhizn iskusstva*, 1925, Nos. 18, 20, 22, 23, 26, 27.
46. See *Vestnik teatra*, 4 January 1921, No. 78–79, p. 15.
47. See Fevralsky, A., op. cit., pp. 247–249.
48. *Zrelishcha*, Moscow, 1923, No. 60, p. 1.

49. *Vstrechi*, p. 298.
50. Ibid., p. 306.
51. Erenburg, I., *A vsyo-taki ona vertitsya* (Moscow–Berlin, 1922), p. 114.
52. Letter to Meyerhold dated 5 March 1924, published in *Novy zritel*, Moscow, 1924, No. 18, p. 16.
53. Ibid., pp. 16–17.
54. *Sobranie sochinenii*, Vol. 8., (Moscow, 1966), pp. 336–337.
55. *Vstrechi*, p. 311; Zharov, M., op. cit., pp. 174–178.
56. Previously unpublished article in Trabsky, A., (ed)., op. cit., p. 218.
57. *Novy zritel*, Moscow, 1924, No. 29, pp. 13–14.
58. For a further account of *D.E.* see Hedgbeth, L., 'Meyerhold's *D.E.*', *The Drama Review*, Vol. 19, No. 2 (T-66), pp. 23–36.
59. See Lunacharsky, A., op. cit., Vol. I, pp. 374–376.
60. See Faiko, A., 'Tri vstrechi', *Teatr*, Moscow, 1962, No. 10, pp. 121–122.
61. *Meyerhold II*, pp. 93–94 (*Braun*, p. 206).
62. Quoted in *Rudnitsky*, p. 331.
63. Faiko, A., op. cit., pp. 121–122.
64. Garin, E., op. cit., p. 101.
65. *Teatr*, Moscow, 1937, No 1. p. 44.
66. See *Rudnitsky*, pp. 287–301.
67. *Pravda*, 19 January 1924, p. 9.
68. Reported in *Novy zritel*, Moscow, 1924, No. 7, p. 6.
69. *Izvestia*, 11–12 April 1923.
70. *Meyerhold II*, p. 57.
71. Ibid., pp. 56–57.
72. See *Rudnitsky*, p. 303.
73. See *Braun*, pp. 318–322.
74. *Rudnitsky*, p. 315.
75. Ibid., p. 302. For an extended analysis by Rudnitsky of *The Forest* see *Teatr*, 1976, No. 11. pp. 97–110, No. 12, pp. 95–106.
76. See Meyerhold's speech 'Meierkhold protiv meyerholdovshchiny' (14 March 1936) in *Meyerhold II*, pp. 330–347.
77. *Rudnitsky*, p. 340.
78. Zharov, M., op. cit., p. 184.
79. Markov, P., *O Teatre*, Vol. 3 (Moscow, 1976), p. 289.
80. Alpers, B., op. cit., p. 48.
81. *Rudnitsky*, p. 342.
82. Markov, P., loc. cit.
83. Quoted in Markov, P., *Pravda teatra* (Moscow, 1965), p. 43.
84. See especially *Vstrechi*, pp. 278–289, *Meyerhold II*, pp. 373–418.

Chapter Eight

1. *Rampa*, Moscow, 5–10 February 1924, p. 7.
2. 'Meierkhold govorit', *Tarusskie stranitsy*, cit., p. 306.
3. Letter to M. P. Pogodin dated 10 May 1836 in Gogol, N. V., *Polnoe sobranie sochinenii* (A.n.S.S.S.R., Leningrad, 1940–1952), Vol. XI, p. 41.
4. *Avtorskaya ispoved*, Gogol, op. cit., Vol. VIII, p. 440.
5. Korenev, M., 'K postanovke *Revizora*' in Nikitina, E. (ed.), *Gogol i Meyerhold* (Moscow, 1927), p. 78.
6. See *Meyerhold II*, pp. 145–146.
7. 'Otryvok iz pisma k odnomu literaturu', Gogol, op. cit., Vol. IV, p. 99.
8. Korenev, M., op. cit., p. 77.
9. 'Razvyazka *Revizora*', Gogol, op. cit., Vol. IV, pp. 121–137.
10. *Meyerhold II*, p. 132, (*Braun*, p. 220).
11. Quoted by *Rudnitsky*, p. 352.
12. *Gogol i Meyerhold*, cit., p. 85.
13. For details of Meyerhold's division of Gogol's text see Garin, op. cit., pp. 136–137.
14. *Meyerhold II*, p. 119.
15. Markov, P., *O Teatre*, Vol. 3, cit., p. 382.
16. See *Meyerhold II*, pp. 110, 112; Garin, op. cit., p. 123.
17. Korenev, op. cit., p. 79.
18. Bely, A., 'Gogol i Meyerhold' in *Gogol i Meyerhold*, cit., pp. 27–29. (The ball takes place in Part One, Chapter 8 of *Dead Souls*).
19. See *Meyerhold II*, p. 132, (*Braun*, pp. 220–221).
20. Grossman, L., 'Tragedia-buff' in *Gogol i Meyerhold*, cit., p. 42.
21. Lunacharsky, A., op. cit., Vol. 1, p. 402.
22. Talnikov, D., *Novaya revizia Revizora* (Moscow–Leningrad, 1927), p. 52.
23. Lunacharsky, loc. cit.
24. 'Otryvok iz pisma k odnomu literaturu', cit., p. 101.
25. Garin, op. cit., p. 148.
26. Quoted in *Rudnitsky*, p. 357.
27. Ibid., p. 353.
28. Radlov, S., *Desyat let v teatre* (Leningrad, 1929), p. 148.
29. Gnesin, M., *Statyi, vospominania, materialy* (Moscow, 1961), p. 198.
30. *Vstrechi*, pp. 336–337.
31. For a comprehensive bibliography see Danilov, S., *Revizor na stsene* (Leningrad, 1934).
32. See *Rudnitsky*, p. 379.
33. See *Vstrechi*, pp. 416–422.

Chapter Nine

1. See *Perepiska*, pp. 249, 412.
2. Ibid., p. 414.

3. Ibid., pp. 265, 267.
4. Tretyakov, quoted in *Slyshish, Moskva?!* . . . (Moscow, 1966), p. 198.
5. For an account by Alexander Fevralsky of this project see ibid., pp. 197–204.
6. *Sovremenny teatr*, Moscow, 1928, No. 9, p. 184.
7. Ibid., 1928, No. 10, p. 203.
8. See *Meyerhold II*, pp. 165, 322–323. For Pushkin's letter see Bogoslavsky, N. (ed.), *Pushkin-kritik* (Moscow–Leningrad, 1934), p. 63.
9. See Asafiev, B., 'O muzyke v *Gore umu*', *Sovremenny teatr*, 1928, No. 11, p. 223.
10. V. Blyum, quoted in *Rudnitsky*, p. 385.
11. See Gladkov, A., 'Meierkhold govorit', *Novy mir*, cit., p. 228; *Meyerhold II*, pp. 322–323.
12. Announced in *Novy zritel*, Moscow, 1928, No. 47, p. 16. The controversy is covered in detail in *Komsomolskaya Pravda*, Moscow, 31 August–4 December 1928.
13. See interview with Meyerhold in *Komsomolskaya Pravda*, 4 December 1928, p.4.
14. Interview in *Komsomolskaya Pravda*, 28 December 1928, p. 4.
15. See Markov, P., op. cit., Vol. 2, pp. 59–75.
16. *Meyerhold II*, p. 177.
17. Loc. cit.
18. See *Rudnitsky*, pp. 398–409.
19. See Katanyan, V., *Mayakovsky – literaturnaya khronika* (Moscow, 1956), p. 369.
20. *Sovremenny teatr*, Moscow, 1929, No. 15, p. 235.
21. Quoted in *Rudnitsky*, p. 424.
22. *Vstrechi*, pp. 387–396.
23. *Novy zritel*, Moscow, 1929, No. 40, p. 5.
24. For a detailed analysis of the play and production see Markov, P., op. cit., Vol. 3, pp. 601–611.
25. Zoshchenko, M., (ed.), *Almanakh estrady* (Leningrad, 1933), p. 6.
26. See Fevralsky's commentary in Mayakovsky, V., *Teatr i kino* (Moscow, 1954), Vol. II, pp. 505–508.
27. For English translations of *The Bath House* see Daniels, G., op. cit., McAndrew, A., *Twentieth Century Russian Drama* (New York, 1963).
28. *Rudnitsky*, p. 421.
29. See Mayakovsky, op. cit., p. 509; *Rudnitsky*, p. 416.
30. Quoted by *Rudnitsky*, p. 420.
31. For a personal account of the tour see Ilinsky, I., op. cit., pp. 231–237.
32. See *Sovetsky teatr*, Moscow, 1930, No. 5, pp. 34–35, No. 11–12, pp. 44–45.
33. Erenburg, I., *Sobranie sochinenii v 9 tomakh*, Vol. 8 (Moscow, 1966), p. 340.
34. Annenkov, Yu., *Dnevnik moikh vstrech* (New York, 1966), Vol. II, pp. 85–87; *Perepiska*, pp. 310, 423.

35. Kirshon, V. in *Sovetsky teatr*, Moscow, 1931, No. 4, p. 18.
36. Ibid., p. 12.
37. *Meyerhold II*, p. 248.
38. See the account by Vishnevsky's wife, Sofia Vishnevetskaya in *Vstrechi*, pp. 405–414.
39. Ibid., pp. 556–557.
40. For an English translation of *A List of Benefits* see McAndrew, A., op. cit.
41. See Chushkin, N., *Gamlet – Kachalov* (Moscow, 1966), pp. 257–259.

Chapter Ten

1. See Ilinsky, I., op. cit., pp. 251–253.
2. Reported by Gliarov, M. in *Rabis*, Moscow, 1933, No. 11, pp. 34–35.
3. Ilinsky, op. cit., p. 244.
4. *Theatre Arts Monthly*, New York, 1935, November, p. 874.
5. *Meyerhold II*, p. 285.
6. Yuzovsky, I., *Zatem lyudi khodyat v teatr*, (Moscow, 1964).
7. *Rudnitsky*, pp. 457–458.
8. *Vstrechi*, p. 476.
9. *Vstrechi*, pp. 500–501; *Meyerhold II*, pp. 286–287.
10. *Meyerhold II*, p. 288, (*Braun*, pp. 274–275).
11. *Rudnitsky*, pp. 464–465.
12. See *Teatr i dramaturgia*, Moscow, 1934, No. 2, pp. 35–39.
13. *Meyerhold II*, pp. 287–292 (for the complete text of this and a second letter to Shebalin see *Braun*, pp. 274–278).
14. *Molodaya gvardia*, Moscow, 1934, No. 8, p. 131.
15. *Meyerhold II*, p. 299.
16. *Sovetsky teatr*, Moscow, 1935, No. 1, p. 12.
17. Quoted in Lapkina, G., *Na afishe-Pushkin* (Leningrad–Moscow, 1965), p. 55.
18. See Bogdanov-Berezovsky, V., *Vstrechi* (Moscow, 1967), pp. 102–106.
19. 'Meierkhold govorit', *Tarusskie stranitsy*, cit., p. 307.
20. *Meyerhold II*, p. 309, (*Braun*, pp. 288–289).
21. *Rudnitsky*, p. 475, *Meyerhold II*, p. 310.
22. See Yuzovsky, I., *Razgovor zatyanulsya za polnoch* (Moscow, 1966), pp. 245–262.
23. 'Meierkhold govorit', *Novy mir*, cit., p. 228.
24. See Hayward, M., Labedz, L. (ed.), *Literature and Revolution in Soviet Russia 1917–62*, (Oxford U.P., 1963), Chapters 4 and 5.
25. 'Sumbur vmesto muzyki' (28 January 1936); 'Baletnaya falsh', (6 February, 1936).
26. See 'Meierkhold protiv meierkholdovshchiny', *Meyerhold II*, pp. 330–347.
27. For the text see *Meyerhold II*, pp. 348–358, (*Braun*, pp. 289–300).
28. *Sovetsky teatr*, 1936, No. 4–5, p. 2.
29. For details and rehearsal notes see *Meyerhold II*, p. 362–369.
30. See *Meyerhold II*, pp. 373–418; Gladkov, A., 'Iz vospominaniy o Meierkholde'

in *Moskva teatralnaya* (Moscow, 1960), pp. 366–376; Lapkina, G., op. cit., pp. 108–112.

31. See *Rudnitsky*, p. 485.
32. *Iskusstvo kino*, 1964, No. 4, pp. 68–69.
33. See *Vstrechi*, pp. 562–564.

Conclusion

1. See *Vstrechi*, p. 565.
2. See *Rudnitsky*, p. 259.
3. Ibid., p. 487.
4. Quoted in *Vstrechi*, p. 589.
5. *Rezhissyor v sovetskom teatre* . . . (Moscow–Leningrad, 1940).
6. *Tyomny genii* (New York, 1955), pp. 406–410.
7. *Teatr*, 1974, No. 2, pp. 39–44.
8. 'A.V.', Gnilaya pozitsia', *Izvestia*, 20 December 1937, p. 4.
9. These details of the deaths of Meyerhold and Raikh are accepted by members of his family. In the preface to *Vstrechi s Meierkholdom* (p. 13) Meyerhold is said to have been arrested 'due to false denunciation'.

Bibliography

—————◆—————

What follows is a comprehensive list of works devoted wholly to Meyerhold or containing significant reference to him. Newspaper and periodical articles are not included; for these the reader is referred to the footnotes above plus the full documentation of the works of Rudnitsky and Ripellino cited below. For a complete bibliography of all Meyerhold's writings and utterances published up to March 1974 see *Bibliograficheskiy ukazatel knig, statei, perevodov, besed, dokladov, vyskazyvaniy, pisem V. E. Meierkholda* (compiled by V. P. Korshunova, M. M. Sitkovetskaya, Moscow, 1974).

Alpatov, M. V. and Gunst, E. A.: *Nikolai Nikolaevich Sapunov*, Moscow, 1965.
Alpers, B. V.: *Teatralnye ocherki* (2 vols.), Moscow, 1977.
Alpers, B. V.: *Teatr revolyutsii*, Moscow, 1928.
Alpers, B. V.: *Teatr sotsialnoy maski*, Moscow–Leningrad, 1931
Annenkov, Yu.: *Dnevnik moikh vstrech* (2 vols.), New York, 1966.
Art in Revolution. Soviet Art and Design since 1917 (Arts Council exhibition catalogue), London, 1971.

Barna, Y.: *Eisenstein*, London, 1973.
Bassekhes, A. I.: *Teatr i zhivopis Golovina*, Moscow, 1970.
Beketova, M. A.: *Aleksandr Blok – biograficheskiy ocherk*, Petrograd, 1922.
Bezpalov, V. F.: *Teatry v dni revolyutsii 1917*, Leningrad, 1927.
Blok, A. A.: *Sobranie sochineniy* (8 vols.), Moscow–Leningrad, 1960–1963.
Bogdanov-Berezovsky, V. M.: *Vstrechi*, Moscow, 1967.
Braun, E.: *Meyerhold on Theatre*, London–New York, 1969.
Brukson, Ya.: *Teatr Meierkholda*, Leningrad, 1925.

Carter, H.: *The New Spirit in the Russian Theatre 1917–1928*, London, 1929.
Chushkin, N. N.: *Gamlet – Kachalov*, Moscow, 1966.
Cinema in Revolution (trans. D. Robinson), London, 1973.

Dana, H. W.: *Handbook on Soviet Drama*, New York, 1938.
Danilov, S. S.: *Revizor na stsene*, Leningrad, 1934.

Davydova, M. V.: *Ocherki istorii russkogo teatralno-dekoratsionnogo iskusstva XVIII – nachala XX vekov*, Moscow, 1974.

Deich, A. I.: *Golos pamyati*, Moscow, 1966.

Eizenshtein, S. M.: *Izbrannye proizvedenia v shesti tomakh*, Moscow, 1964–1971.

Erenburg, I. G.: *Lyudi, gody, zhizni*, Moscow, 1961.

Fevralsky, A. V.: *Desyat let teatra Meierkholda*, Moscow, 1931.

Fevralsky, A. V.: 'Mayakovsky v borbe za revolyutsionnyi teatr' in *Mayakovsky i sovetskaya literatura*, Moscow, 1964.

Fevralsky, A. V.: 'Meierkhold i Shekspir' in *Vilyam Shekspir-issledovania i materialy,*, Moscow, 1964.

Fevralsky, A. V.: 'Misteria-Buff' in *Spektakli i gody* (ed. A. Anastasiev, E. Peregudova), Moscow, 1969.

Fevralsky, A. V.: *Pervaya sovetskaya piesa*, Moscow, 1971.

Fevralsky, A. V.: 'Prokofiev i Meierkhold' in *Sergei Prokofiev: Statyi i materialy*, Moscow, 1965.

Fevralsky, A. V.: 'Stanislavsky i Meierkhold' in *Tarusskie stranitsy*, Kaluga, 1961.

Fevralsky, A. V.: *Zapiski rovesnika veka*, Moscow, 1976.

Fokin, M.: *Protiv techenia*, Leningrad–Moscow, 1962.

Freidkina, L. M.: *Dni i gody VI. I. Nemirovicha-Danchenko*, Moscow, 1962.

Fülop-Miller, R. and Gregor, J.: *The Russian Theatre, its character and history*, London, 1930.

Garin, E.: *S Meierkholdom*, Moscow, 1974.

Ginzburg, S. S.: *Kinematografia dorevolyutsionnogo Rossii*, Moscow, 1963.

Gladkov, A. K.: 'Iz vospominaniy o Meierkholde' in *Moskva teatralnaya*, Moscow, 1960.

Gladkov, A. K.: 'Meierkhold govorit' in *Novy mir*, 1961, No. 8, translated as 'Meyerhold Speaks' in *Novy Mir 1925–1967* (ed. M. Glenny), London, 1972.

Gladkov, A. K.: 'Vospominania, zametki, zapiski o V. E. Meierkholde' in *Tarusskie stranitsy*, cit.

Gnesin, M. F.: *Statyi, vospominania, materialy*, Moscow, 1961.

Gogol i Meierkhold (ed. E. F. Nikitina), Moscow, 1927.

Golovin, A. Ya.: *A. Ya. Golovin: Vstrechi i vpechatlenia. Pisma. Vospominania o Golovine*, Leningrad–Moscow, 1960.

Gvozdev, A. A.: *Teatr im. Vsevoloda Meierkholda (1920–26)*, Leningrad, 1927.

Hoover, M. L.: *Meyerhold – The Art of Conscious Theater*, University of Massachusetts, 1974.

Houghton, N.: *Moscow Rehearsals*, New York, 1936.

Houghton, N.: *Return engagement*, New York, 1962.

Ilinsky, I. V.: *Sam o sebe*, Moscow, 1962.

Istoria sovetskogo dramaticheskogo teatra, Vols. 1–4 (ed. K. L. Rudnitsky), Moscow, 1966–1968.
Istoria sovetskogo teatra, Vol. 1 (ed. V. Ye. Rafalovich), Leningrad, 1933.

Khersonsky, Kh. N.: *Stranitsy yunosti kino*, Moscow, 1965.
Khodotov, N. N.: *Blizkoe – dalyokoe*, Leningrad–Moscow, 1962.
Kogan, D.: *Golovin*, Moscow, 1960.
Kobrin, Yu. V.: *Teatr im. Meierkholda i rabochiy zritel*, Moscow, 1926.
V. F. Komissarzhevskaya: pisma aktrisy, vospominania o ney, materialy, Moscow–Leningrad, 1964.
Kugel, A. R.: 'Meierkhold' in *Profili teatra* (ed. A. V. Lunacharsky), Moscow, 1929.

Lapkina, G. A.: *Na afishe – Pushkin*, Leningrad–Moscow, 1965.
Levitsky, A. A.: *Rasskazy o kinematografe*, Moscow, 1964.
Leyda, J.: *Kino: A History of the Russian and Soviet Film*, London, 1960.
Lunacharsky, A. V.: *Neizdannye materialy. Literaturnoe nasledstvo*, Vol. 82, Moscow, 1970.
Lunacharsky, A. V.: *O teatre i dramaturgii*, Vol. 1, Moscow, 1958.

Malyutin, Ya. O.: *Aktyory moego pokolenia*, Moscow–Leningrad, 1959.
Markov, P. A.: *O teatre* (4 vols.), Moscow, 1974— .
Markov, P. A.: *Pravda teatre*, Moscow, 1965.
Martínek, K.: *Mejerchold*, Prague, 1963.
Maskarad Lermontova v eskizakh Golovina, Moscow–Leningrad, 1941.
Matskin, A. P.: *Portrety i nablyudenia*, Moscow, 1973.
Mayakovsky, V. V.: *Teatr i kino* (2 vols.), Moscow, 1954.
Meierkhold, V. E.: *Perepiska*, Moscow, 1976.
V. E. Meierkhold: Sbornik k 20–letiyu rezhissyorskoi raboty i 25–letiyu aktyorskoi deyatelnosti, Tver, 1923.
Meierkhold, V. E.: *Statyi, pisma, rechi, besedy* (2 vols.), Moscow, 1968.
Meyerhold, V. E.: *Ecrits sur le théâtre* (3 vols., trans. B. Picon-Vallin), Lausanne, 1973— .
Meyerhold, V. E.: *La rivoluzione teatrale* (trans. G. Crino), Rome, 1962.
Meyerhold, V. E.: *Teoria teatral*, Madrid, 1971.
Meyerhold, V. E.: *Textos teóricos* (2 vols., trans. J. A. Hormigón), Madrid, 1970–1972.
Meyerhold, V. E.: *Theaterarbeit 1917–1930* (trans. R. Tietze), Munich, 1974.
Meyerhold, V. E.: *Le Théâtre théâtral* (trans. N. Gourfinkel), Paris, 1963.

Nemirovich-Danchenko, V. I.: *My Life in the Russian Theatre*, London, 1937.
Vl. I. Nemirovich-Danchenko – Teatralnoe nasledie, Vol. 2, Moscow, 1954.

Ocherki istorii russkoy sovetskoy dramaturgii (2 vols.), Leningrad–Moscow, 1963 and 1966.

Pertsov, V.: *Mayakovsky v poslednie gody*, Moscow, 1965.
Pertsov, V.: *Mayokovsky – zhizn i tvorchestvo* (2 vols.), Moscow, 1957 and 1958.
Petrov, N. V.: *50 i 500*, Moscow, 1960.
I. N. Pevtsov – sbornik (ed. K. N. Derzhavin), Leningrad, 1935.
Pikovaya dama – sbornik statey i materialov, Leningrad, 1935.
Pozharskaya, M. N.: *Russkoe teatralno-dekoratsionnoe iskusstvo kontsa XIX, nachala XX vekov*, Moscow, 1970.
Polotskaya, E. A.: 'Chekhov i Meierkhold' in *Literaturnoe nasledstvo*, Vol. 68, Moscow, 1960.
Pyast, V. A.: *Vstrechi*, Moscow, 1929.

Redko, A. E.: *Teatr i evolyutsia teatralnykh form*, Leningrad, 1926.
Revizor v teatre im. Meierkholda, Leningrad, 1927.
Ripellino, A. M.: *Il trucco e l'anima*. Turin, 1965.
Ripellino, A. M.: *Majakovkij e il teatro russo d'avanguardia*, Turin, 1959 (also published in French as *Maiakovski et le théâtre russe d'avant garde*, Paris, 1965).
Rodina, T. M.: *Aleksandr Blok i russkiy teatr nachala XX veka*, Moscow, 1972.
Rostotsky, B. E.: *O rezkissyorskom tvorchestve V. E. Meierkholda*, Moscow, 1960.
Rubtsov, A. B.: *Dramaturgia Aleksandra Bloka*, Minsk, 1968.
Rudnitsky, K. L.: *Rezhissyor Meierkhold*, Moscow, 1969.

Sayler, O. M.: *The Russian Theatre under the Revolution*, Boston, 1920.
Sitkovetskaya, N. M.: 'V. E. Meierkhold do Oktyabrya' in *Vstrechi s proshlym* (ed. N. B. Volkova and others), Moscow, 1972.
Sollertinsky, I. I.: *Kriticheskie statyi*, Leningrad, 1963.
Sovetskiy teatr: dokumenty i materialy – Russkiy sovetskiy teatr: 1917–21 (ed. A. Z. Yufit), Leningrad, 1968.
Sovetskiy teatr: dokumenty i materialy – Russkiy sovetskiy teatr 1921–27 (ed. A. Ya. Trabsky), Leningrad, 1975.
Stanislavsky, K. S.: *My Life in Art*, Boston, 1924.
Stanislavsky, K. S.: *Sobranie sochineniy v vosmi tomakh*, Moscow, 1954–1961.
Stroeva, M. N.: *Rezhissyorskie iskania Stanislavskogo 1898–1917*, Moscow, 1973.

Talnikov, D. L.: *Komissarzhevskaya*, Moscow–Leningrad, 1939.
Talnikov, D. L.: *Novaya revizia Revizora*, Moscow–Leningrad, 1927.
Teatralny oktyabr – sbornik I (ed. A. A. Gvozdev and others), Leningrad–Moscow, 1926.
Telyakovsky, V. A.: *Vospominania*, Leningrad–Moscow, 1965.
Tretyakov, S. M.: *Slyshish, Moskva?!*, Moscow, 1966.

Uchitel Bubus: spektakl Teatra im. Meierkholda (ed. V. Fyodorov), Moscow, 1925.

Van Gyseghem, A.: *Theatre in Soviet Russia*, London, 1943.
Volkov, N. D.: *Meierkhold* (2 vols.), Moscow–Leningrad, 1929.

Volkov, N. D.: *Teatralnye vechera*, Moscow, 1966.
Vstrechi s Meierkholdom (ed. M. A. Valentei and others), Moscow, 1967.

Yelagin, Yu.: *Tyomny geniy (Vsevolod Meierkhold)*, New York, 1955.
Yuriev, Yu. M.: *Zapiski* (2 vols.), Leningrad–Moscow, 1963.
Yutkevich, S. I.: *Kontrapunkt rezhissyora*, Moscow, 1960.
Yuzovsky, Yu.: *Razgovor zatyanulsya za polnoch*, Moscow, 1966.
Yuzovsky, Yu.: *Spektakli i piesy*, Moscow, 1935.
Yuzovsky, Yu.: *Zatem lyudi khodyat v teatr*, Moscow, 1964.

Zakhava, B. E.: *Sovremenniki*, Moscow, 1969.
Zharov, M. I.: *Zhizn, teatr, kino*, Moscow, 1967.
Znosko-Borovsky, E. A.: *Russkiy teatr nachala XX veka*, Prague, 1925.
Zolotnitsky, D. I.: *Zori teatralnogo oktyabrya*, Leningrad, 1976.

Index